World Order for a New Millennium

WORLD ORDER FOR A
NEW MILLENNIUM
Political, Cultural and Spiritual Approaches
to Building Peace

A. Walter Dorn, Editor

St. Martin's Press
New York

ISBN 0-312-21635-1
Library of Congress Cataloging-in-Publication Data

World order for a new millennium : political, cultural, and spiritual
approaches to building peace / A. Walter Dorn, editor.
       p. cm.
  "The book is a result of a conference titled 'The evolution of
world order: building a foundation for peace in the third
millennium,' which was held in Toronto from 6 to 8 June 1997" -
- Intro.
  Includes bibliographical references and index.
  ISBN 0–312–21635–1 (cloth)
  1. International relations. 2. International organization.
3. Peace. I. Dorn, A. Walter.
JZ1308.W67 1999
327.1'72—dc21   99–13634
                                              CIP

Design by Binghamton Valley Composition
First edition: December, 1999

10 9 8 7 6 5 4 3 2 1

Dedicated to readers everywhere who, as citizens of one world, strive to turn their ideals into realities, their enlightened thoughts into fruitful actions and their differences into a harmony of unity.

Contents

Message from the Secretary-General of the United Nations

Kofi Annan
United Nations Secretary-General

Editor's note: This message was sent by the Secretary-General to the World Order Conference of June 6–8, 1997, which was where most of the papers in this volume were first presented.

I am pleased to send greetings to all those gathered in Toronto this weekend for the Conference on the Evolution of World Order. With that theme in front of you, you have a great deal to discuss and think about in three days.

One of the guiding beacons of the work of the United Nations recently has been its commitment to sustainable development. On both the national and international levels the surest foundation for peace, stability and security is economic and social development. Peace-keeping and peace-building may catch the headlines, but in terms of resources and of the changes in peoples lives, the development work of the United Nations is far more significant.

Partnership and cooperation are crucial elements here. Governments, the private sector, local authorities and non-governmental organizations must develop and improve their working links with each other and the United Nations, and the United Nations must enhance its cooperation with regional bodies and other institutions and intensify dialogue with civil society and the business community.

A new global social and economic agenda is in the making. The major United Nations conferences of this decade—on environment and development, human rights, population policy, social development, women and human settlement—have accomplished a great deal to clarify and focus thinking on some of the major challenges facing society. As these conferences have repeatedly demonstrated, there is a very lively interest at the grass-roots level in what citizens can do to contribute to development. That is good news indeed, for without citizen participation, government efforts to improve people's lives stand little chance of lasting success. Sustainable development—that must be one of the primary focuses of the Untied Nations in coming years. When people live in a society where they have something to contribute and something to gain, they have no interest in taking up weapons. When a state can be an active, respected participant in world trade and international affairs, the government can concentrate on constructive matters. In short, sustainable development is essential for sustainable peace. That is after all the raison d'être of the United Nations.

Foreword

Daisaku Ikeda
President, Soka Gakkai International

Dr. Anatol Rapoport, one of Canada's most renowned peace scholars, has pointed to three global challenges with which humanity must come to grips: abolishing war as an institution; ensuring the viability of the biosphere; and reducing the disparity between the affluent and the destitute parts of our world. These are indeed fundamental crises that, if not resolved, will continue to undermine the prospects for lasting peace.

To meet these challenges, Dr. Rapoport further offered this important insight: "the proposals for reorganization, democratization and redefinition of goals all converge on turning the UN into a global organization of people rather than of states." It has been my own consistent assertion that a fundamental shift in emphasis, from national interest to the interest of humanity as a whole, is of paramount necessity, and I thus find myself in wholehearted agreement with Dr. Rapoport.

In our multidimensional task of creating peace, we must, of course, tackle the concrete problems of systems and order, bringing the full analytical powers of the scientific method to bear on questions of economics, of balancing conflicting interests and powers. Such efforts toward tangible systemic reforms are indispensable.

At the same time, however, I believe that, to be lasting and meaningful, such efforts must be integrated with, and supported by, a fundamental inner reformation within individuals. This should include such realms as human spirituality, consciousness and values, as well as the way we view and relate to the natural world. These twin reforms, of external systems and of inner values, are mutually reinforcing and together represent a genuinely holistic approach to peace. It is for this reason that I enthusiastically welcome this book, which seeks to integrate the political and the spiritual dimensions of the quest for global peace and a just world order.

It has traditionally fallen to religion, ethics and education to foster the spirit of non-violence and compassion; to extend individual consciousness to embrace the whole of humanity; to bring about a general reform in people's values systems, worldviews and lifestyles.

In the Buddhist scriptures, which give voice to the age-old wisdom of the East, we find the image of the ideal ruler, the Wheel-turning King who governs worlds with truth and justice. Appearing together with this King is a Buddha called Maitreya, whose name is derived from the Sanskrit "mitra"—"friend"—and expresses his desire and determination to be friend to all people. The Wheel-turning King can be said to symbolize reform in the social, political and economic realms, and Buddha Maitreya, spiritual enlightenment and a revolution of human values. The simultaneous advent of these two figures in the scriptures is symbolic of the fact that an ideal society can best be brought into being through the harmonious and mutually supportive functioning of these two aspects: politics based on truth and justice, and the solidarity of citizens acting in the spirit of friendship.

After the Buddha's passing, there lived, in the third century B.C.E., a sovereign who magnificently embodied the fusion of these two aspects. He is known as Ashoka the Great, the third ruler of the Maurya dynasty and the first king to unify India. British historian Arnold Toynbee expressed an abiding respect for Ashoka, calling him a king among kings.

It was Ashoka's deeply held belief that victory based, not on force, but on the dharma, or supreme truth, is true victory. "Dharma" is a Sanskrit term indicating the principle or energy inherent in the universe that supports and sustains the life-activities of all beings. King Ashoka sought to assure that all of the policies of his reign were in harmony with dharma.

Since the essence of the dharma is the compassionate energy of the cosmos, it is only natural that his policies were attempts to give concrete form to that compassion. Thus, based on the teaching of non-killing and non-violence, he renounced war and established a peaceful reign. His benevolence was directed not only toward human beings but toward nature and all living beings. He founded hospitals for people as well as animals, which provided various medicines; his programs also included afforestation and the digging of wells.

In order to enhance the economic well-being of his subjects, he improved transportation systems, extending trade routes to the Greek states, Egypt and the Middle East. At the same time, he applied Shakyamuni Buddha's principle of the equal distribution of wealth and made offerings to the poor designed to reduce income disparity.

As an individual Ashoka was a devout follower of Buddhism. His desire for the peace and welfare of society arose from his faith in the compassionate teachings of Buddhism. But he never attempted to make Buddhism the state religion and instead protected freedom of belief for all. He sought to encourage the kind of human and social ethos that can assure the flourishing of the whole of society, including its most intimate units: families and local communities.

At the heart of King Ashoka's successful governance was his emphasis on a revolution of spiritual values; his policies were based on the universal value of compassion for humanity and all living beings.

From this distance of time it is, of course, impossible to apply literally all of the lessons of King Ashoka. But we can derive important hints for the ideal society of the future from his remarkable fusion of reform of the inner, spiritual realms coupled with concrete and practical measures for the welfare of his people.

In this sense, I heartily applaud the objectives of this book, which brings together the wisdom of experts whose work spans both the "hardware" aspects of politics, economics and science, as well as those engaged in the "software" side of religion, philosophy, education and ethics. I am convinced that this book, which boldly faces the challenges of global issues, will be a significant milestone toward the construction of a solid basis for world peace.

Acknowledgments

The World Order Conference, the basis for this book, was organized with the help of many people who deserve to be heartily thanked. Michael Greenspoon, the Associate Chair, provided able and dependable assistance. Helen Izumi, Secretary of the Conference, gave selflessly, fully and cheerfully of her time and tireless effort. Professor Helmut (Ken) Burkhardt, the Convenor of the Conference, was a solid and dependable "rock" upon which the conference planning could go forward. The members of the Organizing and Publications Committees provided excellent ideas and feedback. Professor Derek Paul did a conscientious and careful job editing the proceedings of the Conference, which made the job of editing this volume much easier. Ross Wilcock gave constructive advice and created an inspiring and helpful Conference Web Site (www.pgs.ca /woc). Mark English and Colin Puffer did much of the detailed and exacting secretarial work to put the conference papers into proper format for this volume. The people who helped review manuscripts also deserve warm appreciation: Eric Fawcett, Eric Mullerbeck and John Valleau. Sandra Kisner painstakingly prepared the index to the present volume. The support of Sandra and her colleagues in the Peace Studies Program, particularly Professors Judith Reppy and Matthew Evangelista, is much appreciated. It was a pleasure to work with all the authors of the papers in this volume—remarkably there were no disagreements, which is hopefully a good omen for the new millennium! Financial support from Soka Gakkai International is much appreciated, as is the support and encouragement from its Canadian representative, Mickey Masuda. We are also grateful to the UN Secretary-General for sending a message to the conference.

Introduction

A. Walter Dorn
Cornell University

The dawn of a new millennium—the third according to the world's first universally recognized calendar—beckons us to take the "long-term" view of our world and the ways we have ordered it. This is not only because a thousand-year span covers a lot of human history,[1] but because we owe it to ourselves and to future generations to review honestly the mixed and often painful experiences of the past world order, to take stock of any progress and to think boldly about the kind of future world order we would like to see created.

Throughout human history, world order has rarely, if ever, been built upon peace and justice. History provides abundant examples of strong-arm order imposed on sprawling empires and only a few examples of non-violent order through global understanding and peaceful cooperation. Fortunately, there is evidence of a sort of evolution as shown by the gradual improvement in the ethical standards of the great powers in each era. The early Egyptian empires were built on brutal conquest and abject slavery, justified by the alleged divinity and infallibility of the Pharaohs. The Romans created an imperial order based on force (the Roman Legions) in *pax Romana,* with taxation under threat of dire punishment. *Pax Britannica* was based on the rule of British law, which extended the rights of British subjects in the United Kingdom to subjects of the British Empire, but still depended on the military to enforce an official policy of exploitation in the colonies. Before the First World War, the British and other European empires relied on the "balance of power" between them-selves, an unstable and impermanent type of world order in which nations weaved themselves into a web of military alliances to become stronger in order to deter attack. This system kept the peace for decades, but made the inevitable conflagration even more horrendous.

The League of Nations, created after World War I as the world's first international organization mandated to keep the peace, was an attempt at a different system, one based on collective security—especially interna-tional solidarity against an aggressor—as well as cooperation among states on a wide range of political, social and economic issues. But states could not raise themselves to act according to the higher idealism of the League Covenant and reverted to the notion of balance of power in the face of bold aggression by Japan, Italy and Germany. At the end of World War II, U.S. President Franklin Roosevelt strove to build on the liberal ideals of his predecessor Woodrow Wilson to create a world order (*pax Americana,* if you like) based on democracy and global cooperation, fos-tered through international organizations. The League was superceded by a strengthened world organization, the United Nations. The UN's mem-bership eventually became virtually universal, a goal never attained by the League. But the balance-of-power concept remained the dominant one in the painful period that followed World War II. In the Cold War, this con-cept was brought to its ultimate climax in the notion of mutually assured destruction (appropriately called MAD), which kept the nuclear equiva-lent of the sword of Damocles hanging over humanity on a slender thread. Unfortunately, the raw-power concept still holds much sway in military circles, especially in the United States, where American military "supremacy" is still seen as the paramount and permanent goal.

With the end of the Cold War, made possible by the progressive and enlightened leadership of Soviet President Mikhail Gorbachev, there were many positive developments. The UN played a central part in that positive change, showing the awe-inspiring progress in a decade that can come about through concerted international effort.

The UN verified the withdrawal of Soviet troops from Afghanistan; it mediated the negotiations ending the Iran-Iraq war; it oversaw the tran-sition of Namibia to independence, climaxing 70 years of international involvement (Namibia was first placed under the League of Nations man-date system in 1920); the UN supervised South African elections to finally end the ugly and brutal apartheid system; it helped bring greater peace and democracy to Central America, in particular by helping end the bloody and brutal internal wars in Nicaragua, El Salvador and

Guatemala; it brought about peace in a war-torn Cambodia, having to assume near-complete control of several government departments during a difficult transition period leading up to that country's first democratic elections; the UN supervised elections in Haiti and parts of the former Yugoslavia; it guarded aid routes in Somalia and obtained the release of many hostages in the Middle East. The UN was a major contributor to the development of peace in Croatia and Bosnia and in providing the experience necessary to implement the peace accords. In addition, the UN authorized the repulsion of aggression in Kuwait and supervised the destruction of Iraq's weapons of mass destruction.

Undoubtedly, the present international system, and the UN in particular, have had many failures and abundant shortcomings—as do all human systems and organizations. To the UN's embarrassment, it didn't resolve the Somalia conflict and didn't prevent or even mitigate the genocide in Rwanda, though it might have been able to do so. The UN and the international community as a whole face great challenges in the world today, including extremism in Afghanistan, the continuing violence in Central America, the "political wars" in Cambodia and Haiti, and protracted conflicts in the former Yugoslavia, the former Soviet Union, Africa and other parts of the globe. It is, then, all the more remarkable that the UN succeeds, though it is underfunded, underresourced and undersupported, often confounded by power politics in the Security Council and bypassed by the international financial institutions at a time when economic questions are of great concern. The continued determination to make the UN work despite all these daunting challenges is a clear manifestation of the power of the human spirit!

The dawn of a new millennium provides us with the special opportunity to think about further progress and to formulate grand visions. With the end of the Cold War, we have, for the first time in hundreds of years, perhaps in all human history, no global power blocs menacing one another—though many threats undoubtedly remain. We now have the unique opportunity to build a foundation for peace and to establish a more just and stable world order, in its many dimensions. We are encouraged to look at our past and present world order, analyze its flaws and envision a future order that we might like to see. This book attempts to do exactly that.

Thus, with their feet firmly planted on the ground of historical reality but with their eyes looking into the distance at the goals ahead, the authors of the chapters in this book have sought to provide the reader with diverse yet harmonious visions for our global future. They accepted the challenge to paint the "big picture," suitable for a new millennium.

Professor Anatol Rapoport provides us with a clear conceptual basis for past, present and future world order, where "the rules" are either imposed by force, developed by trade or fostered through integration. The gradual evolution over time of "international law"—based mostly on the latter two factors but relying on armed force to some extent—is reviewed masterfully by Professor Jennie Hatfield-Lyon. The fact that most nations abide by international law most of the time raises the question: why behave? Some reasons are suggested in my paper on treaty compliance, which points to interdependence as a main factor. Countries are dependent on each other in many ways, not least of which is economic, even if they have quite different economic systems. Professor Myron Gordon provides a sweeping overview and critique of the main economic approaches that nations have adopted. Professor John McMurtry warns of the dangers of the move to adopting global free-trade and investment treaties without, at the same time, creating regulations to help save the environment, encourage cultural diversity and improve upon global labor standards.

The military has traditionally played a major role in world order. For most of human history, "might made right" and the nation with the strongest armed forces could have the final say. But such an approach, which relies on weapons and threats, is fraught with danger. Alan Phillips, M.D., shows us how close we came to global catastrophe in the age of nuclear weapons, not by intention but by accident. Major-General Leonard Johnson offers us the refreshingly optimistic logic that our future need not follow the pattern of the past: international war is on the decline and may even become obsolete in the next century. But the burden of armaments, we all recognize, still rests heavily on our shoulders, especially in the developing nations that can least afford it. Col. Brian Mac-Donald, realizing that some levels of military force are justified, introduces two new indicators that measure militarization and that can alert us to the misuse of military funds for internal suppression, especially the "Praetorian index," a term and concept that he has coined.

These global problems—of a military, economic or other nature—require global solutions. The papers of the third section are unified in their belief that the United Nations, despite all its faults and limitations, still remains the first and foremost avenue to improve the general condition of this world. Christopher Spencer gives us a broad overview of these many problems and suggests how the UN could and should be involved. Dr. Rosalie Bertell finds inspiration in recent UN-sponsored agreements that can be important building blocks for a better world order for humans and the environment. Perhaps the greatest step to mitigate the worst of human crimes, genocide and crimes against humanity, is the creation of an International Criminal Court, which is succinctly described by Fergus Watt, who closely followed the negotiations for the ICC Statute and was present at the Rome signing ceremony. Finally, in that section, I work my "crystal ball," which is set to "optimistic" mode, to predict how the UN will evolve over the next 5, 25 and 50 years.

But lest we think that world order is only about nations and international institutions, the second part of the book is there to set us straight. The contributions of our varied cultures, religions and non-governmental bodies, many of which are dedicated to fostering peace and developing a harmonious world order, are extremely important. Prof. Cynthia Chataway tells us how the U.S. government has increasingly looked to NGOs for assistance in diplomacy, a domain that was traditionally the proud preserve of government diplomats. An appreciation of gender and cultural issues can help us look at our world in a more balanced way and to work more productively to improve the state for all its inhabitants, as demonstrated by activist Shirley Farlinger. Professor Guy Bourgeault challenges us to educate not only our children but also ourselves, to seek a higher ethics—one in which we realize that the globe is our neighborhood—and to act as worthy global citizens.

The major religions of the world have, at their core, the notion of the spiritual unity of humanity under God or under a great cosmic order. Archbishop Ted Scott provides a Christian commentary on making the change from a mental notion to a living reality in the actions of people, companies and nations. The Jewish faith, which combines a considerable amount of painful history with sacred scripture, also calls for peace within the individual as well as in the world, as Rabbi Marty Lockshin describes to us. Dr. Yoichi Kawada, from Japan, enlightens us on the links between inner and outer peace: from our purified emotions we can create peace in our homes, our communities, our nations and our world. This message is amplified by Daniel Vokey, who also advocates the practice of meditation. The First Nations perspective, presented by Gawithra of the Younger Bear Clan of the Cayuga Nation, reminds us that the world is much more than just human: our environment is a part of our existence and it can, in fact, help us find peace, so long as we don't try to dominate or possess it. A sympathetic consideration of our natural environment is just one consideration of many that Dr. Hanna Newcombe sees as important in the development of a common global understanding, "a world religion"; others are new truths, from the sciences as well from the religions, that need to be recognized and honored. Similarly, the Bahá'í religion, reviewed by practitioners Cheshmak Farhoumand and Dr. Charles Lerche, does not deny the validity of other approaches—scientific, institutional or religious—but seeks to embrace other approaches and faiths. It provides a very precise view of the future world order, based on a benevolent world government. Whether such can be established in the coming century or even millennium may not be certain, but our continuing support of the current instrument of global governance and harmony, the United Nations, is essential, writes Sri Chinmoy. His vision is of an expanding world harmony that is founded upon spiritual principles, sympathetic to many approaches, and anchored in harmonious cooperation through the United Nations and by individuals everywhere. Thus, the second part of the book builds a bridge between the institutions of governance and the guiding vision, showing how the age-long vision of "peace on Earth and goodwill to all" can and should continue to animate our institutions as we seek to build a just and peaceful world order.

The book is a result of a conference titled "The Evolution of World Order: Building a Foundation for Peace in the Third Millennium," which was held in Toronto from June 6 to 8, 1997. From the 50 papers presented at the conference, some 20 were chosen and others added to form this book, which seeks to be wide ranging in its coverage, cohesive in its visions and complementary in its approaches. In this way it seeks to live up to its calling to be a "book for a new millennium."

A. Walter Dorn
Ithaca, New York

NOTE

1. In my opening address at the World Order Conference, I took a cavalier attitude toward the millennium, saying, tongue in cheek: "A millennium here and a millennium there; pretty soon you're talking about a long time!" But I assured my audience (and the readers now) that my intent is solemn!

Part I

Political and Institutional Approaches

The Evolution of World Order

Chapter 1

Conceptions of World Order

Anatol Rapoport
Science for Peace, University of Toronto

Various conceptions of "order" coexist today. They all have in common some idea of social control. However, modes of control that underlie the different conceptions of a world order differ radically.

Three modes of social control were succinctly described by Kenneth Boulding, who subsumed them respectively under "threat," "trade" and "love." Threat or coercion is the prevailing mode of control in totalitarian or authoritarian societies. People are supposed to be induced to behave as the authorities desire by the threat of punishment meted out for disobedience. "Trade" or "exchange" is the mode of control applied in relations among equals. Unlike threat, embodied in a declaration like "If you don't do as I say, I will punish you," an exchange implies reciprocal commitments: "Do this for me, and I will do that for you." People work, not because they are threatened with whipping if they don't, but because they are paid.

Boulding eventually replaced the term "love" by "integration," which has no sentimental or romantic connotations, but means essentially the same as "love," as this word is used in Boulding's description of a mode of social control. A society based on "love" in this technical sense is characterized by an expanded range of public goods. A public good, by definition, is something that is accessible to everyone regardless of ability to pay, simply because everyone is entitled to it. For example, children are fed and protected not because they can threaten those who neglect them and not because they can pay, but simply because they are children. It is this example that probably suggested the term "love" to Boulding. However, in a more general context, certain amenities are not generated by affection such as normal parents feel toward their children. Instead they are subsumed under "human rights" in people-oriented social systems. Members of a society receive them not because they can pay for them and not because they can threaten with reprisals if they are deprived of them, but simply because they are members of the society. Corresponding to the threat system is a world order based on "hegemony." Corresponding to the trade system is a world order based on "balance of power," at times coupled with so-called "collective security." Corresponding to the love system is a world order based on "common security," an idea quite different from that of collective security. I will explain the difference later.

A clear example of a world order based on hegemony was the Roman Empire. The last centuries of its existence were marked by what is called, sometimes nostalgically, *pax Romana*. Peace in the conquered regions was kept by military monopoly. At times analogous terms were used to describe the hegemony of Great Britain over its vast imperial domains (*pax Britannica*) and later, with reference to the geopolitical aspirations of the United States after World War II, *pax Americana*.

A conception of a world order based on collective security has an interesting history. An example dating from the fifteenth century is the attempt of King George of Bohemia to unify Europe in 1464. It is described in a publication by the Czechoslovak Academy of Sciences in 1964, marking the 500th anniversary of King George's project.[1] In the preamble of the document we read:

> In the name of our Lord Jesus Christ . . . Let this be known to one
> and all for all eternity. We learn from the writings of ancient histori-
> ans that Christianity once flourished and was blessed with men and
> goods, spreading far and wide that it held in its womb one hundred
> and seventeen rich kingdoms, that it also brought forth so many peo-

ple that for a long time it held a large part of pagandom including the Holy Sepulchre; in those days there was no nation in the world which would have dared to challenge Christian rule. But we all know how lacerated it is today, how broken, impoverished, and deprived of all its former brilliance and splendour it is.

The proposed treaty contained specific provisions for establishing a permanent peace in Europe. We read:

> In order to strengthen peace among others faithful to Christ, we hereby provide and order that if discord or war should occur between other Christian princes, our below described assembly shall dispatch in our name and at our mutual expense envoys whose task will be to restore concert between the parties to dispute. . . .

Comments by the Czechoslovak Academy of Sciences on this 1464 document are noteworthy. We read:

> The most prominent place is occupied by proposals whose purpose was to exclude war from human society. War against the Turks is not mentioned once. . . . Mankind of the fifteenth century was shown prospects of a world without wars in which even the apparently insurmountable antagonism between the Christians and Moslems appeared to be replaceable by a situation for which we can hardly find a more fitting, modern-day term than "peaceful co-existence." This is clearly indicated in the final part of Article 13, which expressly envisages the possibility of peace between Christendom and the Turks.

Doubtless publication of the document was motivated at least in part by its supposed advocacy of "peaceful coexistence," which in 1964 was a favorite buzzword on the Soviet side, just as "mutual assured destruction" was on the U.S. side. The reference to Article 13 of the proposed treaty, however, is puzzling unless the publishers had not read it. In that article we read:

> . . . we . . . pledge and swear to our Lord Jesus Christ, to his most glorious mother, the Virgin Mary, and to the Holy Catholic Church that we shall defend and protect the Christian religion and all its oppressed faithful against the vilest prince of the Turks . . . and we

shall not cease to pursue the enemy, if our assembly deems it expedient, until he is driven out of Christian territory or until it is jointly resolved to conclude peace, which may be done only if the security of neighbouring Christian states is deemed ensured.

In other words, rather stringent conditions were set as prerequisites of peace with the Turks.

Obviously the arrangement proposed by King George reflected a perception of a common enemy, the fast-growing Turkish empire. Constantinople had been captured only 11 years previously. As a matter of fact, alliances between social and political units were most commonly formed with the same aim in view. Families joined together to form clans to meet the threat of other clans. Clans joined to form tribes, tribes to form chiefdoms, then states. All of these regularly formed alliances aimed against rival alliances.

The notion of balance of power arose in the wake of the Thirty Years' War. That cataclysm is often interpreted as a religious war between Catholics and Protestants. It is noteworthy, however, that France, a Catholic country, participated on the side of the Protestants. The crucial issue, it seems, was not a rivalry of theologies (or ideologies, as we would say today) but a struggle for power. Protestant monarchs mobilized against the hegemonical system established in the Middle Ages by the Church—a threat system based on the widespread fear of eternal damnation and only partially on military potential. Although Louis XIII of France was a Catholic monarch, he must already have put power ahead of salvation, anticipating his son's famous declaration "L'état, c'est moi!" In 1648 the Treaty of Westphalia reflected the victory of the balance-of-power conception of a world order, whereby power was consolidated by the state in the person of the monarch. The total sovereignty of the state was embodied in the principle that the religion of a state was to be determined by its prince.

Eighteenth-century Europe was characterized by a chronic struggle for power. Most states were more or less absolute monarchies, and power was conceived as the range of authority of a dynasty. Witness the predominance of dynastic issues in the so-called cabinet wars of the eighteenth century: the War of the Spanish Succession, the War of the Austrian Succession, the War of the Bavarian Succession, the War of the Polish Succession.

In 1795 the German philosopher Immanuel Kant published his famous essay on perpetual peace, in which he argued that war would die as an institution if monarchies became republics. For without monarchs there would be no struggle for power (which at that time was thought to be embodied in dynastic hegemony). Ironically, the essay appeared in print as war was already raging between the newly established French republic and allied European monarchies. The so-called French Revolutionary Wars merged with the so-called Napoleonic Wars. Napoleon tried to unify Europe by force of arms, again against a common enemy, namely, England. He did succeed in unifying Europe, but, unfortunately for him, not on his side against England but against him. It was not England but Imperial France that was cast in the role of the common enemy. Victory of the Allies in the Napoleonic Wars was a victory of the balance-of-power system against a hegemonical world order.

The notion of collective security arose in the wake of that victory. The common enemy was now no longer a designated state or alliance. Instead, it was the perceived threat to a world order based on monarchical power. At the Congress of Vienna in 1815 all the major European powers, including France, where monarchy had been restored, joined in a "universal" alliance aimed at suppressing revolution, wherever it might break out. Soon, however, that system broke down.

One of the reasons for the breakdown appears to be the transformation of nationalism from a revolutionary to a reactionary force. Nationalism (along with patriotism, its nurturing sentiment) arose in Europe in the framework of the French Revolutionary Wars. A contributing factor was the replacement of standing armies by conscription.

The eighteenth-century European soldier was trained to become an automaton. In a typical battle of that time, the infantry often formed a hollow square. The soldiers faced outward and fired on command barked by officers inside the square. The soldier's job was to execute these commands by rigid jerky movements, learned in close-order drill. Indoctrination such as is practiced today with the view of instilling strong motivation was not part of the soldier's training. The length of service was typically 25 years. In war, the soldier often did not know whom he was fighting, let alone why. The French soldier of the Revolutionary and Napoleonic wars was a recruit. There was no time to turn him into an automaton, and there was no need to do so, since he was strongly motivated to fight. At first he fought for the achievements of the Revolution, then for France embodied in the person of Napoleon. The inculcation of nationalism and patriotism "took" and soon infected all Europe.

Nationalism retained its revolutionary flavor until the last decades of the century. It was manifested, for example, in the Italian Risorgimento, a movement aimed at unifying Italy manifested in the struggle against Hapsburg domination. In 1849 Hungarian nationalists also revolted against Austria. That movement was suppressed by Russia, a belated discharge of the responsibility to the Holy Alliance established at the Congress of Vienna in 1815. The Polish revolt against Russia in 1830 was led by revolutionary nationalists. It is interesting to recall that also in Germany nationalism was at first regarded as what we would call today a "left-wing" rather than a "right-wing" orientation. A group of liberal German intellectuals meeting in Frankfurt in 1848 demanded, along with democratic reforms, including constitutions, unification of Germany, thus irritating the assorted kings, princes and princelings of the crazy quilt that was called Germany at that time.

It was in response to the rise of internationally oriented socialist labor movements in Europe that nationalist and patriotic sentiments were co-opted by the political right. These sentiments became the ideological basis of the world order based on absolute sovereignty of the nation-state and the rationale of so-called balance of power.

It is interesting to speculate why balance of power was taken so seriously by Europeans as a principle of maintaining a stable world order. I believe this has something to do with the impression that Darwin's theory of evolution, driven by natural selection, made on the liberal bourgeoisie, which in the wake of the French Revolution supplanted the aristocracy as the dominant social class. The principle of "survival of the fittest" nurtures the rationale of universal perpetual competition as the driving force of "progress." Incidentally, it nurtures also the ideology of the military caste. Here is what a German general wrote on the very eve of World War I:

> The struggle for existence is the life of Nature, the basis of all healthy development. All existing things show themselves to be the result of contending forces. So it is in the life of man. The struggle is not merely a destructive but a life-giving principle.[2]

We see in this glorification of violence an echo of the Hobbesian view of human nature manifested in the war of everyone against everyone. This is the way the military caste and their ideological hangers-on interpreted the "struggle for existence, survival of the fittest" principle. Thomas Hobbes, however, did not share the bloodthirsty enthusiasm of the militarists. He supposed that if it were allowed to continue, everyone would perish. The remedy he offered was hegemony—the surrender of individual liberty to an absolute monarch who would protect the life of the individual by total control over his activity. This solution was the imposition of a threat system on organized society.

The liberal bourgeoisie, however, except for those directly engaged in the burgeoning arms industry, had little use for violence and threat. Their god was trade, profits, accumulation of capital. Their conception of the struggle for existence and survival of the fittest was business competition, unfettered and ruthless but not bloody. So the idea of balance of power appealed to them as a means of restraining the drum beaters and trumpet blowers. It was supposed that balance of power would dim perspectives of easy victory and so inhibit war. Well, it didn't. The very efforts to establish balance of power or to restore it after it was disturbed led to a feverish arms race, which exploded in the four-year butchery of World War I.

The League of Nations was, in a way, a revival of the Bohemian king's covenant of 1464. The "world" was still Europe. The people of what we now call the Third World did not have a say, and the two major powers outside of Europe, United States and Japan, had no use for balance of power as a guarantee of security. They aspired to hegemony in their respective spheres of influence, the former in the Western Hemisphere, the latter in East Asia and the Pacific. The members of the League of Nations still invoked the image of a common enemy, but now it was no longer a designated enemy, like Turkey was in the fifteenth century, but a hypothetical "aggressor," whom all the "peace-loving" states were expected to chastise and bring to heel.

As we know this scheme died helpless, when Mussolini started his much publicized program of restoring the Roman Empire by attacking, with his tanks, planes and chemical weapons, the Ethiopian tribesmen armed with spears. The "peace-loving" powers could not even agree on cutting off Mussolini's oil supply. Nor could they agree on a way of stopping Hitler's program of "unifying" Europe under Germany's hegemony. The carnage of World War II followed.

The United Nations, still in existence, represents an attempt to establish a world order in which preservation of peace is a primary instead of a secondary concern. Unlike the League of Nations, United Nations membership is universal. Any collection of people that calls itself a country (some 185 groups have been recognized as such) can belong and is accorded formally equal status in the General Assembly. This means that people that had no voice at all on the world stage before World War II now have a voice. The other difference between the old League of Nations and the United Nations is that along with the commitment to collective security both the idea of hegemony (now supposed to be exercised by the five recognized nuclear powers) and the idea of common security (which I will presently define) are imbedded in it. Actually these two ideas are incompatible. Unless one of them survives, while the other withers and dies, the United Nations probably will be dissolved.

Here is what the preamble to the United Nations Charter says:

> We the peoples of the United Nations determined to save the succeeding generations from the scourge of war, which twice in our lifetime has brought untold sorrow to mankind and to reaffirm our faith in fundamental human rights of men and women and of nations large and small, and to establish conditions under which justice and respect for the obligations arising from treaties and other sources of international law can be maintained . . . have resolved to combine our efforts to accomplish this aim.

Is this latest attempt to unify humankind still inspired by fear or hatred of a common enemy, a modern version of the "vilest Prince of the Turks," against whom the King of Bohemia attempted to unify the Christian princes? Yes, there are passing references to "suppressing acts of aggression," and wars were sanctioned by the Security Council against North Korea in 1950 and against Iraq in 1990 on this ground. However, the marked difference between this effort and previous ones was the stress laid on *establishing conditions* of lasting peace. Even more crucial is the recognition that these conditions are not only necessary for eliminating war from human affairs but are also totally interdependent. Four of these conditions were recently named or implied in various resolutions of the General Assembly of the United Nations:

1. Disarmament
2. Environmental protection
3. Human rights
4. Social justice

To effect or protect any of the four, *global effort* must be established, and this implies ultimately limitation of national sovereignty, the sacred cow of international relations since the Treaty of Westphalia at the end of the Thirty Years' War in 1648. It is not possible to solve global problems without limiting national sovereignty.

1. Disarmament is virtually meaningless unless it is total and universal. It does what it is supposed to do, namely, remove the scourge of war, only if it is total and universal.
2. Global environmental problems know no national boundaries. No one can escape global change of climate or the pollution of the oceans and the atmosphere.
3. A violation of any individual's human rights entails a disregard for everyone's human rights.
4. Social justice must be universal to justify being called that.

Pursuing the goal of *common* security (as distinguished from "collective security," envisaged by the Bohemian king and by the League of Nations) entails the recognition of undissolvable interdependence of these human problems. No person, no nation can be secure unless all are secure. Therefore the problems cannot be attacked separately. Consider the tight connection between armaments and the degradation of the environment. Radioactive wastes alone, a by-product of the nuclear war industry, will continue to degrade our home in space for thousands of years.

Of special significance is putting social justice on the global agenda. If social justice means anything at all, it refers to some aspect of equality. For example, "equality before the law" means that in case of confrontation between people or between a person and the state, the decision of the issue depends on the merits of the case, not on the identity of the plaintiff or the defendant. Another aspect of equality refers to equal access to public goods. Social progress can be defined as broadening the scope of public goods. Practically everywhere and always everyone has access to air. Even the most ardent worshippers of the free market have not yet thought of a way to privatize the atmosphere so as to make the price of breathable air a matter of supply and demand. Practically everywhere fire protection and police protection are public goods. The fire department doesn't ask you for the number of your credit card when you ask them to put out a fire nor send you a bill for putting out a fire in your house. In the most advanced societies (by the definition of progress I have offered) education at least to some level and medical care are public goods. In short, equal accessibility to public goods is a vital sign of social equality and, by implication, of social justice.

Social justice, as a goal urged by the United Nations, refers to striving for equality between entire peoples, that is, a global attack on global poverty. Such an attack cannot be launched without radically changing the current trade patterns and financial arrangements between the affluent and impoverished worlds. It cannot be launched without expressly disavowing national policies of the sort proposed shortly after World War II by an advisor to the U.S. government, George F. Kennan. He was also the first to formulate the so-called containment strategy, which dominated U.S. foreign policy for almost a half century. I quote:

> . . . we have about 50% of the world's wealth, but only about 6.3% of its population. In this situation we cannot fail to be the object of envy and resentment. Our real task in the coming period is to devise a pattern of relationships which will permit us to maintain this position of disparity without detriment to our national security. . . . We need not deceive ourselves that we can afford . . . the luxury of altruism. . . . We should cease to talk about . . . unreal objectives such as human rights, the rising of living standards and democratization. The day is not far off when we are going to deal in straight power concepts.[3]

Here you see the connections between disarmament, human rights and social justice clearly spelled out. Preservation of disparity between the United States and the Third World is obviously incompatible with disarmament, if we are going to think in terms of power concepts. Thus, if a privileged position in access to resources is to be preserved, as Kennan once proposed, disarmament becomes unthinkable. Also think of what disarmament would do to arms trade, a major channel for the flow of resources from the Third World to the First, instead of the other way. If maintenance of disparity is to be maintained, human rights and democratization are unreal objectives. Even degradation of the environment, though not explicitly mentioned, is relevant to the proposed policy. For instance, the imposition of monoculture agriculture on impoverished countries results ultimately in desertification.

Clearly Kennan's recommendation to the makers of U.S. foreign policy was based on aspiration to hegemony. This aspiration was reflected in the Monroe Doctrine (U.S. claim in 1824 of hegemony in the Western Hemisphere) and even in earlier pronouncements.

The same conception of world order was expressed in religious instead of geopolitical terms by a United States senator after victory over Spain in 1898.

> We will not repudiate our duty. . . . We will not abandon our opportunity in the Orient. We will not renounce our part in the mission of

our race, trustee under God, of the civilization of the world. . . . We
will move forward to our work . . . with gratitude . . . and thanksgiv-
ing to Almighty God that He has marked us as His chosen people,
henceforth to lead in the regeneration of the world.
    Our largest trade henceforth will be with Asia. The Pacific is
our ocean. The Power that rules the Pacific . . . is the Power that rules
the world. And with the Philippines, that power is and will forever be
the American Republic.[4]

The hegemonic conception of a world order appears to have been pre-
dominant in the thinking of the American power elite. During the Cold
War, however, the balance-of-power model was also prominent among
more sober geopoliticians. Great hopes were laid on so-called deterrence,
a way of preventing a war of total destruction by threatening total destruction, that is, investing in a monstrous doomsday machine, which admit-
tedly can perform its function only if it is never used. There were also
attempts to justify a multipolar world as a successor to the bipolar one.
This would involve unimpeded proliferation of nuclear weapons. Some
argued that such a world would be "more stable" than a bipolar one,
invoking some analogy from theoretical mechanics.
    In one respect the advocates of hegemony (assuming the responsibil-
ity of a world policeman) and the partisans of the "classical" balance-of-
power world order are of one mind. Both are energetically castigating the
idea of common security, as it is implied in the formulation of global
imperatives by the United Nations.
    In an article in *Foreign Affairs* entitled "Saving the UN," U.S. Sena-
tor Jesse Helms writes:

> As it currently operates, the United Nations does not deserve contin-
> ued American support . . . [it] is being transformed from an institu-
> tion of sovereign nations into a quasi-sovereign entity in itself. The
> transformation represents an obvious threat to US national inter-
> ests. . . . This situation is untenable. The United Nations was origi-
> nally created to help nation-states facilitate the peaceful resolution
> of international disputes. However, the United Nations has moved
> from facilitating diplomacy among nation-states to supplanting
> them altogether. . . . Boutros Ghali has said as much. In his Agenda
> for Peace he declared . . . "The time of absolute and exclusive sover-
> eignty . . . has passed. Its theory has never matched reality. . . . "
> Such thinking is in step with the nearly global movement toward

greater centralization of political power. . . . This process must be
stopped. . . . UN reform is much more than saving money. It is about
preventing unelected bureaucrats from acquiring ever greater powers at the expense of elected national leaders. It is about restoring the
legitimacy of the nation-state . . . the UN bureaucracy mistakenly
believes that caring for the needs of all the world's people is . . . its
job. . . . There must be a termination of unnecessary committees and
conferences. . . . In addition to wasteful conferences like the Beijing
women's summit . . . the United Nations continually sponsors work-
shops, expert consultations, technical consultations, and panel discussions. . . . Most of these can be terminated at a savings of
millions of dollars. . . . The time has come for the United States to
deliver an ultimatum: Either the United Nations reforms, quickly
and dramatically, or the United States will end its participation. . . .
Withholding US contributions has not worked. In 1986 Congress
passed the Kassebaum-Solomon bill, which said to the United
Nations in clear and unmistakable terms, reform or die. The time has
come for it to do one or the other.[5]

As Kennan once wrote in a classified document, "the time has come to deal
with straight power concepts." It seems the champions of conventional
geopolitical wisdom, alias realpolitik, have unmasked their batteries.

We are on the threshold of a new millennium. This sort of awareness
occurred only once before, a thousand years ago. Before that people
didn't think in terms of millennia. In fact, as recently as the sixteenth century, Europeans thought the world had only a century or two until Judgement Day. On the eve of the second (that is our) millennium, the end was
widely expected to come immediately. In our day, the end of the world is
not expected to be ushered in by a trumpet blast and rising of the dead.
We have a more realistic picture of it foreshadowed by the gruesome massacres of our century magnified a thousand times by products of awe-
somely sophisticated science. And it is also to science that many of us
look to show us the way to avoid it. Now ordinarily knowledge generated
by science is thought of as an arsenal of techniques. Such is the knowledge that created the undreamed-of technology of our age with its vast
potential for both good and evil. Such is the knowledge that created modern medicine, which doubled the span of human life. Many place their
hopes on generation of knowledge that would forestall conflicts or facilitate conflict resolution and so prevent the disasters associated with war. In
my opinion, this is not enough, because war is not merely an extreme

variety of a quarrel, or an extreme expression of enmity like attitudes generated by ethnic prejudice, or a strife about how to divide a pie, like conflicts between labor and management. War is an institution that has evolved through human history and in the process of this evolution has adapted itself to a large variety of social environments. It is like an organism that has a life of its own and effective defense mechanisms against attempts to put an end to its existence. Knowledge about how to kill this organism involves more than discovery of techniques.

The four global goals inspired by the ideals expressed in the preamble to the United Nations Charter spell out the sort of change in the way of thinking that has become imperative if we are to live through the next millennium. These goals have essentially dispensed with a human common enemy as the prime motivation for integration of small units into larger ones. The notion of the common enemy still exists in global thinking, but this enemy is no longer human. The enemy of disarmament is not a person or such as "the vilest Prince of the Turks," nor a conglomerate of persons, such as an ethnic group or a nation. The common enemy is the war system itself with its vast infrastructure of supporting institutions. These can be destroyed without harming a single person. The common enemy of environmental protection is not human. It is an ideology that puts imperatives of power ahead of the obligation to bequeath a livable home in space to our children. The common enemy of human rights is not "somebody," but thinking habits that split humanity into "us" and "them." Finally, the enemy of social justice is the existing system of trade and finance that puts security of profits ahead of welfare of populations. Changes in ways of thinking that Einstein regarded as prerequisites to integration of humanity are already gathering momentum. It remains to mobilize the collective will to put new thinking to work.

NOTES

1. Czechoslovak Academy of Sciences, *The Universal Peace Organization of King George of Bohemia: A Fifteenth-Century Plan for World Peace* (Prague: Czechoslovak Academy of Sciences, 1964).
2. F. von Bernhardi, *Germany and the Next War* (New York: Longmans, Green, 1914).
3. Policy Planning Study (PPS), February 24, 1948, *FRUS* 1948, I (Part 2).
4. Cited in R. J. Bartlett, *The Record of American Diplomacy* (New York: Alfred A. Knopf, 1956), pp. 385–88.
5. "Saving the UN," *Foreign Affairs* 75, 5 (1996), pp. 2–7.

Chapter 2

The Historical Development of International Law[1]

Jennie Hatfield-Lyon

Faculty of Law, Queen's University,
Kingston, Ontario

Modern international law developed from a series of organized patterns of behavior to deal with specific matters such as commerce, diplomatic relations and rules of warfare. Underlying this development was a basic understanding of the advantages of reciprocity where mutual self-interest dictated a constant pattern of adherence to these rules. Indeed, much of modern international law has evolved from the give-and-take of merchants and tradesmen. The *lex mercatoria* of medieval times consisted of commercial and trade practices that have provided the substratum for the evolution of much of the current law of international trade and commerce, particularly maritime practice. One of the strongest areas of compliance was diplomatic practice, which extended through various areas of the world and has been complied with for very extensive periods of time. Excepting the Iran hostage crisis in 1979–80, this was one of the more effective areas of international law. A major preoccupation of states, which are traditionally the primary actors (as well as groups of individuals influencing states' conduct) on the international plane, has been to maximize their position of power, prestige, wealth and authority through war and conquests. The beginnings of international law are, therefore, invariably traced to rules of warfare, the conduct of belligerents over the battlefield and the humanitarian concern for the treatment of the sick, the wounded and non-belligerents.

The perception of international law as the "Law of Nations," or *jus inter gentes,* although descriptively correct, has tended to blind the reality that all law, whether operating at the local, regional, national or international level, is in fact concerned with human welfare and with the well-being of individuals in society. The importance of the individual has become recognized as one of the pillars of international law that in past analysis has been obscured by the concentration on the nation-state.

ANCIENT SOURCES OF INTERNATIONAL LAW

Recorded evidence from historical sources, such as the scriptures from India, China and Egypt, confirm the preoccupations of sovereign states to respect and preserve, on a reciprocal basis, basic elementary norms for their mutual survival. For instance, evidence recently has been found of a treaty dating as far back as 1269 B.C. (it is believed to be a peace treaty) whose clear text indicates that it was signed by Huttusillis III, the King of Hittites, and Ramses II, the Egyptian Pharaoh, pledging eternal friendship, lasting peace, territorial integrity, non-aggression, extradition and mutual help.

Similarly, the Indian epic Mahabharata (which includes the Bhagavad Gita), a narrative at least five thousand years old, carries a full chapter describing the role of diplomacy in the conduct of war and the necessity to accord diplomatic immunities to messengers and representatives of the kings sent abroad. These areas of international law today still show a great deal of vitality and a surprising level of compliance. It must, nevertheless, be admitted that the ravages of war, the demise of ancient civilizations, such as those of the Indus, Nile and Harappa and others, no doubt may have deprived history of valuable evidence of the systematic development of much of the ancient international law practiced in those periods. In Europe, in the period of the Greek city-states, the relations between the various communities reveal evidence of international law in practice although it was of limited regional scope. Roman international law was that of the hegemonic model described in the previous chapter by Professor Rapoport.

MODERN SOURCES

The modern development of international law as a distinct discipline goes back, however, only to the period of the formation of the modern state system in Europe during the past five hundred years. This development had a limited precedent taken from the Greek city-states. For example, there evolved legal practices in the relations between the various independent municipalities distinct from the laws followed in their internal relations. This "inter-municipal law" was considered by Professor Paul Vinogradoff to be an important forerunner to the evolution of modern international law. It is an evolution that began during the period, roughly speaking, of the dissolution of the Holy Roman Empire.

The growth of international law was considerably influenced by at least two factors in this period. The role of the Holy Roman Empire as a temporal and political authority was a factor unifying the many feudal states of Europe at that time. The rediscovery of Roman law also influenced the evolution of modern international law concepts.

The feudal structure of most of Western Europe during the medieval period, in fact, facilitated the ability of the Holy Roman Empire and the papacy to exercise enormous influence to play a role in maintaining the unity of Europe. The discovery of the New World, the Renaissance of learning and the Reformation of the prevailing religious stronghold on Europe effectively opened up a new chapter in the conceptual development of modern international law. The evolution of independent secular states necessitated scholars to evolve new theories. The works of French scholar Jean Bodin (1530–1596), the Italian political strategist Machiavelli (1469–1527) and the English writer Thomas Hobbes (1588–1679) were focused principally on the authority, that is, the *sovereignty,* of the state and on theories reconciling those notions with the reality of international law evolving in the relations between them.

The unifying factor of religion in the European feudal system had to give way to take into account the evolution of a community of independent sovereign states. Jurists began to draw upon the "Law of Nature" or natural law notions of a superior authority in order to explain the law governing the relations between nations. Among the early writers who began to write systematically on the interrelationship of the "Law of Nature" and the earlier customs of the Greek city-states, modern notions of Roman law, and the medieval canon law, theology and other disciplines were Spanish writers Vittoria (1480–1546) and Suarez (1548–1617) and the Italian Professor at Oxford, Gentilis (1552–1608). These early seventeenth- and eighteenth-century writings of jurists also bear witness to the influence of political changes taking place in Europe.

POST-WESTPHALIA DEVELOPMENTS

The modern state system began to evolve as a legacy of the Peace of Westphalia (1648) which ended the Thirty Years' War in Europe. Nothing really came close to the powerful influence that religion played in medieval times when that influence was removed after the emergence of independent nation-states in Europe. Among early writers, much of the credit for a systematic formulation of the various fundamental principles as a science of international law goes to the Dutch scholar, jurist and diplomat Huigh de Groot (1583–1645). He produced the first systematic treatise on the subject, a two-volume study entitled De Jure Belli ac Pacis (The Law of War and Peace). De Groot, popularly known as Hugo Grotius and rightly called the father of the modern law of nations, was considerably influenced by the writings of earlier scholars, especially Gentilis and Ayala. It is his classification of the subject and its treatment under various chapter headings that has survived until today in the works of Oppenheim and others.

It is important to understand that the twentieth-century political scene with which we are familiar presents many distinct features that were nonexistent before. For example, there were no formal international institutions or international organizations convened on a regular basis or even on an ad hoc basis. The few occasions when nations of Europe met to adopt a peace treaty or negotiate a regime upon the termination of a war did not evolve any organizational body. However, the post-Westphalia state system, though struggling for the much-needed organizing concepts, did survive to achieve a modicum of stability and order and to permit the community of nations to live in some peace.

These concepts include formal notions of "equality" among states, the notion of "sovereignty" as a manifestation of the ultimate authority within a state unit and so on. The sovereign is traditionally viewed as "supreme," in terms of competence, to do whatever it wants unless it has "agreed" otherwise. While concepts such as these are useful, they are problematic in that it is difficult for the theorist to explain how "the sources of international obligation" or "the binding nature of any international law" arise except by the *consent* of the sovereign state. It can be argued that if the binding character of such a normative system is dependent on the consent of every independently governed state, and if its principal aim is to restrain the sovereign from committing "unjust" wars or violating the basic human rights of its populations, it cannot rest on such a perilous basis as the individual ruler's will, which constantly changes to reflect his or her self-interest. In order to escape this difficulty, the early classical publicists resorted to fundamental notions of natural law as the basis of the authority of international law. This view was, in turn, vigorously challenged as purely transempirical in nature and, therefore, claimed to be invalid by positivist theories of law.

Theories of positivism explain the rationale behind the binding character of international law in terms of the consent of the state given either expressly, as in treaties and international agreements, or implicitly by conduct, as in the case of customary law. However, as Brierly pointed out:

> There need be no mystery about the source of the obligation to obey international law. The same problem arises in any system of law and it can never be solved by a merely juridical explanation. The answer must be sought outside the law and it is for legal philosophy to provide it.[2]

The evolution of international law over the past several centuries lies mostly in the realm of the practical: what activities are acceptable or justifiable and what other actions or activities are unacceptable or unjustifiable in the views of the society taken as a whole. It is but natural that this complex issue arises more sharply in the context of war and use of force than in any other inter-state relationship or activity. The doctrine of just war is but an aspect of the larger question of the just or proper manner of conduct for a sovereign state in any particular type of situation.

MODERN DEVELOPMENTS

Efforts to establish some sort of impartial third-party mechanism for deciding contested state behavior are marked by many to be the beginning of the development of the evolution of modern international law. However, it was only with the peace conferences, at The Hague in 1899 and 1907 that progress toward a peaceful system of institutional resolution of international disputes began to take some concrete form.

LEAGUE OF NATIONS

Those efforts were continued after World War I, culminating in the establishment of such mechanisms within the context of the League of Nations in Geneva (1919). Independently of the establishment of the League, the earlier successful example of the establishment of the Permanent Court of Arbitration at The Hague (1907) gave impetus to the creation of the Permanent Court of International Justice (1926), also at The Hague (in the same building, the "Peace Palace"), which became the precursor to the present International Court of Justice (1945) at the same place.

THE UNITED NATIONS

The establishment, following the end of World War II, of a comprehensive United Nations System changed the course of events in the world today. The Charter of the UN incorporated the Statute of the World Court, thereby making the International Court of Justice the "principal judicial organ of the United Nations" as well as one of the six organs of the United Nations System.

The United Nations brings to bear a half century of experience. These have been years of unprecedented change in international society. The political map of the world has now been redrawn with the emergence of new states, and UN membership now stands at 185 nations. International peace and security is still at risk as a result of the continued reliance on nuclear weapons by major powers and political instability in many of the newly independent states and in the newly democratic Eastern European states. Science and technology have opened up abundant opportunities for rapid resource development, bringing in its wake urgent concerns of environmental quality, preventing pollution and safeguarding the future of the planet itself. Human rights have taken a fundamental and deeper meaning. The role and purpose of international law, thus, remain fundamentally of critical concern in the modern world.

To begin, a brief description of the UN itself and of the UN system is, therefore, in order. The UN itself has six major organs: the General Assembly, the Security Council, the Trusteeship Council, the Economic

and Social Council, the International Court of Justice and the Secretariat.
Related to the UN are 15 organizations, known as "specialized agencies,"
that carry out special functions in technically distinct areas, such as communications, finance, health, environment, labor, science and education
and similar activities. They are independent bodies, each with a separate
constitution and a distinct membership of governments. Some of these,
such as the Universal Postal Union (UPU) (now affiliated with the International Telecommunications Union (ITU)) and the International Labor
Organization (ILO) antedate the establishment of the UN itself. Their
main purpose is, through international cooperation in almost all fields of
human activity, to foster a peaceful international environment. The arenas
of international negotiation and deliberation on these and other global
issues of common concern to all of humanity—both under the auspices of
the United Nations and independently of that body—have thus become
more frequent, and more representative. Today, virtually every sovereign
independent state, whether it is a tiny island, a statelet, a city-state such as
Singapore or a huge territorial unit such as China, is represented in and is
a member of the United Nations. A few non-member states, such as the
Holy See and Switzerland, also participate, as "observers," in the deliberations of the United Nations.

Within the political structure of the UN, the General Assembly of the
United Nations is the largest body, in which each member state is represented. By a one nation-one vote formula, the Assembly, aptly described
as the "town meeting of the world," examines, debates and promotes
global consensus on virtually any and every issue of common concern to
humanity. For many of its smaller and newer members, the Assembly
offers an indispensable arena for establishing contacts and forging common understandings. The Assembly, except under certain specified circumstances, can adopt recommendations but not legally binding
decisions (for example, see Articles 13 and 14 of the Charter of the UN).
In particular, the Charter mandates the General Assembly to consider the
general principles of cooperation in the maintenance of international
peace and security (including the principles governing disarmament and
the regulation of armaments) and to make recommendations with regard
to such principles. In addition, under Article 12, the Assembly is authorized to promote the progressive development of international law in general, and toward that end, in 1948, the International Law Commission was
established.

Unlike the General Assembly, the Security Council of the United
Nations—which has a limited membership of 15, composed of 5 perma-

nent members (China, France, Russia, United Kingdom and United States) and 10 non-permanent members elected periodically every two years by the Assembly—has the primary responsibility of maintaining international peace and security. Chapters VI and VII of the Charter of the UN describe the considerably detailed system established for this purpose. A decision under Chapter VII, especially under Article 39 of the Charter, concerning acts of aggression or violations of Charter principles, entails far-reaching legal consequences. In Chapter VII, the UN envisages a fairly simple system of sanctions for purposes of enforcing the decisions of the Organization, declared under Article 25 of the Charter, as legally binding on *all* member states. The overriding character of decisions made by the Security Council under Chapter VII of the Charter has raised fundamental questions about the need to reform the UN system in general and the decision-making procedures of the Security Council in particular.

However, the decision-making procedures of the Security Council described in Article 27 envisage the collective responsibility of those five permanent members and accords to them a right of veto. The UN's dependence on the unanimity of the five permanent members for its effectiveness arouses at once public disdain for its weakness, as well as hopes that its realistic strength would only prevail when, in the real world of unequal but sovereign independent nations, maintenance of international peace is contingent upon a shared perception of common responsibility and obligation.

This skeletal description of the decision-making apparatus established in the aftermath of the Second World War is sufficient to drive home the crucial fact that prohibition of war as an instrument of national policy is sought to be achieved simultaneously with the establishment of an effective and dependable third-party system for settlement of disputes. The Security Council of the United Nations is designed to serve this purpose and the elaborate provisions in Chapters VI and VII of the Charter were designed to serve that goal. However, the Cold War, ensuing soon after the establishment of the UN, emasculated the initial agreement among the major powers to cooperate and work together in the common interest of preserving international peace and security. The end of the Cold War was hailed as an opportunity to make the original goals feasible.

The past weakness of the UN system, even in the events since the end of the Cold War, means that the global community today still does not have effective mechanisms for peaceful settlement of disputes. The question of the lawfulness of a state's use of force, in the absence of objective fact-finding procedures and impartial decision making, becomes invariably tangled in confusion as to who was attacking (the aggressor) and who was defending (in self-defense) in an armed-conflict situation. Given the purely voluntary nature of international adjudication, invocation of "vital national interests" in defense of questionable conduct or the use of political question doctrine, are often the means by which states shield conflicts from impartial third-party scrutiny. The effectiveness of international legal norms, therefore, remains elusive.

CONCLUSION: TOWARD THE DEMOCRATIZATION OF INTERNATIONAL LAW

One can regard international law in general as the reflection of the conscience of mankind. Thus is the conscience of the king being replaced increasingly by the conscience of mankind. The emergence of non-governmental transnational bodies in recent years is, in part, a response to this weakness of the UN system. It is also due to an awareness that non-state, non-official private organizations and pressure groups whose primary loyalty is to a common cause, rather than to any one or more sovereign state(s), can be highly effective; this has prompted many agencies and institutions to organize across state boundaries. Witness the role of Amnesty International, Greenpeace and the International Committee of the Red Cross in mobilizing world public opinion on issues touching the conscience of the international community. Increasingly, these non-governmental bodies are assuming a legitimate role and, thereby, a meaningful role in the development and implementation of international law norms. "We the Peoples" of the United Nations must take responsibility for our destiny into our own hands if the states, which are supposed to represent us, fail in their responsibilities.

NOTE

1. This question is dealt with at length in the next chapter.

Chapter 3

Carrots, Sticks and Bombs: Securing Disarmament Treaty Compliance without a World Police

A. Walter Dorn[1]
Cornell University

What makes nations comply with agreements they have signed? There is no world police force to monitor, let alone enforce, compliance with international standards. Still, it remains true that most states comply with most of the agreements they have signed most of the time. This history of disarmament treaties since the Second World War provides a suitable example of a set of treaties and patterns of behavior for analysis of state practice. By exploring the issue of state motivations for compliance with disarmament treaties, we can help explain the mechanisms of compliance in general and, hence, find ways to improve upon them.

To begin with, a sense of *national honor* provides the foundation for all treaty compliance, though sometimes it's a rather shaky foundation. Like individuals, nations feel, to a greater or lesser degree, a sense of obligation to live up to their commitments. In international law, this sentiment is summarized in the Latin edict *pacta sunt servanda* (treaties must be respected). The 1925 Geneva Protocol, the first of the modern multilateral disarmament treaties, invokes only such national honor as a compliance provision: the protocol states that it is "a part of International Law, binding alike the conscience and the practice of nations."

Rarely since the end of the Second World War have nations openly disregarded or deliberately ignored treaties to which they are party. Even North Korea, while it was refusing access to inspectors of the International Atomic Energy Agency (IAEA) and thus contravening its obligations under the Non-Proliferation Treaty (NPT), was careful to put forward a series of excuses and thus to claim to be in compliance. True, the excuses were generally invalid, but not once did the isolationist nation say that it had decided to disregard or ignore the treaty. In recent times, Iraq provides the most frequent examples of flagrant treaty violation, but still it has excuses and it claims to be acting lawfully.

This shows the need for an impartial forum to make judgements about whether a state is in compliance or not. Catching and pursuing a nation that is cheating on a treaty requires that the international community first make an objective determination of non-compliance in an authoritative and respected body. The alternative is always weaker—unilateral determinations usually by unfriendly countries. Therefore a fundamental compliance mechanism is *international verification,* the objective determination of compliance by a competent and respected international body. Even when there are no immediate suspicions of treaty violations, impartial verification can help increase confidence. This attitude is embodied in the Russian proverb "trust but verify." It is necessary, however, for states to have faith in the capabilities, technical and managerial, of the international verification organization (IVO) that carries out the monitoring. Also, the verification procedures should be non-discriminatory. A problem often arises in IVOs about how to focus energy, resources and attention on suspected states without being labeled discriminatory. The answer is that the IVO should conduct "baseline" inspections in all states parties in an impartial and equal fashion but, when it has gained credible evidence of a violation, it should conduct in-depth investigations.

The organization must also have a means of publicizing its decisions regarding compliance. The international media, for instance, has closely followed the work of the United Nations Special Commission (UNSCOM), created by the Security Council in 1991 to monitor Iraqi destruction of its weapons of mass destruction. The media coverage has led to increased international attention and understanding, even though the reporting is often biased, inaccurate, incomplete and sensationalistic. Unfortunately, more attention was not paid to the UN Secretary-General's investigations of Iraqi non-compliance in 1984–86, when Iraq used chemical weapons against Iran, in disregard of its obligations under the Geneva Protocol (which it had signed and ratified).

International verification organizations usually rely on the regular submission of reports or declarations by parties on their own activities. In recent disarmament treaties, these are followed by agency inspections whose purpose is to verify the national submissions. But these are not always sufficient to detect non-compliance. Obviously, Israel was not confident in the reports given by Iraq to the International Atomic Energy Agency (IAEA) when it bombed the Osiraq reactor in 1981. In that case, Israeli doubts were well founded, though its unilateral actions remain questionable. Since 1991, the IAEA Director-General has insisted that the IAEA should receive sensitive information if such information/intelligence is in the possession of member states, even if it involves sharing secret satellite reconnaissance. In this way special inspections and more-intrusive procedures can be initiated by the organization.[2]

There remains a great deal of resistance among some nations, notably the United States and the United Kingdom, to give international bodies the right to follow through to the end of the verification process, that is to make a determination of compliance or non-compliance. In the negotiations for a 1993 Chemical Weapons Convention (CWC), the United States insisted, until near the end of the negotiations, on the view that decisions "as to whether a Party is complying" should not be put to a vote in the CWC's administering body, the Organization for the Prohibition of Chemical Weapons.[3] The final text provides that the Conference of the States Parties (CSP) of that organization shall "review compliance with this convention" (Article VIII, para. 20).[4] Still, the United States maintains that, while compliance matters may be discussed, the final decision rests with each state individually. It is difficult to believe, however, that the responsible organs under the CWC (for example, the CSP) will refrain from passing decisions on non-compliance and that these decisions will not be taken as being legally authoritative. A precedent of an international body passing judgement on a disarmament treaty is the IAEA's governing body's declarations in 1991 and 1993 that Iraq and North Korea, respectively, were in violation of their safeguards agreements and hence the NPT (which incorporates the safeguards agreements by reference).[5]

Even when objective verification, the sine qua non of an effective compliance system, is combined with the full force of international condemnation, it may not be sufficient to deter violations. Witness, for instance, the Iraqi violations of the Geneva Protocol verified by an objective source (the UN Secretary-General in ad hoc investigations in 1985–87). While it can be argued that nothing short of military force could have stopped the Iraqi regime, international pressure at a much earlier stage would have been wise and entirely warranted.[6]

Pressure can be of various sorts, most easily categorized as "carrots and sticks." These tools in the hands of the international community are the incentives for compliance (the benefits, or carrots) and disincentives for non-compliance (the penalties, or sticks). Treaties that include provisions for these carrots and sticks become more robust. It is therefore worthwhile to examine in some detail the range of benefits and penalties to be incorporated in treaties or applied in an ad hoc fashion.

Nations may derive *long-term general benefits* from disarmament treaties. In the first place, by joining a treaty regime, they contribute to the establishment and development of international standards of behavior. The presence of order and norms in international affairs is essential for the internal functioning and national security of states. For instance, the CWC, which establishes a global norm against chemical-weapons production, is a concrete step toward removing the threat of chemical attack. Hence, nations will in general feel less threatened and more secure.

In addition, very practical and *specific benefits* can accrue from joining a treaty. The 1963 Partial Test Ban Treaty (PTBT) removed the threat of radioactive fallout in the atmosphere from nuclear weapons tests of the nuclear powers, to the relief of citizens everywhere. The CWC provides that a nation being attacked by chemical weapons may receive assistance from the international community in defending against the attack.

Naturally, the removal of a specific incentive for compliance can be seen as a penalty. States signatory to the Non-Proliferation Treaty (NPT) gain increased access to nuclear technology and by withdrawing from the treaty those benefits will be lost. This can become more complicated, as shown by the case of North Korea. By threatening to withdraw, North Korea actually gained new, presumably safer, nuclear technologies as part of a "$4 billion carrot."[7]

The application of sanctions to redress non-compliance is an important and frequently used form of *penalty* after the end of the Cold War with the "unfreezing" of the Security Council. The sanctions may be economic (for example, boycotts of goods such as oil), financial (freezing foreign accounts), transportation (refusal to land planes in the nation's territory or the creation of no-fly zones), military (for example, arms embargoes), sports/cultural (refusal to permit such interaction) and non-cooperative in a variety of other fashions (for example, suspension of cooperation in research and development). A multi-billion dollar "stick" was used against Iraq in the form of a prohibition of oil exports pending the complete and final destruction of all its weapons of mass destruction. Later, the combined carrot and stick approach was used when Iraq was permitted to sell certain quantities of oil for humanitarian supplies in the UN's "Oil for Food" program.

In other cases, however, the application of sanctions by the Security Council has been shown to be deficient in many ways (see criteria below). The UN Secretary-General cited some difficulties: the "imprecision and mutability" of sanctions as currently practiced by the Security Council, the lack of "objective criteria for determining that their purpose has been achieved," the need to protect innocent victims and to compensate neighboring states or economic partners of targeted countries. The Secretary-General also proposed the development of a mechanism within the UN Secretariat to assess the effects of sanctions before and during their application with the intent of "fine tuning" them.[8] If human ingenuity can produce "smart" bombs to locate small targets, then they should be able to devise "smart" sanctions for maximum effectiveness and minimum collateral damage.

Very few treaties in the disarmament field (or any other area in international law for that matter) give specific penalties for non-compliance.[9] Nations, especially the major powers, have been hesitant to codify international behavior and would prefer the flexibility of responding on a case-by-case basis. Most of the treaties provide for recourse to the UN Security Council, an action that may or may not strike fear in the hearts of leaders of non-complying nations. In particular, the Security Council would be useless in the face of non-compliance by one of the veto-carrying permanent members or any state being protected by one of them.

If the world is to move closer to the rule of law globally, the range of responses to non-compliance will have to be spelled out. Such responses should be guided by the three principles of impartiality[10] (justice is blind), proportionality (severity of punishment is proportional to severity of the crime) and automaticity (application of penalties as soon as a determination of non-compliance has been made).[11]

A fourth principle that should gradually be added to the list is "individuality," or individual accountability. Some would argue that international punishment can never be fair or satisfactory until individuals, as opposed to nations or in addition to them, are made the object of punishment. Shifting from national to individual responsibility would mean that leaders of nations are personally held accountable for the behavior of their nations and those under their command. There's a long way to go on this score, but some powerful precedents are being developed in the human rights field, especially in the war crimes tribunals created for the former Yugoslavia and Rwanda and, more recently, the International Criminal Court.

There is a much easier way to introduce the notion of individual accountability into the disarmament process: by requiring states to pass domestic legislation prohibiting its citizens from violating the provisions of the treaty. The Biological Weapons Convention includes vague wording along these lines, requesting state parties, "in accordance with its constitutional processes, [to] take any necessary measures to prohibit and prevent the development [of biological weapons]." Some states have passed specific legislation (for example, Australia, the Netherlands, the United States) while others have deemed it unnecessary (for example, Canada). The Chemical Weapons Convention goes much further by requiring the enactment of *penal legislation,* for the first time in the history of arms control.[12] The CWC provides that states shall "prohibit natural and legal persons . . . from undertaking any activity prohibited to a State Party under this Convention, including enacting penal legislation . . . " (Article VII, para. 1).

One obvious limitation of mandatory domestic (penal) legislation is that an independent judiciary is necessary for this mechanism to be of any restraining value. In some states, which may also be the most likely to engage in non-compliance, the legal system is unable to pronounce judgement against the wishes of the leader of the state, much less enforce its decisions. However, the requirement for penal legislation may have some effect, if only to embarrass the judiciary or to raise concerns for the future in the minds of the current leaders.[13] Another drawback, which is much less obvious, is that the necessity to enact penal legislation forces some states to delay the ratification proceedings because of the substantial time and effort required to develop all the legislation.[14] However, this process of increasing complexity is something that we should welcome despite the difficulties.

These then are the fundamental compliance mechanisms: objective verification, incentives and punishments and domestic implementation provisions (especially penal legislation). Other, perhaps less important, compliance mechanisms can be briefly discussed, but the following is by no means an exhaustive list.

Graduated exposure. Once non-compliance is suspected, the process usually follows a typical scenario: *consultation* with the suspected party, formal recommendations in a governing body, possible demands for on-site inspections, increased *public exposure, referral* to the UN Security Council, collective measures (perhaps) or last-minute solution (for example, the North Korean-United States bilateral agreement in 1993). These measures are provided for in almost all of the treaties signed since 1967. More precise means of graduated exposure are not usually specified in treaties. This is an area where in-depth academic study could be very helpful—using precedents in other areas of international law (for example, in labor conventions and the International Labour Organization).

Domestic implementing agency. By including in the treaty provision that each state party must establish or designate an agency within the government to be responsible for overseeing national compliance and for liaison with the international verification organization, a constituency within the government is created that is formally, at least, committed to upholding the treaty and promoting its smooth operation. Alternatively, the implementing body may provide a means for observing a lack of commitment after inquiries and requests have been made by the international organization. Such a "National Authority," as it is called in the CWC, can also be expected to help facilitate inspections and to become involved in the licensing process (for example, of dual-use chemicals).

Dispute settlement mechanisms. A prime example is referral to the International Court of Justice. When mechanisms are provided, then minor irritants, such as some differences in treaty interpretation, can usually be overcome without involving an international tragedy or an escalation of tension, or in the worst case, the outright abrogation of—or withdrawal from—the treaty.

Amendment and review provisions. If a state feels that the provisions of the treaty are unjust or require modification, there should be a mechanism for amendment and for treaty review conferences where, at the least, such views can be voiced. Review conferences of the Biological Weapons Convention, held every five years, have helped further transparency and confidence-building measures. Withdrawal clauses. Provisions for withdrawal are often included in treaties and may provide some benefits. First, they may serve as an incentive for a nation to sign a treaty since it would not feel trapped indefinitely, especially when it can withdraw when "its supreme national interests are jeopardized." Second, there may be restraints on withdrawal. For instance, the Non-Proliferation Treaty (NPT) has a three-month time lag between the declaration of withdrawal and the date upon which it takes effect. Recently, this provision provided much-valued time for the international community to exert pressure on North Korea to prevent that nation from withdrawing.[15]

In the twenty-first century, the international community will have many new opportunities to make the treaties more robust with the inclusion of a range of novel and evolving compliance mechanisms. In this way, we can hope that international law will gradually acquire the force of national law and be more strictly monitored, enforced and obeyed. This brief overview shows that there is a range of tools or mechanisms that can be used to promote compliance in the absence of a world police force. Such a force may, however, be necessary eventually if nations are to carry out deep reductions in their armaments and defenses and if the stated goal of "general and complete disarmament under strict and effective control" is to be genuinely achieved.

NOTES

1. With acknowledgement to the stimulating discussions held in the Markland Group, especially its President, Doug Scott, over many years. See also the book by Markland Group members: D. Scott, G. Alexandrowicz, W. Dorn, M. Greenspoon, J. Hatfield-Lyon and G. Morris, *Disarmament's Missing Dimension: A UN Agency to Administer Multilateral Treaties* (Science for Peace/Samuel Stevens, Toronto, 1990).

2. See Statement of Dr. Hans Blix, United States Senate Committee on Foreign Relations, *Hearings before the Committee on Foreign Relations,* 102nd Cong., 1st sess. (S. Hrg. 102–422), October 17 and 23, 1991, U.S. Government Printing Office, Washington, DC. There has been substantial opposition from member states to the idea of establishing a new information unit within the IAEA Secretariat and the idea was shelved. Rather, the current

approach is "to treat such cases pragmatically in the context of [IAEA] work in the Safeguards Department, in relation also to the Director-General's own office" (Letter from David R. Kyd, Public Information Director, to Andrew Fulton, October 27, 1994).

3. "The report of a fact-finding inquiry should not be put to a vote, nor should any decision be taken as to whether a Party is complying with the provisions of the Convention"; UN Doc. CD/500, Annex 1.A.5. This wording was carried over into the Rolling Text as a footnote, e.g., CD/1116 of January 20, 1992 (Art. VIII, para. 20(d), footnote 2).

4. Furthermore, the Executive Council "shall consider . . . concerns regarding compliance, and cases of non-compliance, and, as appropriate, inform States Parties and bring the issue or matter to the attention of the Conference" (Art. VIII, para. 35).

5. The Board of Governors declared Iraq in non-compliance with its safeguards agreement on July 18, 1991, based on a report of the Director-General (GOV/2530), which drew the same conclusion. In a similar manner, North Korean non-compliance was determined on April 1, 1993 (GOV/2645).

6. In 1984 and 1985, when Iraq was found by the Security Council to have used chemical weapons and therefore to have violated the Geneva Protocol, there were no serious efforts made to punish Iraq, which was considered at the time an "ally of the West" in the front against Islamic Iran. See also note 9.

7. A case study of the international community's efforts to secure North Korean compliance with the NPT is reviewed in A. Walter Dorn and Andrew Fulton, "Securing Compliance with Disarmament Treaties: Carrots, Sticks and the Case of North Korea," *Global Governance,* 3 (1997), p. 17.

8. UN Secretary-General, "Supplement to an Agenda for Peace: Position Paper of the Secretary-General on the Occasion of the Fiftieth Anniversary of the United Nations," UN Doc. S/1995/1 of January 3, 1995. A brief summary and commentary was provided in the *Globe and Mail* on January 6, 1995.

9. The Non-Proliferation Treaty and the Chemical Weapons Conventions are the two main examples. In those cases penalties include the loss of rights and privileges under the Convention.

10. This would involve, for instance, increased use of the International Court of Justice.

11. To his (very rare) credit, Senator Jesse Helms (R-N.C.) proposed in 1985 that the U.S. impose sanctions automatically on any state caught using chemical weapons. In 1988, French President Francois Mitterand proposed that the UN endorse an international embargo of "products, technologies, and . . . weapons" against any such state (*Washington Post,* September 30, 1988, p. A21).

12. There are notable precedents of mandatory penal legislation to be found in the Torture Convention, the Genocide Convention and the 1949 Geneva Conventions.

13. It might also be noted that, in some states (e.g., Canada), legislation is not binding on government officials unless it contains a clause that specifies that the legislation is "binding on the Crown."

14. The CWC entered into force in April 1996, 180 days after the sixty-fifth ratification had been deposited.

15. North Korea suspended its notice of withdrawal one day before it was to take effect.

Chapter 4

Economic Bases for World Order: Corporate Capitalism and/or Market Socialism?

Myron J. Gordon[1]
University of Toronto

The world order that emerges in the next century will depend materially on its economic foundations. The great debate over the last 150 years has been over the comparative merits of a pure capitalist and a pure socialist system. The former relies of private ownership and markets to control and coordinate economic activity. The latter relies on public ownership and bureaucracy. Both have failed in practice. England in the middle of the 19th century, and other countries after it, turned to a system of welfare capitalism that is now being transformed into corporate capitalism.

In this chapter I examine the main features and consequences of six economic systems. Two are the theories of a pure capitalist system and a pure socialist system. Another two are the actual performances of pure capital-

ist and pure socialist systems. The last two systems are a welfare-corporate capitalist system and a market socialist system. These last two are
systems that we now enjoy or suffer depending on your point of view, and
variations on them are what the future is likely to bring. Our understanding of these two systems is served by first considering the other four, and
we will do that first.

PURE CAPITALIST AND SOCIALIST SYSTEMS

The two main distinguishing features of a pure capitalist system are (a)
private ownership of the means of production, and (b) reliance on markets
for the administration of the economy. By contrast, a pure socialist system has (a) public ownership of the means of production, and (b) reliance
on a bureaucracy to administer the economy. Neoclassical (that is, establishment) economists have constructed a theory of a perfectly competitive
capitalist system that is a utopia. Everyone is free to buy, produce and
work at whatever she wants. All wage and profit rates are fair. There is no
unemployment, insecurity, and so on. Similarly, establishment socialist
economists in the former Soviet Union have constructed the theory of a
pure socialist system that also is a utopia.

Both groups of economists recognize that the real world falls short of
their respective utopias. Neoclassical economists tell us that the gap is due
to market imperfections. In doing so they offer us a more attractive vision
of the future than the great theologians. The latter, with few exceptions,
recognize that human imperfections make a heaven on Earth practically
impossible, but neoclassical economists assure us that heaven on Earth
requires only that we overcome market imperfections. I presume that the
establishment economists in the former Soviet Union claimed that their
utopia required only that imperfections in the bureaucracy be overcome.

THE EVOLUTION OF ACTUAL CAPITALIST SYSTEMS

In fact, neither pure system has existed in practice for any length of time,
and neither is a viable option for the future. To see why that is so, and to
understand what options we really have, we must look at each of these
systems within the context of their historical development. European capitalism had its origins in feudal society. Feudalism in Europe arose in the
centuries following the fall of the Roman Empire, to provide security

against the raids of marauding tribes. Tribalism was the alternative economic system at the time. The typical feudal manor was a closed system that also provided economic security through its technology of production and social arrangements. However, the agricultural surplus that increased with the progress of feudal society was realized most effectively through the rise of capitalism. That is, the surplus was converted to armaments, jewelry and other manufactures through sale to the towns with their market economy. The towns in turn financed the rise of national monarchs and eventually nation-states; in other words, the progress of feudal society required the relative growth of capitalism. The contradictions in this process transformed, corrupted and ultimately destroyed feudal society. It culminated in the transition to capitalism between the fifteenth and eighteenth centuries, a unique and remarkable event, since that transition did not occur under roughly similar circumstances in other places. One striking example of the transition not occurring is seventeenth-century China.[2]

Capitalism is a very effective engine of economic growth, but it is also a terrible engine of economic insecurity, and without high growth the insecurity is intolerable. This insecurity was moderated during the transition from feudalism to capitalism, both by the growth made possible by the transition and by the cushion provided by the underlying feudal society. The transition was completed in Great Britain by about 1850, and by that date the country was to come as close as it ever was to having a pure competitive capitalist system. Feudalism was gone and the welfare state had not been established. About 1850, Charles Dickens's novels and Karl Marx's *Capital,* each in its own way, described the consequences of that system for the mass of the people. Marx drew his information from the reports of parliamentary committees on child labor, the employment of women, and the housing and health of the people. These reports warned that unless drastic corrective action was taken, the British working class would be physically destroyed by the competitive capitalist system that was in place.

Over the years 1850 to 1950, the leading capitalist countries suffered both the privation and insecurity of fluctuations in employment and output, and periodic wars of increasing scale. However, the dominant story was the rise of the welfare state, the extraordinary growth in prosperity for both capitalist and worker, and the phenomenal growth in the managerial and professional middle class. The private arrangements to find economic security proved to be unsatisfactory, and social security was found in numerous ways, including pension plans, unemployment compensation, socialized medicine and public housing. Progressive taxation and full-employment expenditure policies, undertaken to increase aggregate demand, were among the other features of the welfare state. Toward the end of this period, the theoretical rationale for the welfare state and its related developments were discovered by the great econmist John M. Keynes. The formal recognition and acceptance of the welfare state, due to Keynes, made the years 1945 to 1970 a golden age in capitalist development. It was a period of stability and growth, rising expectations and their realization.

THE MODERN CORPORATION AND WELFARE-CORPORATE CAPITALISM

The 1970s, however, inaugurated a reversal in the rise of the welfare state. The leading capitalist countries have since experienced various combinations of high unemployment rates, high inflation rates, unprecedented government deficits and increasing inequality. The experience of the Third World countries and the countries of the former Soviet Union has been far worse. Now more than ever, the rich get richer and the poor get poorer. The progress of technology seems to contribute more to ravishing the environment than protecting it, particularly in the Third World. The internationalization of real and financial capital proceeds at a breathtaking pace, and the ability of national governments to manage their economies in the interest of their people declines correspondingly. The buzzwords are globalization, downsizing and the end of work.

The causal factor in all of these developments has been the rise of the modern corporation. The eighteenth and nineteenth century enterprises of Adam Smith and Karl Marx had the factory and its offices located in the same or in adjoining buildings. Over the last century the progress in travel, transportation, communication, data processing and in the practice of management have resulted in the global corporation. It participates in all of the world's important markets, while moving production almost at will from one low-wage country to another in order to minimize production cost.

Perhaps more important, the primary if not sole activity of the enterprises of the eighteenth and nineteenth century was production. The modern corporation, by contrast, engages primarily in a wide range of non-production activities in pursuit of monopoly power. These activities include research and development for the purpose of improving existing products, discovering new products and reducing production costs. They include selling and advertising to increase sales and the markup of price over production costs. They include labor relations to persuade or intimidate workers to produce more or accept lower wages. They include political contributions, lobbying and corruption of government officials in order to obtain natural resources on favorable terms and other favors of government. They include the employment of lawyers, accountants and financiers to avoid and evade taxes and to influence tax legislation. I could go on. These activities may be harmless apart from their cost and their consequences for the distribution of income. They may be beneficial or they may be malignant in their consequences for society. Regardless, what they all have in common is the pursuit of the profits to be gained from monopoly power.

The importance of these monopoly activities is illustrated quite dramatically by looking at the financial statements of Microsoft, a leading high-technology company. For the year ending in June 1997, it had sales revenue of $11.358 billion, while the labor and material cost of producing the products sold was only $1.085 billion. The cost of research and development was $1.925 billion, while sales and marketing expenses were almost 50 percent larger at $2.856 billion. General and administration expenses came to $362 million, and income before deducting income taxes was $5.314 billion. Notice that the labor and material cost of producing the goods sold during the year was less than 10 percent of the value of those goods, while the expenditures to maintain and increase its monopoly power came to 45 percent of sales revenue, and profits amounted to 47 percent of sales revenue. The profit of over $5 billion was earned with an investment in inventory, equipment and buildings of less than $2 billion. The market value of Microsoft's common stock was over $160 billion, reflecting the extraordinary growth opportunities created by its monopoly power.

Microsoft is only a somewhat extreme example of the costs incurred and the profits generated in the pursuit of monopoly power by the large modern corporation. The measure of monopoly power, called the *degree of monopoly,* is the ratio of value added to the wages of production workers. Value added is sales volume, less the cost of the materials used in production. The Annual Survey of Manufactures of the U.S. Bureau of Census collects these data. Over the years 1899 to 1949, the degree of monopoly in the manufacturing sector of the U.S. economy fluctuated in a narrow range around 2.5. Over the years 1949 to 1994, it rose dramatically to 5.2. In 1994, production cost accounted for only 20 cents of every dollar of profit. Profit on capital and the cost of monopoly activities absorbed the other 80 cents. The system we now live in may be called welfare-corporate capitalism. Under it, the role of the state in providing for the welfare of the population is gradually diminishing, while the role of the corporation in generating growth, monopoly profits, inequality and unemployment is expanding. It is to be hoped that this process is cyclical and not secular, and a desirable balance between the two forces can be achieved. Recent election results in England, Germany and elsewhere suggest that is what the people want.

MARKET SOCIALISM: THE CHINESE MODEL

Let us now consider the historical development of market socialism in China. For over a hundred years prior to 1949, when a socialist government came to power in China, rule by imperialist foreign governments and provincial warlords had reduced the country to a state of poverty, corruption, violence and degradation that defied description. Over the next five years, the new government moved rapidly toward a pure socialist system. Ownership of practically all wealth was transferred to the government, and a bureaucracy determined the production and distribution of output. These changes accomplished wonders in terms of equality of income, full employment, and improvements in education, health care and other services. Production of basic commodities such as grain, cloth and steel also increased dramatically.

However, the progress that took place under this centralized bureaucratic system made further progress increasingly difficult. A modern economy requires hundreds, no, thousands, of different types of steel, and even greater variety in cloth, food and other classes of products. Growth and technological progress required change. A central bureaucracy could not possibly acquire all of the information needed to administer the economy effectively. This was particularly true under the primitive state of Chinese technology in travel, communication, data processing and enterprise management. It also could not bring about a high rate of technological progress, since central control required that workers and managers do only what they were told to do: the freedom and motivation to improve, innovate, or work harder would disrupt the system. The Great Leap Forward and the Cultural Revolution were disastrous attempts to catch up with the West within the framework of a pure socialist system.

In 1978 China decided to expand the role of the market in administering the economy without giving up government ownership. It also decided to acquire technology and to some degree capital from the West through joint ventures, wholly owned foreign companies and private enterprise. What were the consequences of this decision?[3]

In agriculture, the use but not the ownership of the land has been privatized. In this way each peasant family cannot be separated from the income from its plot of land. The security of state ownership was combined with the material incentives of the market, and the result was spectacular. Prior to 1978 the growth rate in agricultural production was about 2.1 percent per annum, little more than the population growth rate. Since then the growth rate has been over 6 percent and now all but a small fraction of the Chinese people eat well. In addition, the movement of peasants to the city has only been as fast as they could be absorbed without undue hardship.

The high infrastructure investment and low productivity of urban industry made it unprofitable to expand urban industry at a higher rate than the natural growth rate in the urban population. Consequently industry was brought to the countryside. Employment in township and village enterprises rose from 22 million in 1978 to 135 million in 1996. The quality and quantity of the output have improved correspondingly. In bringing industry to the countryside Deng Xiaoping succeeded where Mahatma Gandhi and Mao Zedong failed. Now more than half the families in the countryside have income from township and village enterprises or urban employment in addition to farm income. The increased prosperity of the peasant families near the big cities and along the coastal plain has been stunning.

The story with regard to urban state enterprises is mixed. Total output has grown impressively, but about half the enterprises by number suffer losses that are absorbed by the state. One reason is their failure to modernize. Another is that redundant workers and poor managers are dismissed only as fast as they can be absorbed elsewhere in the economy. These enterprises, as well as the profitable ones, continue to pay generous pensions and other benefits. Policies to curtail or make profitable these enterprises are being developed slowly and carefully. It has not been found possible to transform the equipment, technology and management of *all* of Chinese industry in one generation.[4] Consequently, joint ventures and private enterprises grow faster and lead the way in importing foreign technology.

In aggregate, the prosperity of the urban as well as the rural population is increasing at an impressive rate. Civil rights as well as human rights have also improved significantly over these years. China is still a poor country, and its people do not have the civil rights that exist in wealthy capitalist countries. Furthermore, the inequality of income, crime, prostitution and corruption that we find in capitalist market systems have also increased considerably. However, their levels do not approach what we observe in Indonesia, India, Egypt, Brazil and other large Third World countries. Most important, China does not have the widespread grinding poverty and the private and unofficial violence against the poor that exists in so many countries.

What is going on in China may, as some claim, be nothing more than a transition to capitalism, so that within 25 years China will be a capitalist country that enjoys the blessing of the United States. It is also possible that China and some other countries will find market socialism an attractive long-run alternative to welfare-corporate capitalism. It is to be hoped that this great social experiment can continue without being aborted by foreign intervention.

THE FUTURE

The previous pages make clear that at present I can see nothing beyond welfare-corporate capitalism and market socialism as the economic systems through which the world order will evolve over the next century. However, the path each of these systems will follow is by no means certain. With respect to welfare-corporate capitalism, welfare and not the corporation must become the prime concern. In Southeast Asia, Russia and other countries of the former Soviet Union, as well as practically all of South America and Africa, we see the terrible consequences of the subordination of national governments and their concern for the welfare of their people to multinational corporations. Even some establishment economists now recognize that the complete international mobility of real and financial capital must be restricted.[5] Far more restriction is needed. The participation of multinational corporations in the markets of a country and in the extraction of its natural resources must be controlled by that country in its national interest. The failure of a country to pursue its national interest wisely and efficiently is no justification for submitting to the sovereignty of foreign corporations. They invariably support corrupt and inefficient governments in the Third World.

Our concern for the environment and the quality of life is also served by subordinating the corporation to national welfare and control. We have seen how the modern corporation is driven by a growth imperative. The inequality, unemployment and greed fostered by that growth imperative imposes it on the countries in which they operate and overrides concern for the environment and quality of life.

China, no less than the countries of the West, perhaps even more so, is subject to a growth imperative. Its growth over the past 20 years has been the highest among the large and important countries, and the consequences for the environment have not been good. These developments raise a number of questions. Has China gone too far in sacrificing the socialist concern for equality, security and the quality of life? Is the subordination of all other concerns to growth the inevitable consequence of *market* socialism, or are there other explanations?[6] The answers to these questions may become clearer only with the passage of time.

NOTES

1. The ideas presented here are developed in greater detail in M. J. Gordon, "China's Path to Market Socialism," *Challenge: The Magazine of Economic Affairs,* January-February 1992, pp. 53-56, and in the last chapter of M. J. Gordon, *Finance Investment and Macroeconomics: The Neoclassical and Post-Keynesian Solution* (Aldershot, Eng.: E. Elgar, 1994).

2. This transition from feudalism to proprietor capitalism, and its evolution to the welfare-corporate capitalism we have today, is described in greater detail in the last chapter of Gordon, *Finance, Investment and Macroeconomics.*

3. The consequences are described in greater detail Gordon, "China's Path to Market Socialism," and in Myron J. Gordon, Yue Li, and Zhilong Tian, "The Future of Market Socialism in China," in *Taxation in Modern China,* ed. Donald Brean. (New York: Routledge, 1998).

4. Periodically, the government announces that it will accelerate the elimination of unprofitable enterprises, even at the cost of large-scale unemployment. Workers at unprofitable enterprises are now facing sharper reductions in compensation in order to encourage progress. However, there is little increase in the outright unemployment experienced in Third World capitalist countries. Few of the unprofitable companies are actually driven into bankruptcy.

5. The Chief Economist of the World Bank is among the economists who have come out for restrictions on capital mobility. See Joseph Stiglitz, *More Instruments and Broader Goals: Moving Toward the Post-Washington Consensus,* World Institute for Development Economics Research, United Nations University (Helsinki: 1998).

6. In this connection, it should be noted that concern for national independence

and security may contribute materially to China's desire for growth. When China looks abroad, it sees large U.S. military bases in South Korea, Japan, Okinawa and the Philippines. It sees the United States cultivate relations with Taiwan, Vietnam and other countries of the region. It hears powerful voices in the United States shed crocodile tears about human rights in China and call for the "liberation" of Taiwan and Tibet from Chinese oppression. China's leaders may see economic development as a means for maintaining national independence and security.

Chapter 5

World Order by Trade and Investment Decree: The Global Corporate System

John McMurtry
*Department of Philosophy,
University of Guelph*

For many years, the primary block to a just world peace seemed to be the Cold War and the dominance of the military paradigm in waging it. The military institution's arms-race priorities and bottomless financial demands cut across the warring Soviet and U.S. empires as a common pathological structure—draining public treasuries, terrorizing the world's peoples with global nuclear devastation, and killing and maiming Third World civilians as the actual victims of armed-force attack.[1]

Now the Cold War is over. Only one military superpower remains, and like Hobbes's Leviathan, it appears to have maintained a Hobbesian state of international peace. The long nightmare of permanent nation-state conflict by means of threats and campaigns of competitive mass homicide has, at the end of the second millennium, given way to multilateral trade and investment agreements. World order has emerged from a century of massacre on the basis of open and equal market competition. Or so it seems.

So pervasively have the images of a "new world order" been borne across the world by the corporate mass media that normally thoughtful people have come to assent to this one-sided tale—as if in the accommodating hope that international power holders have learned at last to compete across borders without sacrificing the lives of masses of ordinary people.

I suspect that Mikhail Gorbachev was led by this vision, and it is certainly evident that many intelligent anti-war citizens have been similarly influenced. John Kenneth Galbraith, for example, has regretted that in recent years "the rich have won the war against the poor," but advises that "we must live with the [rising] divergences in wealth and income" of the transnational market system because globalization "reduces tensions between countries" and "has a positive influence on employment in [poorer] countries."[2]

THE SHADOW SIDE OF THE END OF THE COLD WAR

What is not recognized by this dominant acceptance of corporate capital's triumph in the Cold War is its shadow meaning—that when one side of a superpower contest collapses, the other side is left in a vacuum of no resistance to the prescription of its agenda across the globe.

The development of a civil commons of social programs after 1945 in virtually every society across the world was never an intrinsic element of this capitalist agenda. Subsidized food and lodging, livable minimum wages, socialized health care, universal pensions, income security and social assistance, free higher education, public broadcasting, policed environmental controls, workplace and occupational safety, and legislated secure employment were never really accepted by the corporate sector, but were generally seen as "interferences in the free market" and "socialist." They were accepted because they were believed to be "necessary to show that capitalism has a conscience" and proof that a free-market system could "beat the Reds at their own game." The tremendous growth of national social programs after the World War II was always in the context of this all-out competition with the communist bloc or other social alternative. It demonstrated that capitalism was not only better for those who had money to invest, but also better for society's wage workers and the poor.

Another feature of the pre-1989 world was that the markets, natural resources and built infrastructures of nations were not unconditionally open to foreign corporate exploitation and control "free of national barriers." In ideology at least, access to host societies' wealth by dominant foreign corporations was to be negotiated with the countries concerned on an asset-by-asset basis. Investing transnational corporations had to promise some substantial economic benefits to these societies to be given market shares in their economies, to be awarded the right to extract their valuable natural resources, and to access or buy their built heritages and physical infrastructure with the same rights as native citizens. Unless the relationship was colonial occupation, there were returns they had to guarantee in exchange for these enormously valuable rights—reinvestment of a percentage of profits in the host society, domestic job creation equivalent in value to sales (as in the Canada-United States Auto Agreement), and technology transfer in the area of manufacture, depending on the domestic asset that was to be exposed to foreign takeover, exploitation or control.

Again, these terms of access to other societies' markets, environmental resources and industrial infrastructure were not terms that transnational corporations chose on their own, or even agreed with in principle. Just as the non-priced goods of the social sector violated the basic principles of unfettered market doctrine, so did the demand that both public-sector control and costs of production be increased by "performance requirements" imposed by host societies. These terms were seen as based on a "protectionist" premise and—more to the point—they very substantially increased cost inputs for investing corporations and left host societies with the power to require corporations to comply with their domestic interests, or be denied access to their wealth and resources.[3]

"Protectionism," a concept whose meaning bears reflection, is second only to the evil of socialism in corporate ideology. Communism is beyond the pale. All are firmly believed to be best eradicated.

Nevertheless, societies' control of their own markets and their natural and physical capital, which enabled performance requirements to be negotiated with foreign corporations, were tolerated in the conditions of a world competition of alternative social paths. If domestic economies had been simply taken over by foreign corporations with no limit to their exploitation of host societies' natural resources, buyout of their economies, and expatriation of their profits, home populations might well have come to the conclusion that corporate capitalism was not in their interests and opted for another social alternative. In consequence, negotiated terms of access to the markets, natural wealth and strategic assets of domestic economies evolved in the years of social model competition, and no war was declared on these "mixed economies" by big business. But this evolution of the civil commons in the twentieth century turned out to be a temporary concession. After the Cold War, social programs and performance requirements for transnational capital were attacked without letup as "protectionist," "discriminatory" and "barriers to free trade." A "new world order" was pervasively promoted as "inevitable" and "the only alternative."

Social programs were defunded and stripped by a process of public-sector bankrupting—ironically, the same strategy as was deployed to bring down the Soviet Union. With the one, an arms race that could not be paid for was the strategy. With the other, the bankrupting of government proceeded by three avenues: accumulating compound interest on public debts by military-binge expenditures, unprecedented interest-rate increases by central banks, and steep tax reductions for corporations and high-income individuals. Together, these emptied public treasuries and stacked up public debts to such levels that not even the interest could be paid without raising annual deficits. The new condition of unpayable public debt was blamed throughout on "excessive social spending," though rises in social programs typically accounted for less than 10 percent of the debt increase.[4]

So at the end of the century, an unopposed corporate agenda had "structurally adjusted" the world into a condition in which social sectors and independent powers of elected governments had been more or less effectively reduced to impotence across the world. This was a "triumph of capitalism" that was more important than the victory over the alien Soviet system, for it broke the financial capacities of societies to further develop or even maintain their social programs and—through new "free trade" treaties—removed the rights of public authority to negotiate terms for access to their markets and resources.

REPLACING RESPONSIBLE GOVERNMENT BY THE
CORPORATE AGENDA: THE PURE-TYPE MODEL OF
THE MULTILATERAL AGREEMENT ON INVESTMENT

The loss of society's right to develop independent social sectors and to negotiate the terms of foreign corporate access to its domestic wealth was, in 1998, a still largely hidden underside of "the global market revolution." When peoples awake to it, they are likely to demand that the governments that represent them regain their societies from transnational corporate control. This is why there has been such a flurry of transnational trade and investment treaties since 1989 to lock all the nations of the globe into the new system. The North American Free Trade Agreement (NAFTA), the World Trade Organization (WTO) and the 1992 Maastricht Treaty of Europe (prescribing borderless capital movement and the control of national monetary and fiscal policy by a central bank accountable to no elected body)[5] are the three lead prongs of this new global corporate system.

But one might never have known the full dimensions of the corporate agenda had not the WTO initiated through the transnational Organization for Economic Cooperation and Development (OECD) the omnibus trade and investment regime calling itself the Multilateral Agreement on Investment (MAI), whose secretly negotiated structure was leaked in February of 1997.

The MAI was a creature of the WTO, which regulates the world's trade but not its investment. The MAI had as its initial purpose the legal binding of all 29 nations of the Paris-based OECD to an unconditional trade *and* investment regime that could not be altered. Once signed by the world's leading economies, it was to be extended to all WTO countries, as a condition of continued investment in their countries. Where NAFTA could be abrogated on 6 months notice, the MAI would require first 5, and then 15 years of compliance with no right to leave.

What the MAI sought to add to already existing WTO regulations was a sweeping new power. In addition to the WTO-granted right of transnational corporations to the *movement* of their commodities across national borders with no recourse of societies to limit this access to their markets, the MAI sought to add the further unconditional right to directly *own and control* the internal economies of host societies with no limiting condition permissible under law.

Overall, the MAI is governed by the same one-sided logic of corporate rule that we have witnessed since the Canada-United States Free Trade Agreement of 1989. Its goal is to institute a global regulatory framework that overrides all national, regional and municipal jurisdictions, policies and statutes wherever they conflict with the right of foreign corporate ownership of and market access to everything of economic value in host economies across the world.

The sole focus of the MAI and whatever form it assumes next is the protection of the rights of foreign capital. No other rights are recognized.

The master principle of the model is the blanket right to "national treat-ment" of transnational corporations in host societies. Under the terms of the MAI's prototype structure, foreign corporations must never be "dis-criminated against" by any government on any level on any account, such as their contribution to the well-being of the host society. Serving the interests of the home society is deemed protectionist by the logic of this model and therefore, is unacceptable.

To accomplish the full color of this blanket right to the internal wealth of all societies across all borders and existing legal frameworks, a re-engineering of the affected societies is required. Accordingly, the pro-totype MAI inscribed in its detailed articles the possession by transna-tional corporations to the following unabridgable rights, concealed beneath a trade-lawyer jargon that few have sought to penetrate:[6]

- to export their commodities or services across all borders of locale or nation to other societies' markets with no conditions attached;
- to unilaterally purchase and own any built structure or produc-tive capacity of any other signatory nation with no requirement to sustain its viability, employment level or location in the home country;
- to own any salable natural resource of other countries and to have national right to any concession, license or authorization to extract its oil, forest, mineral or other resources with no obliga-tion to sustain these resources, or to use them in the interest of the host society;
- to profit from any commercial enterprise with no requirement to reinvest in the enterprise or any other enterprise in the country in which the resources have been received and the profits earned;
- to create credit and thus increase domestic money supply with no restriction on the amount of new currency demand so created in the host economy, however inflationary to the economy or bankrupting to domestic citizens;
- to bid for and own any privatized public infrastructure, social good or cultural transmission without any limit of foreign con-trol permitted by law;
- to access any domestic government grant, loan, tax incentive or subsidy with the same rights as any domestic firm with no means test, locale requirement or public-interest distinction permitted;
- to be free of any and all performance requirements of job cre-

ation, domestic purchase of goods, import-export reciprocation, and technology or knowledge transfer to the host society;
- to repel as illegal any national standards of human rights, labor rights or environmental protection on goods produced in and imported from other regions or nations. (This process protection disqualifies as discriminatory even packaging information that reports to consumers the method of manufacture of what they eat.)[7]

If any one of these sweeping rights for transnational corporations is denied as an entailment of the MAI program or the larger world corporate agenda it embodies, the testing response to the denial is: Which of these blanket rights is limited, and by what binding article? It is only in this way that the fog of obfuscation and rhetoric cultivated around this system of transnational coup d'etat can be penetrated.

CORPORATE RIGHTS TO RULE, PUBLIC OBLIGATIONS TO OBEY

Under the proposed prototype for future corporate world order, all provision by domestic governments of goods to their citizens by public ownership or control are construed as monopolies. Monopolies of knowledge by corporate copyright, in contrast, are specially excepted as non-monopolies. This double standard is significant because monopoly designation entails special legal restrictions on pricing and distribution of goods that would be "an interference with business freedom to transact" on private corporations. Any public non-profit monopoly in health care, education or other universally accessible life good is, therefore, to be bound by the obligation to act "solely in accordance with commercial considerations in the purchase or sale of its good or service" ; in particular to be prevented from the "abusive use of prices" that might adversely affect the market share of foreign corporations; and, in general, to be liable for damages for any "lost opportunity to profit from a planned investment" that might be incurred by public involvement in providing citizens with goods in which private foreign corporations could assert a market interest.

Worker buyouts of enterprises, or return of their ownership to host-society investors, are, moreover, not to be permitted any favorable loan, tax or start-up cost by public authority, since this would constitute a "discriminatory treatment against foreign investors." "Educational products" as well as any other product, except military—the one article of trade

given full protectionist walls by this and other recent trade-and-invest-
ment treaties—are also prohibited from any limit on foreign control or
domination. Any requirement for long-term commitment of investment in
any strategic area, such as the nation's natural resources or high-employ-
ment sector, are, moreover, forbidden. Any other condition that reduces
the right of foreign transnationals to move their profits and assets from
the home society to other jurisdictions with lower environmental, labor,
corporate-tax or safety standards is likewise prohibited by this transnational framework of new world law.

The regulating principle of these blanket rights and powers to be
granted carte blanche to private, transnational corporations is that no
social life-host has under them the legal right to protect the ownership or
control of its markets, its built assets, its environmental resources or its
public-sector provision of life goods to its citizens if any of these limit
transnational corporate rights to profit from them.

To avoid protests by citizens against such a one-sided bill of rights to
transnational corporations at the expense of societies' established right to
govern themselves, the MAI's planning and drafting were not reported by
any government or, with rare exception, any mass media in any of the 29
countries involved, including Britain, France and Canada during their
national election campaigns. To round out its assertion of overriding
rights to multinationals at public expense, all the costs of this new regime
to privilege transnational corporations above governments and elec-
torates—that is, the costs of its planning, negotiation, enforcement, adjudication *and* liabilities for infraction—like all other institutions of this
global corporate agenda, are to be paid for out of the public purse.[8]

CONCLUSION

The general logic of overriding the established sovereignty of nations is
complemented in the new global corporate system by a systematic exclusion of human rights and evolved environmental standards. The President
of the U.S. Council for International Business made this position clear in a
letter to U.S. officials on March 21, 1997: "We will oppose any and all measures to create or even imply binding obligations for governments or business related to the environment and labour." [9] It is important to understand
this business-led refusal to recognize human or other life rights in the context of the internationally lawless nature of these sweeping trade and investment treaties in general. For incredible as it may seem, there is no binding

term of the MAI or the WTO or the NAFTA which anywhere recognizes a single article of the entire body of human rights or international law which the world's nations have developed during the twentieth century.

To restore sanity to the perfectly one-sided "world order" being currently prescribed to global society, a minimum condition must be inscribed as binding in every trade or investment agreement. Already signed international laws need to be recognized as prior obligations of the contracting parties and their enterprises, upon which their right of access to other societies' markets, assets and resources is conditional. If any contracting party or corporate enterprise within its territory does not comply, they should be made subject to barriers against their access to other societies' domestic markets and assets. This long overdue rule of law in the global market revolution would not solve the problem of the loss of sovereignty of peoples over their own societies. But it would render world corporate rule less internationally lawless than it now is.

The problem with putting stock in the recent assertions of governments such as Canada's or the United States's that there will be "labor and environmental standards" or other life-protective terms in the MAI or other trade and investment treaties is that despite these public-relations exercises, no established international human rights, labor or pollution-control laws are, as mentioned, specified in any such treaty. This is because there is no evident intention of requiring transnational corporations to comply with life-protective international law. As mentioned above, trade negotiators are, in fact, doing their utmost to ensure that no such standards are made binding.[10]

At the same time, we would be more than naive if we were to believe that this latest phase of the post-1989 program of world rule had been overcome simply because its most recent and most sweeping model, the MAI, had been temporarily turned back by a dramatic uprising of international NGOs and intellectuals across the world against its dictates. For no significant political or corporate leader has yet renounced the MAI program, whatever name it might next have, and it is, in truth, only the latest vehicle of a rapidly instituted global regime.[11]

In the end, we face a turn of history in which corporate-financed and -publicized political parties serve corporate masters in a dizzyingly fast-track replacement of the democratic rule of law across the world. In this new order, the legal capacity of any government or any law that limits transnational corporations' control over the world's markets and all their wealth becomes increasingly illegal. The MAI has been the latest incarnation of what is, in the end, a form of world rule.

NOTES

1. Analysis of the military institution as a pathological structure of group intention and action is provided by my *Understanding War* (Toronto: Science for Peace, 1989).
2. Ben Laurence and William Keegan, "Galbraith on Dangers of Unbridled Optimism," *Guardian Weekly*, June 28, 1998, p. 18.
3. A systematic analysis of the principles of corporate capitalism and their relationship to social sectors and to performance requirements is provided in my *Unequal Freedoms: The Global Market as an Ethical System* (Toronto: Garamond Press, 1998).
4. I analyze this process of public debt creation after 1980 as an overall strategic pattern in my forthcoming book, *The Cancer Stage of Capitalism* (London: Pluto Books, 1999).
5. See Stephen Frank Overturf, *Money and European Union* (New York: St. Martin's Press, 1997), appendix 2, for a direct reproduction of the terms of the Maastricht Treaty.
6. All of these facts are drawn from a draft of the Multilateral Agreement on Investment, Paris, January 13 Draft, 1997.
7. This prohibition of requiring or reporting the "process" of production of products is also enshrined in the parent WTO regime. Packaging information disclosing genetically altered foodstuffs, for example, is not information that governments can require without exposure to WTO trade sanction. The proceedings of trade panels are, moreover, confined to trade bureaucrats and are secret. The MAI panel proceedings, to cite the government of British Columbia's description, "are closed. Interested citizens have no right to intervene; there is no substantive appeal procedure; and, if a party decided to withdraw as a result of a bad decision, MAI rules would continue to apply for at least 15 years." (Submission to the Sub-Committee on International Trade, Trade Disputes and Investment of the House of Commons Standing Committee on Foreign Affairs and International Trade regarding the Proposed Multilateral Agreement on Investment, November 26, 1997, p. 13.
8. The prototype draft of the MAI included reservations from specific countries on specific clauses that are no longer available in subsequent releases—for example, Norway's reservation with respect to the MAI's inclusion of "authorizations, licences and concessions for the prosecution, exploration and production of hydrocarbons," a right of the home country that Norway's negotiators, mindful of Norway's reliance on public control of public oil resources for the funding of its social infrastructure, sought to exclude (Ibid., Definitions 2.b.9).
9. Cited in Tony Clarke, *The Corporate Rule Treaty* (Ottawa: Canadian Centre For Policy Alternatives, 1997) p. 9.

10. In response to criticism that the MAI should include the rights of others than transnational corporations, the former Canadian Liberal Party politician and now OECD Secretary-General, Donald Johnston, replied with the well-worn economist dismissal: "That's nonsense" (Canadian Press, "OECD Head Unfazed by MAI Protests," May 26, 1998). The Dutch State Secretary, Van Dok, was no less dismissive of the European Parliament's March 4, 1998, rejection of the MAI on the grounds, among others, that it included no binding provision for "human rights conventions and environmental and social standards." "The EP," she replied, "has nothing to say about it" (reported by participant Erik Wesselius, NGO Consultation, April 3, 1998).

11. As I write, I am provided with a report that an international seminar on the topic in Switzerland has been invaded by police, and its participants arrested, a seminar that a lead participant, the eminent author an and Third World specialist Susan Georg, described as a "group of peaceful and law-abiding people." This event occurred in Cologny, Geneva, on Friday August 28, 1998. The seminar's title was "International Seminar on Globalization and Resistance."

The Military

Chapter 6

A Cold War Retrospective: Mishaps That Might Have Started Accidental Nuclear War

Alan F. Phillips, M.D.
Physicians for Global Survival

There is a widespread feeling that the Cold War was a success. There is also a common notion that if a risk is taken and the result turns out all right then the risk was justified; that the leadership was trustworthy; that bold stances work, and if we have to do it again we can again count on using the same methods. But we are in great danger of drawing the wrong lesson from the end of the Cold War and the wrong conclusion from the nuclear deterrence system that characterized it.

Dependence on nuclear deterrence, or mutually assured destruction (MAD, as it is appropriately called), brought us so close to the brink, even through accident, that we should never dare to depend on it again. We should analyze, in retrospect, what were some of the dangers, mistakes and close calls. Forty years of nuclear weapons operation showed up a number of them. Human errors and unanticipated malfunctions occurred. Not all of these were caught by the built-in "fail-safe" features of the system, but because of intelligent intervention by humans at moments of great stress, none resulted in nuclear war. Good luck was also a necessary factor which helped us survive the Cold War.

Some examples show the great variety of these incidents, and the bizarre character of some of them. They were caused by errors of design, errors in construction (notably electrical wiring errors), errors in interpretation of information, and failures of communication, alone or in combination.

Any one of the events described may have had an extremely low probability of escalating into war, but the laws of chance do not allow the indefinite acceptance of a lethal risk with impunity. Nuclear deterrence is not a safe system. If it is retained as a permanent feature of world order, it is bound to end in disaster. A fairly obvious conclusion? Not for everybody; and it is dangerous when people think otherwise. One failure of deterrence that leads to a major nuclear war is the end of civilization. There would be no second chance. It was by good luck that the world survived the 40 years of Cold War, and we must not count on our good luck holding another time.

A huge system like the American nuclear deterrence system is bound to have mistakes in its design and construction. During prolonged operation these show up. Also it is bound to suffer equipment failures and human errors of many kinds. It did evolve to be fairly safe, as the planners gradually became aware of the power of nuclear weapons. As they came to realize the danger of inadvertent war they incorporated elaborate accessories into nuclear weapons and their delivery systems to reduce the risk. They also knew that failure of a component part might prevent proper warning and the retaliation they planned, so they built in plenty of redundancy. But they were not very quick to learn from mistakes, and they refused to follow the logic of both theory and experience: that the risk of inadvertent war could not be made zero, and therefore the whole MAD doctrine was unacceptable. Some examples of various types of errors show how close we came.

A DESIGN ERROR[1]

On the night of November 24, 1961, at U.S. Supreme Air Command HQ in Omaha, Nebraska, all communication links with the North American Air Defense Command (NORAD) at Colorado Springs and the three early warning radar sites suddenly went dead. For General Power in Omaha there was really only one explanation: enemy action. Failure of the multiple telephone and telegraph links, all at the same time, was almost inconceivable. Air Force bases were alerted and the B-52 nuclear bomber crews started their engines, with instructions not to take off without further orders.

The Omaha staff managed to make radio contact with a B-52 in flight 4,500 kilometers away over Greenland. The B-52 crew contacted the Thule Early Warning site, and reported that no attack had taken place. (Imagine those messages, vital to the survival of civilization, heard only through the static of long-distance air-to-ground radio!) The General could not have known that the redundant communication routes between NORAD and his HQ all ran through one relay station in Colorado, where a motor had overheated, causing a small fire, which interrupted all lines.

A WIRING ERROR[2]

At around midnight on October 25, 1962, a guard at the Duluth base in Minnesota saw a figure climbing the security fence. He shot at it, and activated the sabotage alarm. This automatically set off sabotage alarms at all bases in their area. At Volk Field, Wisconsin, the alarm was wrongly wired, and the Klaxon sounded that ordered nuclear-armed fighter aircraft to take off. This was during the Cuban Missile Crisis, and the pilots believed World War III had started.

The duty officer at Volk Field kept his cool. He called Duluth. By this time the aircraft were starting down the runway. A car raced from the command center and managed to signal the aircraft to stop.

The original intruder was a bear, an American bear (not even a Russian bear!). Once again, good and quick thinking by the officer in charge prevented a possible disaster.

CUBAN MISSILE CRISIS CLOSE CALL[3]

At the height of the Cuban Missile Crisis in 1962, when both Soviet and U.S. militaries were on high alert for any signs of preemptive attack, a U-2 high-altitude reconnaissance flight from Alaska flew unintentionally into Soviet airspace. Because of this known risk, during the crisis the U-2 pilots were ordered not to fly within 100 miles of Soviet airspace. However, on the night of October 26 the aurora borealis prevented good sextant readings and a U-2 plane did stray over the Chukotski Peninsula. Soviet MIG interceptors took off with orders to shoot it down. The pilot contacted his U.S. command post and was ordered to fly due east toward Alaska. He ran out of fuel while still over Siberia. In response to his SOS, U.S. F-102A fighters were launched to escort him on his glide towards Alaska, with orders to prevent the MIGs from entering U.S. airspace. The U.S. interceptor aircraft were armed with nuclear missiles. These could have been used by any one of the F-102A pilots at his own discretion.

COINCIDENCE[4]

An event that could start a war inadvertently might be some sort of coincidence: two or three mishaps or false warnings, leaving such a confused situation that no one manages to guess right.

On November 5, 1956, British and French forces were attacking Egypt at the Suez Canal. The Soviet government had suggested to the United States that they join forces to stop this, and had warned the British and French governments that rocket attacks on London and Paris were being considered. (These were not nuclear-armed rockets, at that date, but NATO could have retaliated with nuclear bombers and attacked Russian cities.) That night, among the many messages received by the U.S. military HQ in Europe were these four:

1. unidentified aircraft were flying over Turkey and the Turkish air force was on alert;
2. 100 Soviet MIG-15s were flying over Syria;
3. a British Canberra bomber had been shot down over Syria;
4. the Russian fleet was moving through the Dardanelles.

These four reports added up to a strong presumption that a war with Russia was starting; but each one turned out to be a misinterpretation of information. A flight of swans over Turkey had been misidentified as aircraft. The Soviet MIGs over Syria were a routine escort for the Syrian president, nowhere near 100 planes; he was returning from a visit to Moscow. The Canberra bomber was forced down by mechanical problems; and the Soviet fleet was engaged in a scheduled routine exercise.

COMPUTERS

Everyone knows that computers can play dreadful tricks, and can fail at most inconvenient moments. The two following examples fortunately did not happen at any very bad moment. The warning displays at the main Command Centers were two windows that normally showed a string of four zeros. This represented the number of missiles, land-based (ICBMs) and submarine launched (SLBMs), detected by the early warning radar. At 2:25 A.M. on June 3, 1980, the windows started showing various numbers of missiles, with always 2s in place of one or more of the zeros.[5] Preparations for retaliation were instituted, including nuclear bomber crews starting their engines, actual launch of Pacific Command's Airborne Command post, and the concrete covers of Minuteman missile silos being rolled back. It wasn't difficult to assess that this was a false alarm, because the patterns of numbers didn't make sense. The cause was a single faulty chip that was failing in random fashion, causing the deceptive display at all the command posts.

While the cause of that false alarm was being investigated three days later, the same thing happened again, and again preparations were made for retaliation.

A WAR GAME

My last example is one of the nearest we have come to nuclear holocaust. Fortunately it happened in 1979 when nothing much else was going on. Just suppose the following had happened during the Cuban Missile Crisis when the U.S. military was on high alert.

At 8:50 A.M. on November 9, duty officers at the four principal U.S. Command Centers all saw on their displays a pattern showing a large number of Soviet missiles in a full-scale attack on the United States.[6] Preparations for retaliation were put in hand. Missile silo lids were rolled back. Air Force planes took off, including the President's National Emergency Airborne Command Post—though without the President! (It seems they did not find him in time!)

With commendable speed, NORAD was able to contact the advanced PAVE PAWS early warning radar and learn that no missiles had been reported. In only 6 minutes the threat assessment conference was terminated. It is said that at 15 minutes the U.S. ICBMs would have been launched.

What had happened was that a technician was trying out a war games tape on one of the back up computers. Two operational computers failed one after the other and automatically switched in their backups. The second backup was the computer the technician had been using. U.S. Senator Charles Percy happened to be in NORAD HQ at the time and is reported to have said there was absolute panic. I think some officers kept their heads remarkably well, fortunately, to make correct checks and be able to cancel the alert so quickly.

The practice of running exercise tapes on computers that could be connected to the operational system ought to have been corrected long before. There were two or three incidents in which exercise tapes caused confusion at the time of the Cuban Missile Crisis.

People sometimes act foolishly, sometimes more wisely than we could ever expect. You cannot foresee everything that might happen.

HOW GREAT WAS THE RISK?

What was the real risk of nuclear war? Any risk of it was too high, but I should like to know whether we needed just a bit of good luck to survive, or whether we were incredibly lucky. You cannot tell, but you can make some guesses.

Suppose each of the 20 mishaps in my paper "20 Mishaps That Might Have Started Accidental Nuclear War" carried a 1 percent risk of disaster. The chance of surviving, 99 percent, sounds pretty good. Now comes the math: if you multiply 0.99 by 0.99 20 times the answer is 0.82, or 82 percent. That is just about the chance of surviving the single pull of the trigger in a game of Russian roulette played with a six-shooter. Add a similar 20 on the Russian side, another pull of the trigger?

Remember that the calculation depends on the pure guess of a risk of 1 percent for each incident, and the known underestimate of 20 events. Some of those events seem to me a lot worse, particularly the computer tape. Suppose that some of them were as bad as 10 percent risks. It would only take 7 events like that, including both sides, to give the world less than an even chance of survival.

The "20 Mishaps" are only a small selection of the mishaps in the accessible U.S. records. Quite a lot more are described in the book *The Limits of Safety* by Scott D. Sagan. The reports of some, perhaps many, may still be "classified," and some must have been unreported, because individuals did not want to admit error, and wanted to maintain the good reputation of their military unit.

My conclusion is that, although most of the time great prudence was exercised by military commanders at all operational levels, the risks of the Cold War were by no means justified. Nuclear deterrence is far too dangerous, and has to be abandoned. We should never put ourselves in a position where we have to resort to it again.

BIBLIOGRAPHY

Britten, Stewart. 1983. *The Invisible Event.* London: Menard Press.

Calder, Nigel. 1979. *Nuclear Nightmares.* London: British Broadcasting Corporation.

Peace Research Reviews, vol. 9, pp. 4–5, (1984); vol. 10, pp. 3–4, (1986). Dundas, Ont.: Peace Research Institute, Dundas.

Phillips, Alan F. "20 Mishaps That Might Have Started Accidental Nuclear War," available from Science for Peace. (To be published in *Splitting the Atom: A Chronology of the Nuclear Age,* 1998 ed. appendix. Santa Barbara: Nuclear Age Peace Foundation.)

Sagan, Scott D. 1993. *The Limits of Safety.* Princeton, N.J.: Princeton University Press.

NOTES

1. Sagan, *The Limits of Safety,* p.176.
2. Ibid., p.99
3. Ibid., pp.135–138.
4. *Peace Research Reviews,* vol. 10, 3, p. 90.
5. Sagan, *The Limits of Safety,* p.231.
6. Ibid., p.228.

Chapter 7

The Decline of International War

Major-General (Ret) Leonard V. Johnson, CD, LL.D
Chairman, Canadian Pugwash Group

I contend that war between great powers has become less likely than at any time in history and that national armed forces and their weapons are fated to disappear before another century has passed. If this is so, then future generations may well achieve security and prosperity without warfare. History is a function of time, and, as Anatol Rapoport once observed, time does not run backward. Societies do not forever bear the dead weight of institutions that no longer serve them, even when they are as deeply rooted as armed forces have become.

Some people still argue that making war is inherent in human behavior and that war is therefore a permanent feature of international relations. Here is an early example of that view: In 1904, at the concluding banquet following the World's Peace Congress in Boston, the American philosopher William James identified human bellicosity as the principal, and permanent, obstacle to peace. "A deadly listlessness would come over most men's imagination of the future if they could be brought to believe that never again would a war trouble human history," he said. "In such a stagnant summer afternoon of a world, where would be the zest or interest?"[1]

However true that might have been in 1904 and for ten years after that, the war spirit was considerably dampened by the carnage of the First World War. It recovered during the Second World War, but was almost extinguished in the United States by the war in Vietnam, when American draftees came home in body bags and television brought the war into American living rooms. Something like that also happened in the Soviet Union after the invasion of Afghanistan in 1979. The wars in Vietnam and Afghanistan were both defeats, be it noted—not for lack of manpower or high-tech equipment but by lack of public enthusiasm for them. Both wars destroyed public faith in the infallibility of political elites where decisions of war and peace were concerned. In the United States, the gross error that was the Vietnam War has been publicly and painfully acknowledged by no less than Robert S. McNamara, former Secretary of Defense and principal architect of that debacle.

Finally, the nuclear standoff of the Cold War brought home to publics the totality of war in which civil populations have been deprived of sanctuary and made prime targets, largely without their knowledge or consent. The folly of nuclear deterrence has also been acknowledged by its most prominent theorists and practitioners, notably Robert McNamara and General Lee Butler, USAF, former commander of U.S. strategic nuclear forces. Growing public opposition to weapons of mass destruction may yet achieve what many have hitherto thought impossible: the abolition of nuclear weapons.

The fragility of public support has become a powerful disincentive to allow casualties on the battlefield, as we saw in the Gulf War and in military opposition to ground intervention in the former Yugoslavia. In both cases, air and missile power with precision-guided munitions were preferred because they limit the exposure of vulnerable ground forces. As we have also seen, in the February 1998 preparations to bomb Iraq to force Saddam Hussein to open his palaces to weapons inspection teams, there was not much public or international support, even among U.S. allies, for bombing and missile attacks, the brunt of which would have been borne by innocent civilians who have already suffered too much and too publicly. It's also likely that an attack on Iraq would destroy what is left of the Gulf War coalition, a political defeat for the West.

War has also lost its economic utility. It is no longer necessary to conquer and occupy territory in order to gain access to the resources of others—mutually beneficial trade does it better. Germany and Japan went to war in the 1930s for Lebensraum and the Greater East Asia Co-Prosperity Sphere and were utterly defeated, only to recover with modernized infrastructure and become economic great powers within two decades. Hong Kong and Singapore prosper without a resource base. It is no longer necessary to possess an empire to be prosperous and a great power, and thus no longer necessary to maintain armed forces to police distant realms. Indeed, territory confers little or no advantage and smaller has become better. It may even be that small and militarily weak states are safer than their great-power neighbors. Because they do not threaten neighbors they are not threatened in turn and they may become highly skilled in the diplomatic arts of dissuasion.

The Royal Navy and nuclear-armed bombers couldn't prevent the dissolution of the British Empire, nor could the Soviet armed forces sustain the Soviet empire against collapse. The world's most powerful armed forces could not have prevented the destruction of the United States had it been attacked with nuclear weapons, nor can they defend the United States against drug barons, terrorists with improvised explosives, commercial espionage, global environmental threats and adverse conditions of trade. Except in the context of the past, when land and sea battles determined the security of states, there are no threats to modern states that justify powerful and expensive armed forces, nor are there offensive purposes that can be legally pursued.

Military security, defined by Samuel Huntington as "security from harm arising from the operations of foreign armed forces directed against the territory or vital interests of the state,"[2] cannot be absolute in the era of missiles and stand-off weapons with precision-guided warheads. These terror weapons, though immensely destructive, can punish an enemy state, but they cannot occupy its territory or destroy its capacity to resist, both necessary conditions of victory. Increasingly, it is being recognized that military security cannot be achieved by making others insecure.

In the realpolitik school of foreign policy, still deeply rooted in governments and political science departments, military power enhances national well-being, fostering patriotism, national pride and confidence, making people feel superior to others. It enhances political influence over other states and access to their markets, and compels obedience to the will of its owner. In this view, military power confers prestige in the community of nations and is the final determinant of the international pecking order, ultimately conferring great-power status. Like Mao Zedong, these self-styled political realists believe that power flows from the barrel of a gun. May it not be that the bellicosity James noted is itself the foster child of military power? In the 1950s, the American sociologist C. Wright Mills wrote that the immediate cause of World War III would be the military preparation for it.

These "realist" assumptions are still widely held, justifying the nuclear weapons of the five permanent members of the Security Council, for example. But diplomacy is no longer conducted solely between states, acting through ambassadors and ministers plenipotentiary. Foreign relations are now conducted between officials at all levels of government departments, corporations and non-governmental organizations of all kinds. Those who wield the levers of power in the new international order would have nothing to gain and everything to lose by a major war.

Clearly, the days of gunboat diplomacy are over. Force is no longer the ultimate arbiter of international affairs, the faithful servant of diplomacy. This is a consequence of modernization and complex interdependence among states. These developments have made obsolete Clausewitz's famous and oft-quoted dictum that "War is a mere continuation of policy by other means." As such, they are hopeful and probably irreversible historical developments.

The conditions that led to global wars in the twentieth century no longer exist, nor can they recur. If so, it seems likely that the powerful armies, navies and air forces of this century will shrink and atrophy in the next. Whatever else they find to justify their existence, it won't be fighting each other.

In the speech I referred to earlier, William James saw hope, not in utopian visions of the abolition of war by a single act, but in *the gradual erosion of the war spirit* by organizing "in every conceivable way the practical machinery for making each successive chance of war abortive." Much has been accomplished toward that, foremost among which are the growth of democracy and human rights.

The spread of modernization in the world and the complex interdependence resulting from it has given peaceful and cooperative relations predominance over force in the hierarchy of foreign policy goals. At the same time, the capacity for mutual annihilation and the destructive power of even conventional weapons have ruled out war between states bound together in a web of mutually beneficial economic and financial ties. The "hard" power of military force is being supplanted by the "soft" power of global interdependence.

It is unfortunately true that civil wars still exact heavy costs in life and property and it is likely that will continue to be the case until emerging states achieve stable governments with a monopoly on the use of force within their borders. As locally destructive as these conflicts may be, however, their effects are limited outside of the regions in which they occur. What has disappeared is war between advanced postindustrial states, the only actors powerful enough to wage global war.

James predicted that "The last weak runnings of the war spirit will be 'punitive expeditions,'" to restore order in dissident parts of the empire, I suppose. The Gulf War was just such an expedition, as were the forays into Panama, Grenada and Chechnya. Military peace-keeping is another "weak running." It isn't too much to hope that the twenty-first century will be a century of peace made permanent by the final disappearance of the war spirit. Peace is no longer a utopian dream but a long-awaited condition whose time has come. In that "stagnant summer afternoon of a world" we'll have to find other delights to provide zest and entertainment. It shouldn't be hard to do that.

BIBLIOGRAPHY

Clausewitz, Carl von. 1968. *Clausewitz on War,* p. 119. Anatol Rapoport, ed. Harmondsworth: Penguin Classics.

Keohane, Robert O. and Joseph S. Nye. 1977. *Power and Interdependence: World Politics in Transition.* Boston and Toronto: Little Brown and Company.

Morse, Edward L. 1969–70. "The Transformation of Foreign Policies: Modernization, Interdependence and Externalization," in *World Politics,* vol. 22. Princeton, N.J.: Princeton University Press.

NOTES

1. William James, "Remarks at the Peace Banquet," in *Highlights From 125 Years of The Atlantic,* ed. Louise Desaulniers (Atlantic Monthly Company, 1977).

2. Samuel Huntington, *The Soldier and the State* (Cambridge: Belknap Press, 1957).

Chapter 8

Indicators of Militarization: Coping with the Specter of Praetorianism

Brian S. MacDonald
President, Strategic Insight

INTRODUCTION

The end of the Cold War has seen a striking decline in world militarization measured by such traditional measures as that of the economy (military expenditure divided by gross national product, ME/GNP), of the government (military expenditure divided by current government expenditure, ME/CGE) and of the population (armed forces personnel per 1,000 total population).

However, this could mask a troubling process as military establishments may shift from a concentration on inter-state conflict as their raison d'être, toward the protection of the state against internal threats. A possible negative result is the development of Praetorianism, the illegitimate use of military power for internal political agendas—including the propping up of undemocratic regimes, or even the overthrow of civilian governments by military coups, and the creation of military-run governments.

The author has examined the hypothesis that an appropriate level of military spending could be determined by applying a financial "benchmark," such as the percentage of GNP devoted to military spending, or ME/GNP.[1] IMF Managing Director Michel Camdessus had effectively suggested such a benchmark (4.5 percent) in a 1991 speech to the United Nations Economic and Social Council meeting in Geneva. The author has concluded that the financial "benchmark" approach was not supportable since it ignored the strategic context in which countries found themselves, and that a "threat/risk assessment" approach provided a superior manner of determining appropriate military force levels, force structures, and military budgets.

A surprising finding was that a number of African countries, with ME/GNP levels much below the Camdessus benchmark, were overspending on their military forces when measured by the threat/risk assessment. A closer examination of their organizations and post-colonial histories led to the conclusion that their militaries followed behavior patterns similar to those of the Praetorian Guard in the later period of the Roman Empire—of taking advantage of their monopoly of the use of military force to make or unmake civilian governments, or to govern their country themselves—to their considerable financial benefit.

Further work to develop a methodology for operationalizing the Praetorian concept led to two new measures: the Spartan Index and the Praetorian Index. The Spartan Index was developed from the traditional social militarization measure of soldiers per 1,000 population, modified to include paramilitary and reserve military personnel, as well as regular military personnel. The Praetorian Index was a new construct that related military spending per soldier to GNP per capita—producing a socioeconomic measure independent of exchange-rate variations and thus usable in cross-country militarization analysis. Taken together, the two indices provide new insights with respect to the governance of military forces, and appear to have value in predicting civil war.

DETAILED MODEL

Three variations of the Spartan Index were developed. The first (SI1), calculated by dividing the total number of military personnel by the total population, produced a ratio of uniformed regular personnel per 1,000 total population; the data source was *The Military Balance,* published by the International Institute for Strategic Studies.

The second (SI2) added paramilitary personnel since in some countries reductions in military personnel were paralleled by equal increases in paramilitary personnel; moreover, paramilitary personnel are often used as part of internal control forces. The third (SI3) included $^1/_{12}$ of the total reserve strength level. Some countries, such as the Republic of South Africa, made use of active reserve personnel who were required to undergo annual training and employment periods of about 30 days per year.

Similarly, three variations of the Praetorian Index were developed. The first (PI1) includes only the personnel component of the military budget. NATO countries provide disaggregated figures for total personnel costs, but others do not.

The second (PI2) adds operations and maintenance portions of total military expenditures to produce what is usually referred to as P, O & M, which was the form used in the study. While NATO countries publish reliable figures on the subdivision of their defense budgets, this is not always the case with other countries, particularly in the developing world. A major concern of analysts has been the problem of "off budget" items that do not appear in reported defense budgets, particularly in the case of equipment imports. Consequently, a partial correlation calculation was undertaken to determine whether published total military expenditures appeared to include imports of military equipment shown in *World Military Expenditures and Arms Transfers (WMEAT),* published by the United States Arms Control and Disarmament Agency; where the partial correlations appeared to indicate this, the value of military imports was removed to determine the P, O & M component.

The third (PI3) is based on total military expenditures per uniformed soldier as a multiple of GNP per capita; financial data was taken *WMEAT* and personnel data from *The Military Balance.*

PI1 and PI2 are effectively independent of currency exchange-rate variations since the financial components of both measures (GNP/capita and ME/soldier) are expressed in the same currency units. PI3, which includes equipment imports, could, on the other hand, be affected by exchange-rate variations. Consequently PI1 and PI2 can be used more reliably for country-to-country comparisons, whereas PI3 is less suited to that end.

SI3 and PI2 were used in the study since the data bases used did not permit personnel costs to be broken out separately. A set of 50 African and Middle East states formed the basis of the study. SIs and PIs were calculated, where data was complete, for the period 1985 to 1994, plus earlier years in some cases.

FINDINGS

The following table provides a three-by-three matrix of the two Index means (PI, SI) for the 1990–94 period, with boundaries set as the overall index mean (20.9 for the PI, and 3.2 for the SI for the sub-Saharan set) plus or minus 0.43 standard deviations—a procedure dividing the set into

Table 8.1: Sub-Saharan Countries, by Praetorian Index and Spartan Index

	Low Praetorian (PI<13.7)	Middle Praetorian (13.7<PI<28.1)	High Praetorian (PI>28.1)
High Spartan (SI>4.3)	Congo (11.8, 7.2)	South Africa (14.7, 5.2)	
	Botswana (10.8, 5.4)		
	Chad (7.4, 5.6)		
	Zimbabwe (8.5, 7.0)		
	Gabon (7.2, 8.7)		
	Guinea-Bissau (3.7, 8.9)		
Middle Spartan (2.0<SI<4.3)	Ethiopia (11.7, 2.2)	Tanzania (22.9, 2.2)	Sudan (39.1, 3.7)
	Guinea (8.8, 3.1)	Central African	Mozambique (35.5, 2.8)
	Zambia (6.9, 2.7)	Republic (19.8, 2.1)	
	Uganda (6.4, 3.4)		
Low Spartan (2.0<SI)	Malawi (11.3, 1.2)	Sierra Leone (24.0, 1.3)	Rwanda (95.8, 0.8)
	Togo (10.7, 1.6)	Niger (23.5, 3.1)	Zaire (40.1,1.5)
	Nigeria (8.8, 1.0)	Burundi (23.2,1.5)	The Gambia (31.5, 1.6)
		Cameroon (23.1,1.1)	Burkina Faso (30.2, 1.5)
		Benin (20.5, 1.4)	Kenya (29.5, 1.1)
		Mali (19.4, 1.8)	Cote d'Ivoire (29.0, 1.2)
		Senegal (17.3, 1.5)	
		Ghana (14.8, 0.8)	

three equal parts on each dimension. The first number in parentheses is the mean PI, and the second the mean SI.

This indicates two principal axes, one characterized by low PI scores and the other by low SI scores, with a smaller number of outliers. This suggests, at first glance, that the two axes might discriminate between countries with an externally oriented national defense posture (low Praetorian scores), and those with an internal control orientation (low Spartan scores). The combination of low Spartan and high Praetorian scores suggests a military orientation not so much to the protection of the state against foreign enemies, as to the protection of the regime against its people.

An analysis of changes in the Praetorian Index over time led to the observation that sudden upward changes in the Praetorian Index appeared to correlate with increased probabilities of subsequent civil war. Rwanda's 1989 PI was 21.7. It began to shoot up in 1990, reaching 59.5, and peaked at 119.3 in 1993—just before the catastrophe—the highest PI of any state examined in the study.

This led to the hypothesis of a "Praetorian Cycle," which begins with a middle or high PI, characteristic either of an authoritarian state, with a military protecting a ruling elite from its own people, or a Praetorian state, with the military itself ruling. If the excesses of the ruling elite become so great that a resistance emerges, the initial response is to increase spending on the existing, relatively small regular military and paramilitary forces, both to ensure their loyalty and to cover the increased O & M costs of a repressive campaign—a pattern that explains the sharp upward spike of the Praetorian Index as a precursor of civil war. When the civil war breaks out the threatened elite adds to the numbers of military and paramilitary troops such that the PI falls and the SI rises.

The post-civil war pattern depends on whether the state evolves towards a democratic form and both PI and SI fall, as in Uganda; back toward the authoritarian or Praetorian form, with a constant or slightly declining SI together with a continuing high PI; into terminal collapse, as in Liberia; or into a frozen post-revolutionary state with the revolutionary army maintained to provide employment for the revolutionary fighters, such that the SI remains high while the PI falls, as in Zimbabwe.

The PI spike phenomenon was also evident in Burundi, Liberia, The Gambia, Sierra Leone, Sudan, Central African Republic, Togo and Zaire as a precursor of civil unrest and conflict. The unrest was contained in Central African Republic and Togo by French troops intervening on the side of the threatened elites, but evolved into civil war in the other states mentioned. Two PI spikes that did not follow the pattern came in Ghana and Burkina Faso and appeared to result from sizeable reductions in military strength that took place more rapidly than defense budget reductions. PI upward spikes that have yet to be followed by full-scale civil war came in 1992–94 in Nigeria, and paralleled the "Praetorian coup" led by General Abacha, and a slower PI spike in Kenya over the 1987–93 period, which paralleled a 275 percent expansion of paramilitary forces. Nonetheless, the PI spike suggests that both countries must now be regarded as "at risk."

IMPLICATIONS FOR POLICY DEVELOPMENT

The post-Cold War period has seen a dramatic increase in internal conflict in states, especially in the less developed world, and in calls for "peacekeeping" and "armed humanitarian" operations to intervene in these conflicts. The limited recent success of such operations stems in part from the traditional peace-keeping paradigm, based on the interposition of a strictly neutral peace-keeping force between combatants who have already agreed to a truce, which does not fit effectively a scenario in which the combatants are intent on continuing hostilities.

In addition, such interventions are unlikely to be completely neutral and may be, in effect, an intervention on one side or the other. Given the diplomatic preference for the status quo ante, such intervention can favor existing governments, which may have been responsible for the conflict in the first place. As a thought experiment we could consider what might have happened had Lt.-Gen. Maurice Baril recommended in 1996 a Canadian-led intervention in eastern Zaire instead of against it. Such an intervention, needing the permission and cooperation of the Mobutu administration, might well have put Canadians on the side of a corrupt and incompetent Praetorian regime, in opposition to the rebels who eventually overthrew it. While the support of corrupt and incompetent Praetorian regimes may have been a feature of post-colonial French foreign policy it hardly seems appropriate to Canada.

Such measures as the Praetorian Index may serve as a "check against gross error" in the development of responses to hasty calls for peacekeeping or peacemaking interventions. They may have even greater value in developing more effective proactive "peace-building" efforts and eliminating the need for reactive peacemaking or peace-keeping efforts.

Some analysts have suggested the use of "donor leverage" in efforts to reduce the size of military establishments in developing countries. Such reductions, however, may fall disproportionately upon junior ranks, particularly in countries moving from a conscription-based military to a professional one, and those professional military establishments can become increasingly top-heavy and dedicated to matters of "perks and privileges" rather than the goals of national defense. Even professional military forces in the developed world are not immune to such tendencies.

In areas such as West Africa, with a comparatively benign local strategic environment, such a process may lead to the evolution from an externally oriented national defense army to an internally oriented "police army." Consequently, a more sophisticated analysis of military governance may be needed than that derived from simple "bean count" analysis of ME/GNP, and soldiers per 1,000 population. During the late Cold War, arms-control theory had begun to move beyond simple quantitative arms-control measures, which characterized the Conventional Forces in Europe (CFE) Treaty, for example, toward qualitative arms control. It may be time for a similar development in militarization analysis, with the use of such measures as the Praetorian Index as a guard against the Praetorian specter.

The potential Praetorian response to demobilization pressures may also bring into question the conventional defense-conversion paradigm, which seeks to reduce financial and social militarization through a variety of "demobilization and reintegration programs," or DRPs. A disturbing finding of recent World Bank studies[2] has been that ex-combatants in Ethiopia, Namibia and Uganda possess minimal skills utilizable in a civilian economy since most if not all of their schooling, or human capital formation period, was spent in civil or revolutionary war, and that DRPs did not adequately address the issue of human capital reformation of ex-combatants and their families. In Uganda, for example, the authors noted that incomes of ex-combatants were less than half that of the national average. In other cases, ex-combatants often carried a social stigma in their communities, where they were feared as "illiterate thugs, conveyors of violence, crime, and sexually transmitted diseases."

An alternative defense conversion paradigm may be appropriate for some developing countries with national militaries encouraged to follow the "assistance to civil authority," or "non-military roles for the military," concept, which can include national-development roles for military forces. A case, little studied or analyzed in either the development or military literature, was the assignment of national-development roles to the Egyptian armed forces after the Camp David accords. In 1986 "development regiments" were created with a total strength of 30,000 personnel and assigned a variety of national infrastructure development tasks. The 1982–86 Five Year Plan assigned them the construction of approximately 40 percent of the total telephone links in Egypt, as well as the development of civilian job skills among the annual conscript intakes. Since military forces in developing countries often have considerable roles and influence in government and their bureaucracies, and considerable power and skill in avoiding complete demobilization, their reorientation to nonmilitary roles may be a means of avoiding the Praetorian alternative.

BIBILIOGRAPHY

Colletta, N .J., M. Kostner, and I. Wiederhofer. 1996. *The Transition from War to Peace in Sub-Saharan Africa.* Washington: The World Bank.

————— .1996. *Case Studies in War-to-Peace Transition.* Washington: The World Bank.

MacDonald, Brian S. 1997. *Military Spending in Developing Countries: How Much Is Too Much?* Ottawa: Carleton University Press.

The Military Balance. London: The International Institute for Strategic Studies.

World Military Expenditures and Arms Transfers. Washington: United States Arms Control and Disarmament Agency.

NOTES

1. This earlier work is described in the author's recent book *Military Spending in Developing Countries: How Much Is Too Much?*, which was a development of contract work conducted for the Africa and Middle East Branch of the Canadian International Development Agency (CIDA).
2. Colletta et al., *Transition*; Colletta et al., *Case Studies.*

The United Nations

Chapter 9

Challenges for the World and for the United Nations

Christopher Spencer
*Former Senior Advisor,
Department of Foreign Affairs and
International Trade Canada*

About five centuries ago, the human race—for the first time in its million-year history—began a comprehensive, disciplined and scientific study of itself and its environment. In the ensuing evolutionary instant, we have discovered enough about the laws of physics to fundamentally change our conditions and status. We have acquired the power to transform our biosphere—and even ourselves—for good or ill. Moreover, this process is not only accelerating, but is now forcing us to take an increasing number of basic, global decisions. These decisions made—or unmade—affect the whole species, and in fact, the whole planet

To deal with those problems of a global nature necessarily means using the United Nations, the only organization that effectively includes and represents all of humankind. With its many imperfections, we are very fortunate to have it. A century ago, not even its embryo existed; today, almost 200 sovereign states would be totally unable to reach agreement to create any institution remotely as useful. We have no choice but to exploit our best global option and tool.

Not only a sense of elementary justice and democracy or even enlightened self-interest, but the hope of success demand that as many citizens as possible become involved, not merely in key decision making that will permanently affect them all, but also in the difficult search for solutions. To succeed we must use institutions that reflect and pool maximum resources of knowledge and ability. If not, vital experience will be ignored, key players excluded, and essential elements omitted.

This does not imply passing all global issues to the UN; we neither need, nor could agree, to give one authority pervasive, let alone binding, powers. Our aim must be to select those issues that the UN seems most suited to address, and then to identify how it might address them. We soon admit that increasing numbers of human problems can only or best be dealt with at the global level, which necessarily means the UN.

Some of the major challenges that the UN must face include the following. They can be divided into four broad groups: human resources, natural resources (the environment), security and economics.

HUMAN RESOURCES

EMPLOYING HUMAN RESOURCES EFFECTIVELY

Behind most current global insecurities lie two profound, interacting distortions. First, humanity appears—at least temporarily—to be exceeding the "carrying capacity" of both its institutions and the biosphere. Our newly acquired abilities have enabled us to expand human impact and numbers significantly faster, and to engage in activities much more destabilizing, than either our ecosystem or traditional social arrangements can absorb. Yet second, our knowledge-based society dissipates almost all the vast human intelligence that might help utilize or constrain these very numbers and profligate activities; only a tiny handful out of almost 6 billion people already alive will ever develop their full potential. Instead we condemn billions of invaluable intellects to marginal lives of un(der)employment—1.5

billion of them condemned to strait-jackets of illiteracy. Yet we continue to add almost 80 million persons annually to the tragic pool of particularly wasted talent, and to the pressure on institutions and resources. Yet these twin crises—continued population growth and wasted human capacity—not only have common roots in poverty and ignorance, but a common solution: human development through knowledge. This means family-planning advice and education made available to all, but particularly women; and all societies voluntarily choosing prudence before progeny. Many women already seek fewer children; and the more education they have, the fewer children they want and the more rights they gain from spouses and society. Men, too, want fewer children as they move up the social ladder; again their greatest asset is education. These programs, so mutually reinforcing, offer such economies of scale/technology that they can best be approached cooperatively on a global basis.

MANAGING MASS MIGRATIONS

Humans now move in unprecedented numbers, not simply because there are more people, but because both the need and opportunity have grown: both push and pull forces are powerful. The UN officially recognizes well over 20 million refugees forced unwillingly out of their own country. Globally, about one person in a hundred is either a refugee or displaced, that is, forced unwillingly to move within their country. Other mass migrations are more ambiguous, particularly the uncontrolled flows in poorer countries from country to city. When either or both the migrant and the locus of migration is unwilling, problems are bound to arise beyond mere acculturation. These increasingly global issues can best be dealt with at the global level.

OPTIMIZING GLOBAL KNOWLEDGE

In a knowledge-driven world, the maximum and most rapid exploitation of accurate information and essential technology should be facilitated, to the general welfare. Assisting in raising the Third World's access to information is a challenge so big and beneficial that it falls on the UN. States can be assisted electronically in gaining access to the world's essential pool of knowledge, particularly to exploit modern technology for rapid and widespread education. The distortions and instability that accompany the global revolution can thus be absorbed as quickly and painlessly as possible, and the Third World can make a major contribution to global sustainable development.

NATURAL RESOURCES (THE ENVIRONMENT)

ENDING MISUSE OF NON-HUMAN RESOURCES

Humanity's fixed global heritage is being destroyed or exploited at an accelerating rate. The net result is ultimately unsustainable. This applies to both renewable and non-renewable resources—those claimed by individuals or organizations, and those seen as our common heritage and/or as valueless externalities. From now on, all exploitable reserves must be at least roughly calculated, valued and used on a broadly sustainable basis. If these difficult aims are to have meaning and some hope of success, global accords and close cooperation are essential; the UN is already taking the lead.

CLEANING UP OUR MESS

Since the scientific revolution, and particularly since the population and technological explosions, certain human activities have done such dangerous and costly damage to the biosphere that mankind has no choice but try to make corrections. At minimum, widespread and/or transboundary environmental disruptions (for example, air pollution, soil erosion/salinization, desertification, water misuse, deforestation) must be controlled or reversed. The scale and wide spread nature of most of these problems, and the limited financial and technical ability of many of those worst affected, require that most can only or best be addressed collectively on a worldwide basis (as by more frequent and effective Earth Summits).

DEALING WITH BIOSPHERIC DISRUPTION

We confront or create serious physical phenomena of global impact, many caused by forces that can only be indirectly influenced or even understood. These may or may not be avoidable, but they can be predicted, or reduced in force or effect. Examples may be climatic (global warming, ozone loss); geological (earthquakes, eruptions); meteorological (floods, storms, droughts); space-originated (asteroids). Any human counteraction must be undertaken collectively by the global community.

DEALING WITH DISASTER

Almost all the challenges identified raise the possibility of catastrophe, however prescient the UN's efforts. World interdependence increases the chances that local events have global effects; the colossal and ever-growing scale of human intrusions on the biosphere make catastrophes both more likely and more serious; and the omnipresent media, combined with the appalling discrepancies in wealth, make assistance politically unavoidable. Geography, resources and technology alone make UN-coordinated action preferable.

COUNTERING MEDICAL CHALLENGES

Two trends cause increasing health concerns. First is the rapid and relentless escalation in the global movement of both people and things. Every conscious transfer also carries the threat of transmitting human, plant or animal disease, and inevitably raises the likelihood of pandemics. Second, the very widespread (over)use of antibiotics and other drugs has produced more resistant mutations and a global race to keep ahead. All this calls for tighter global biological preventive and control measures. Fortunately many can be integrated to a degree with other "security" screening and control of toxic-goods movements. Again, any impervious system demands all-inclusive global coverage.

SECURITY, LAW AND HUMAN RIGHTS

MEETING NEW SECURITY THREATS

The end of the Cold War did not ease, but instead probably intensified, human insecurity. The UN recognizes that dangers to international peace and security equate less with inter-state military violence, and more with other varied and multiple threats to survival. The priority reaction to altered threats must be changes and flexibility in human response. Human perceptions, priorities and institutions must adapt to situations. The necessary process of reaction is so grave, urgent and universal that it must be addressed collectively, as at the UN World Summits.

DEALING WITH FAILURE AND ANARCHY

The collapse of major institutions, both national and international, including failed states, is seen by many as a future headache for the international community. The UN will probably be the only acceptable physician in many cases. Two problems inevitably arise: the degree of global control/help that is acceptable yet sufficient, and the enormous cost and possibly time-scale involved. For many reasons, however, a political/security "black hole" can no longer be left unattended by an interdependent community.

ACCOMMODATING NON-STATE POWER

The authority, wealth and activities of many non-state transnational organizations (corporations, NGOs, ideological movements, and so on) is approaching or exceeding that of sovereign states. The international rules in regard to such bodies remain very limited. One reason is that they may have no genuine nationality and/or can play one state off against another. Somehow such organizations must be persuaded to respect a minimal system of supranational norms, if not jurisdiction. Only the UN System has any hope of accomplishing this.

CONFRONTING VIOLENCE

Since the end of the Cold War, while conflict between states has become rare, intra-state violence has increased. Self-determination, ethnic and religious differences have partly replaced resource gain and even ideology as reasons for inter-human combat. The proliferation and lethality of new weapons alone demands the reduction and eventual elimination of mass conflict. There is a continuum of things the UN can and must do. Through prevention and mediation, varied military or other sanctions, peace-keeping, and other intervention or assistance designed to stabilize or defuse situations, the UN must act as it was designed to do—further the building of global peace. A shrinking world makes peacemaking everywhere enlightened self-interest.

PROMOTING DISARMAMENT

The end of the Cold War brought new hope for peace dividends, but left a world awash in arms, surplus arms-making capacity, and unemployed arms professionals. Traffic increased in both scale and recipients, as prices fell. Control over the development, manufacture and deployment of lethal weapons and substances, particularly nuclear, biological and chemical, has became no longer the preserve of the superpowers and their allies. UN concern and activity has grown, but will be constrained by: continued weapons research, driven by fear, greed and curiosity; global diffusion of both weapons and relevant knowledge; the increasing difficulty of verification; and the vulnerability of complex modern society to disruption. All demand global reaction.

REDUCING HAZARDOUS FRUSTRATION

With the proliferation of weapons comes the profusion of those who could and might use them. The desperation of unemployment, the anger of those masses who perceive themselves deprived in a grossly unequal but more-aware world, and the boldness of ethnic and religious certainties, sow contagious seeds of terrorism, fanaticism and martyrdom. Arming and financing them are the growing numbers and wealth of drug dealers and other international criminals, and new thousands of well-trained and armed international mercenaries. Miniaturization, the diffusion of lethal knowledge and components, multi-use equipment and substances, all impede surveillance, while the vulnerability of energy- and information-dependent society makes it more susceptible to focused attack and blackmail. Counteraction must therefore involve all governments to eliminate sanctuary and safe transit. Counterintelligence must become as airtight and coordinated as possible. Only global coverage is effective.

BUILDING A GLOBAL RULE OF LAW

Every (binding) inter-state agreement constrains sovereignty, and every resolution passed in a universal forum contributes to creating global standards/norms. The general trend is thus for the body of international practice, precedent and law to grow at an unequalled rate. The reason is practical. A world whose international interconnections grow exponentially must establish and maintain relevant rules, controls and principles. The development of international law and tribunals must keep pace with interdependence. If global, the UN is involved.

DEVELOPING GLOBAL RIGHTS

The formation and acceptance of universal human rights and democratic norms raises questions. While some governments argue that human rights are culturally based, in practice the body of those globally accepted is expanding. In any event, any universal code must be developed through the gradual build-up of norms. The process of formulation and acceptance is constantly underway in various UN forums, and has been for many years. Movement, though slow, is clearly forward and increasingly intrusive within states.

ECONOMICS

MAINTAINING GLOBAL FINANCIAL CHECKS

About US$1 trillion worth of international financial transfers take place daily, a high percentage (80 percent?) of which is purely speculative. This reduces governments' degree of control over their fiscal policy and can threaten the stability of major currencies. It has therefore been suggested that a tax be levied on such transfers to damp down their scale. Since the proceeds would amount to billions of dollars, the UN, with its arrears problems, and the Third World, with its debt load and uncertain income, have a direct interest.

OPTIMIZING INTERNATIONAL TRADE

As the volume and value of international trade grows, it raises new problems of negotiation and regulation. In particular, the World Trade Organization will have to deal with the rapidly growing trade in services, chronic problems with agriculture, the issues of international investment and corruption, environmental and labor standards, and the taxing of international trade between parts of "global" corporations. Many economic agreements are already global, and will inevitably grow and become more complex.

ALLEVIATING GLOBAL DISTRESS

The avoidable frustration, hopelessness and anguish of billions of humans, brought about by abject poverty and extreme income divergence, both within and between states, should be rejected—if only in the selfish interest of global stability. The international community through the United Nations has a unique capacity, and so responsibility. We must try; there is no alternative.

In suggesting that the UN tackle these immense challenges, its limitations must be recognized. It has a number of quirks and constraints that will make its work difficult. (1) The UN System comprises a very large and loose network of agencies and other organizations, many with quite independent incomes, memberships and Charters. Effective coordination of all the System's activities, then, would require considerable effort by members states—and the amendment of many charters and agreements. (2) The UN consists of member states—now about 185. No nongovernmental bodies, let alone individuals, can vote in or for the UN. Equally, the UN is not a sovereign entity with its own views; it generally represents the collective will of member states. However, NGOs, business and technical bodies, and even private persons already play increasing roles, formally and informally, in UN decision making, usually indirectly, according to their unique roles and knowledge. (3) The UN Charter gives each member one vote. From microstate to superpower, this results in absurd, very undemocratic anomalies (humans are inherently similar; states never were). Although the smaller the state, the more it clings to the equal-vote anomaly, trends toward more decision by consensus has reduced resolutions by powerless majorities. A fair but practical balance is difficult. (4) General Assembly resolutions cannot bind governments. Only two types of international agreements do that: some Security Council decisions and some parts of binding treaties. Increasing global interdependence is forcing both categories to expand, while also gradually adding moral/political weight and variety to all inter-state agreements. (5) The five permanent members of the Council each have veto power, that is, substantive decisions cannot be taken against their will. This clause did not simply reflect 1945 realities; it almost certainly remains a basic condition for the United States and probably other veto powers to remain UN members (remember the helplessness of the League of Nations as nations bailed out and prepared for world war). Hence present vetoes are unlikely to be dropped even if more permanent members—with or without vetoes—are added to reflect current power realities. (6) The UN System has neither its own military forces nor direct funding sources. Both are now conceivable but very controversial.

In spite of these limitations and weaknesses, the UN remains the only universal body we have, representing the peoples of the Earth, as its Charter eloquently states. It is clear that global problems require global solutions, and this necessarily means involving the United Nations.

Chapter 10

Recent United Nations Agreements: A Force for Change

Rosalie Bertell

International Institute of Concern for Public Health

THE GOOD NEWS AND THE BAD NEWS

Over the last 50 years, the various agencies of the United Nations have evolved rather miraculously into more or less effective agents for global change. This is a remarkable accomplishment made difficult by the multinational and multilingual nature of the UN staff and the escalating nature of its mandate. The world's expectations of it are awesome, and it has endured great financial insecurity. At this crucial time in history, the close of the Cold War and the beginning of the Global Trade War, it is important to rethink the structure of the United Nations, its agencies and their mandates so as to encourage further growth in the direction of sustainability. It is also important to give it a new vision toward which to strive.

Because the United Nations lacked physical coercive power from the beginning, not having a monopoly on lethal weapons and forces as have nation-states, it has developed the more feminine qualities of consensus building and moral persuasion. Recently, through a quick succession of international conferences, the United Nations has been building a strong global consensus for environment, sustainable development, human settlement needs, human rights, population concerns and the rights of women and children. While this consensus has not yet been translated into action, I believe that its vitality will prevail over the other very strong movements within the United Nations to orient the world body to serve the needs of global trade in an aggressive market economy.

As the Western world moves from military competition to exerting firm control over world trade policies, it has been attempting to use the United Nations and its agencies to consolidate its control over intellectual property, patenting of nature and natural processes, and promoting constant national growth scenarios together with production of unlimited amounts of consumer products. Individual governments have played on addictions to gambling and lotteries as a source of money to fund social programs, while these are really a way of exploiting the poor and lowering taxes for the well off. The public's fear of crimes, and criminals addicted to alcohol and drugs, has become an excuse for using greater police force and suppressing legitimate dissent. At the United Nations level, these tendencies have brought both the Uruguay Round of GATT decisions and emergence of the World Trade Organization.

One is reminded of the techniques used by Adolph Hitler in forming Jewish ghettos. He declared that it was necessary to isolate the Jewish people because they had contagious diseases. He prescribed ghettos as a public health policy. Then he controlled the jobs available in the ghettos and the health care available, but left the ghettos free to govern themselves. As jobs were poorly paid, food expensive, living conditions more crowded, and outward mobility prohibited, the problems of contagious diseases, of course, escalated. This reinforced the false logic and exerted pressure on ghetto leaders, who were forced to take the blame for conditions. However, the situation was unsustainable, and Hitler soon reverted to outright murder, without a great public outcry. With today's globalization of money and trade goes a sort of ghettoization of nations, labor exploitation, restriction of worker mobility, control of jobs and health care, and the monetary policy of structural adjustment.

The global trade and economic war we are experiencing offers an unsustainable scenario similar to that of Hitler's. It imposes the "logic" of structural adjustment for struggling nations with developing economies, which in turn brings to the people poverty, sickness and crime, with no escape. The "cure" creates the problem, and the policy will create very unstable situations in the world. Such instability, with the poor growing poorer and the rich growing richer, cannot be "managed" with brute force and suppression for long. When it breaks down, will it tend toward genocide again, or will there be an alternative answer that will rally human support from all parts of the world? There are clear signs that force will be tried. There are also signs of hope for a global breakthrough to new behavior!

The trend toward increased force can be seen in the continued development of rocket technology and efforts to control space; in the continued development of high-tech weapons: robots, space shields, laser beams and electromagnetic-field weapons. I see it in attempts to harness the power of the electrojet in the ionosphere, and in the hardening of communications systems by the GWEN program in North America. Right now the people of Kodiak Island, in Alaska, are being asked by the U.S. military to accept a new rocket launching pad for the interception of "enemy" rockets, and the U.S. military High Active Auroral Research Project (HAARP) is manipulating our ionosphere and undertaking deep Earth tomography. What I believe is at stake, although the time line is not well known yet, is the way we will handle the unsustainable global scenario when the people of the world awaken and realize their plight. Obviously, those who propose the economic policies are the same ones who are preparing for the next war. I believe that the war will be against the people who wish to share in the bountifulness of the Earth! This means the aggressors are well aware that their economic policy recommendations are unsustainable! I do not see that a viable alternative consensus was available to those Germans who disagreed with Nazi policy in the 1930s and 1940s, but today we have some encouraging signs of hope and some other possibilities.

Greed, violence and short-term goals will mean a good life for a few people for a short time, but the ultimate destruction of the global environment and society as we know it. The alternative is widespread behavioral changes, and the adoption on a grand scale of attitudes, values and behaviors that lead to sustainable development. It has been slow in coming, but when one believes that life is stronger than death, one can stand against the tide and keep waiting and working for this change.

A vision of a sustainable development would need to include a healthy social, economic and natural environment. Poverty and unemployment are unsustainable pollutions of the social and economic environment. They have no place in the evolution of a healthy world order, one in which people can enjoy normal development of their potential and have healthy children. One of the means at the disposal of the United Nations to rectify the balance between social/environmental needs and those perceived needs of the economic community that tend to distort holistic development is to strengthen the agencies that directly speak to the social and environmental needs. A second important option is to develop an International Environment Agency to see to the development of health-based regulations and environmental protection laws that cannot be manipulated for trade advantages, and a specialized Court of the Environment to enforce these laws.

TWO INTER-AGENCY DOCUMENTS FOR PROGRESS

On March 5, 1997, the heads of the United Nations Environment Program (UNEP) and the United Nations Children's Fund (UNICEF) signed an important Memorandum of Understanding (MOU) aimed at cooperation between these two United Nations programs in areas fundamental to the attainment of sustainable development. They will mutually support efforts, using the best available scientific and environmental information, that bear on children and child health, to implement programs to ensure the well-being of children. Obviously, a good environment for children will help enable them, as adults, to reach their potential. Currently more than 12 million children die annually from preventable diseases. Pressures against children's survival come from poverty, World Bank policies of structural adjustment, unfair trade practices, unemployment and underemployment of their parents, environmental degradation such as desertification, war and other counterproductive human behavior. Whether or not this coalition of UN agencies will be strong enough to counteract the more aggressive policies of the World Trade Organization will be seen in the future. However, UNEP, in particular, has been building carefully its credibility and reliability especially among environmental and health professionals, and among grass-roots people in economically developing countries. They have broad human support, even though they lack political and economic support.

About a week after the UNEP/UNESCO agreement, on March 14, 1997, the Environment Liaison Center International released its Tilonia Declaration, calling for a people-centered ecologically sustainable development model. This triennial meeting, held in Tilonia, Rajasthan, India, denounced trade and development practices that wipe out local culture, sustainable local practices and identities. This conference, in a remote village of the so-called Third World, has stated: "No sustainable solution to improve, preserve, protect and conserve the environment is possible without the direct involvement of communities in the planning and implementation process. Space must be created for the oppressed communities to participate in decision making." People will no longer be sidelined and used to produce the wealth of others. Even the focus on biodiversity has aroused the passion for cultural diversity and healthy pride in one's heritage. Local leaders are no longer being blamed for all local problems. This desire for grass-roots participation in planning is an exact antithesis of the planning scheme behind the World Trade Organization, which has never sought grass-roots input!

A United Nations International Environment Agency and an International Court of the Environment were both proposed in Agenda 21 of the UN Conference on the Environment and Development (UNCED) in 1992, and approved by the participating nations. Judge Amedeo Postiglione, of the Supreme Court of Italy, has, with the backing of his country, been developing plans for the structure and functions of these two new UN agencies. He needs international support for this endeavor, which is important for maintaining the balance of power with the World Trade Organization. Environmental protection is often called a trade barrier, and a level playing field sometimes means the lowest common denominator for workers' rights and human health concerns.

Women have often been considered an indicator of social rest or unrest. They often act as social-change agents, having generated and organized most social institutions, including schools, hospitals and social-service agencies. Recently, we have had two women heads of the leading United Nations social agencies, Elizabeth Dowdeswell for UNEP and Carol Bellamy for UNICEF. Barbara Ward was influential in putting the environment on the global agenda. The World Women's Conference in Beijing in 1995 was incredibly well attended and, for the first time in history, the NGO Parallel Conference was better attended than the Governmental Conference.

The partners for an emerging coalition of UN agencies, people's movements, non-governmental organizations, and women's movements are now in place. I would rate them as still politically weak in the face of nation-state power and economic (money) power, but they are becoming a real moral force not easily ignored.

HUMAN RIGHTS DOCUMENTS

When the United Nations was first launched in 1945, there was a justice-oriented, poetic vision born with it to nourish its more practical structural components. This vision was embodied in the Human Rights Covenants. It is notable that these rights were not called "democratic," but "human." They applied to every person born into this world and not just to those who had a democratic form of government. The Covenants set a limit on governmental power, no matter what its origin, form or history. Governmental power was clearly declared to be limited by human rights.

This vision has given rise to many organizations, such as Amnesty International and the International Human Rights Lawyers, and the grassroots people of the world have found it a powerful friend. It has given pause to those who would abuse power, and even where it failed to moderate aberrant behavior, it took away all pretense to social approval. Humans can change their behavior, and withhold social approval of behavior, even when that behavior was not questioned in the past. The great human victories in this regard have been over slavery, torture, oppression of women, exploitation of children and destruction of worker health. The struggle goes on to outlaw capital punishment, genocide and rape as weapons of war, and violence as a way to settle differences.

This tactic of sowing a seed of hope and vision along with structural creations has helped all of the UN agencies and given them enormous human credibility with all people. Even in the most restrictive times of the former Soviet rule, United Nations programs could be implemented. Developing nations hold the United Nations as their friend and mentor, and as a sign of hope in a hostile world.

THE EARTH CHARTER

A new seed has been cast in the human community, and if it takes root and grows, it will, I think, be strong enough to assure that sanity will carry the balance of power between the conscientious NGOs and the corporate elite. That "wild card" may well be the Earth Charter, which set sail into the human global forum from the Rio + 5 Conference in March 1997.

This new-vision document can grow over the next decades. If supported, it will not only broaden the concept of good global citizenship, and articulate the values and behaviors acceptable in a developing global community, but it should effectively mold society's expectations. It can also be expected to spawn non-governmental organizations that will take to heart this vision and give it life.

Hopefully, it will also serve to reorient nationalism toward globalism in a world enriched with a countless variety of global villages, each with a distinctive culture and place in the tapestry being created. In turn, this will fulfil the desire to nurture helpful differences in lifestyle, and encourage the formation of bioregional coalitions for handling common problems. It should serve to reduce local governments to maintaining viable local infrastructure and civil order. The reduction of competition should lead to solving differences by legal means rather than by law-of-the-jungle violence, thus at the same time reducing the need for nation-states. National political organization will be relatively less important, and there will be no need to raise standing armies. Capable international police and emergency response teams will be all that are needed to maintain peace within and between the global villages.

My hope for the future of the United Nations rests in structural reform, especially in the strengthening of the social and environmental agencies, in the development of international law, and in the power of the seed sown through the promulgation of the Earth Charter. A copy of the draft Charter is appended to this paper. The Benchmark Draft released in 1997 is viewed as a "document in process," and is intended to serve as a guide and basis for discussion in regional consultations around the world. It is hoped that this Charter will be the basis for a new treaty, a new covenant governing human relationships with the Earth and with all of the living creatures with whom we share this profound gift of life. It is the seminal basis of my hope. The Earth Charter, as with the other documents mentioned, can be a force for change as well as a reason for hope.

ANNEX: THE EARTH CHARTER

(Benchmark Draft, reviewed and presented during the Rio + 5 Forum on March 18, 1997.)

Earth is our home and home to all living beings. Earth itself is alive. We are part of an evolving universe. Human beings are members of an interdependent community of life with a magnificent diversity of life forms and cultures. We are humbled before the beauty of Earth and share a reverence for life and the sources of our being. We give thanks for the heritage that we have received from past generations and embrace our responsibilities to present and future generations.

The Earth Community stands at a defining moment. The biosphere is governed by laws that we ignore at our own peril. Human beings have acquired the ability to radically alter the environment and evolutionary processes. Lack of foresight and misuse of knowledge and power threaten the fabric of life and the foundations of local and global security. There is great violence, poverty, and suffering in our world. A fundamental change of course is needed. The choice is before us: to care for Earth or to participate in the destruction of ourselves and the diversity of life. We must reinvent industrial-technological civilization, finding new ways to balance self and community, having and being, diversity and unity, short-term and long-term, using and nurturing.

In the midst of all our diversity, we are one humanity and one Earth family with a shared destiny. The challenges before us require an inclusive ethical vision. Partnerships must be forged and cooperation fostered at local, bioregional, national and international levels. In solidarity with one another and the community of life, we the peoples of the world commit ourselves to action guided by the following interrelated principles:

1) Respect Earth and all life. Earth, each life form, and all living beings possess intrinsic value and warrant respect independently of their utilitarian value to humanity.

2) Care for Earth, protecting and restoring the diversity, integrity, and beauty of the planet's ecosystems. Where there is risk of irreversible or serious damage to the environment, precautionary action must be taken to prevent harm.

3) Live sustainably, promoting and adopting modes of consumption, production and reproduction that respect and safeguard human rights and the regenerative capacities of Earth.

4) Establish justice, and defend without discrimination the right of all people to life, liberty, and security of person within an environment adequate for human health and spiritual well-being. People have a right to potable water, clean air, uncontaminated soil, and food security.

5) Share equitably the benefits of natural resource use and a

healthy environment among the nations, between rich and poor, between males and females, between present and future generations, and internalize all environmental, social and economic costs.

6) Promote social development and financial systems that create and maintain sustainable livelihoods, eradicate poverty, and strengthen local communities.

7) Practice non-violence, recognizing that peace is the wholeness created by harmonious and balanced relationships with oneself, other persons, other life forms and Earth.

8) Strengthen processes that empower people to participate effectively in decision-making and ensure transparency and accountability in governance and administration in all sectors of society.

9) Reaffirm that Indigenous and Tribal Peoples have a vital role in the care and protection of Mother Earth. They have the right to retain their spirituality, knowledge, lands, territories and resources.

10) Affirm that gender equality is a prerequisite for sustainable development.

11) Secure the right to sexual and reproductive health, with special concern for women and girls.

12) Promote the participation of youth as accountable agents of change for local, bioregional and global sustainability.

13) Advance and put to use scientific and other types of knowledge and technologies that promote sustainable living and protect the environment.

14) Ensure that people throughout their lives have opportunities to acquire the knowledge, values, and practical skills needed to build sustainable communities.

15) Treat all creatures with compassion and protect them from cruelty and wanton destruction.

16) Do not do to the environment of others what you do not want done to your environment.

17) Protect and restore places of outstanding ecological, cultural, aesthetic, spiritual, and scientific significance.

18) Cultivate and act with a sense of shared responsibility for the well-being of the Earth Community. Every person, institution and government have a duty to advance

the indivisible goals of justice for all, sustainability, world peace, and respect and care for the larger community of life.

Embracing the values in this Charter, we can grow into a family of cultures that allows the potential of all persons to unfold in harmony with the Earth Community. We must preserve a strong faith in the possibilities of the human spirit and a deep sense of belonging to the universe. Our best actions will embody the integration of knowledge with compassion.

In order to develop and implement the principles in this Charter, the nations of the world should adopt as a first step an international convention that provides an integrated legal framework for existing and future environmental and sustainable development law and policy.

(Further information about the Earth Charter can be found at <www.earthcharter.org>.)

Chapter 11

Monitoring the Rules: The United Nations and Iraq

D. Marc Kilgour

Director Laurier Centre for Military, Strategic and Disarmament Studies, Wilfrid Laurier University

INTERNATIONAL INSTITUTIONS AND HOW TO CHANGE THEM

Social institutions are "the humanly devised constraints that structure political, economic, and social interaction" (North, 1991). Theorists often evaluate social institutions, and inquire how they could be modified to achieve, for example, greater individual equity or better environmental management. (See, for example, Loehman and Kilgour, 1998.) New institutional arrangements, they have concluded, may be imposed by external authority, or may evolve from the coincidence of mutually fulfilled expectations.

Imposed or not, institutions are always at risk of breaking down unless (most of) the individuals whose actions are constrained are willing to continue to accept those constraints. Institutions can be stabilized by credible threats—individuals may forego personal gains when those gains would be outweighed by a threatened reprisal. Institutions can also be stabilized positively, by the perception of mutual interest that, as Axelrod (1984) argued, can develop when participants use Rapoport's tit-for-tat strategy. For instance, drivers who are in a hurry may obey speed limits because they fear the punishment (and delay) that would follow detection, or because they recognize that prudence behind the wheel is a general benefit to society.

The rules and conventions that constrain the interactions of sovereign states, called international institutions or *regimes,* are in many ways analogous to the institutional arrangements that constrain the actions of individuals. Under the so-called Westphalian system, each state has complete autonomy in the pursuit of its own interests as it sees them. But states can resemble individuals in that actions chosen by one state may benefit itself but harm others. With increasing population, increasing expectations and increasing technical capabilities, this problem is becoming extremely grave, leading many observers to conclude that many regimes must change if humanity is to have a future.

Some international institutions have evolved based on the coincidence of mutually fulfilled expectations, including those governing international trade, for example, or international travel for migration, employment or tourism. These regimes are well established and likely to remain stable, or to evolve slowly. Attempts to establish regimes for environmental management are under way, such as the 1997 Kyoto Protocol limiting emissions of greenhouse gases. Such regimes may begin with wide initial agreement, but their success depends on the continuation of perceived mutual interest, for example in reduction of negative climatic effects caused by greenhouse gas accumulation in Earth's upper atmosphere.

Regimes that have existed for some time, or that are formed on the basis of wide agreement, seem to have a good chance of success. Unfortunately, there are instances when regimes, though sorely needed, seem extremely unlikely to evolve spontaneously, or to develop on the basis of explicit agreement, simply because the manifestly conflicting interests of the participants seem impossible to reconcile. In such cases, many look to the United Nations to impose a regime, as it did in the series of Security Council resolutions referring to Iraq in 1991.

To fulfill the role of guardian of the common interests of humanity, a strengthened UN (or successor organization) must be able to (1) act quickly and decisively to structure a fair and just international regime, and (2) establish and maintain that regime. The first of these requirements—to find just and appropriate rules to apply to each sovereign state—undoubtedly presents the greater difficulty in theory and in practice. But it is the second requirement—to enforce the rules—that is the focus of this chapter. As discussed above, enforcement may be necessary, at least temporarily, for regime change. A state may come to recognize that a system of rules is in its interest; subsequently, only minimal enforcement effort is required. But, states may not come to this recognition quickly, if ever, so enforcement may be a substantial burden, one that may be difficult to support using the existing United Nations structure.

Rule enforcement has two aspects. Rules must be monitored—behavior must be observed, assessed and compared to what the rules prescribe. In other words, violations of the regime must be detected. Then there must be the capability, and the will, to take appropriate action in response to deliberate violations of the rules. This chapter concentrates on UN efforts to monitor Iraq with respect to the rules imposed by the UN Security Council. The United Nations Special Commission (UNSCOM), created for this purpose, was particularly innovative in both structure and procedures, and, as will be argued below, was largely successful in its mission. If enforcement of the rules imposed on Iraq was not successful, the fault lies mainly in lack of capacity and willingness to respond to violations, rather than in weaknesses in UNSCOM's ability to detect them.

THE UNITED NATIONS SPECIAL COMMISSION

United Nations Security Council Resolutions 687, 707 and 715, all passed in 1991, required that Iraq destroy its stocks of weapons of mass destruction and the means for their delivery, and dismantle associated development and manufacturing programs. The United Nations Special Commission (UNSCOM) was created to ensure that these obligations were met, and to develop systems for the ongoing monitoring and verification of related future activities in Iraq. In the nuclear-weapons area, UNSCOM worked with the International Atomic Energy Agency (IAEA), a UN-affiliated body with special expertise in nuclear materials verification.

As an arms-control regime, the Security Council resolutions on Iraq are unprecedented. They call for the elimination of complete categories of weapons, not only current stocks but also the capacity for future development and production. As well, there are no limits (such as annual inspection quotas) on monitoring and verification activities. UNSCOM's operations in Iraq are constrained only by the inherent difficulty of obtaining appropriate personnel and equipment and then carrying out the planning, coordinating, logistics, debriefing and assessment of monitoring missions. Though the Security Council resolutions constitute unilateral arms control, a contrast to the traditional bilateral or multilateral varieties, Iraq's non-cooperation has amounted to a serious constraint on UNSCOM.

UNSCOM grouped its efforts to carry out its mandate into four functionally defined inspection disciplines:

1. Nuclear Weapons,
2. Chemical Weapons,
3. Biological Weapons,
4. Missiles with a range at least 500 kilometers.

Most of UNSCOM's personnel and operations, including on-site inspections, have been associated with one of these four disciplines (rarely more than one). "Special" inspection missions, intended mainly to establish or prepare inspection infrastructure, or to clarify inspection rights and obligations, have also been undertaken.

ON-SITE INSPECTIONS

UNSCOM has carried out hundreds of on-site inspections, the mainstay of its operations. About 40 countries have contributed personnel to UNSCOM on-site inspection teams.

Initially, inspection teams were assembled out-of-country (sometimes as far away as New York), briefed, flown to Iraq immediately prior to their missions, and flown out immediately afterward. About 30 on-site inspection missions were carried out in this way in each of 1991, 1992 and 1993. The frequency of inspection missions then rose sharply to more than 100 in 1995. This sudden increase likely reflects the opening in 1994 of the Baghdad Monitoring and Verification Center (BMVC), an in-country base and accommodation facility for personnel associated with all four inspection disciplines, along with support staff.

Some features of the UNSCOM on-site inspection program have

been fairly constant over time. For example, the proportion of inspections that are discipline-related has remained around 80 percent. But other characteristics have exhibited considerable variation. Discipline inspections, for instance, were mostly against nuclear weapons and missiles initially, then against chemical weapons, then biological, so that totals for all four disciplines are now approximately equal. The average duration of discipline-related inspection missions has been increasing steadily since 1991, a trend unaltered by the opening of the BMVC. The average number of inspectors on a discipline inspection began at about 10 in 1991, peaked at 15–20 in 1993–94, and declined thereafter. (See Kilgour and Cleminson, 1996, for more details.) This pattern must reflect, at least in part, the availability of the BMVC, where inspections with only a handful of inspectors have sometimes been based.

Within an inspection discipline, on-site inspections can generally be categorized as having at least one of the following purposes:

1. *Baseline:* to establish data on the layout and organization of a site and the means of access to it, and on the capacities, capabilities and normal activities at a facility.
2. *Search:* to obtain evidence (direct or circumstantial physical evidence, or documentary evidence) of proscribed or undeclared activity at a site.
3. *Tagging and Inventory:* to record and mark permanently the equipment at a site, and to measure current inventories of expendable materials.
4. *Interrogation:* to interview personnel concerning activities at a site, data interpretation, data anomalies and missing information.

Within each inspection discipline, the proportion of on-site inspections applied to each of these purposes depends on many factors. Baseline inspections, for instance, are usually early in a sequence of missions, and occur later on only if new information has been received.

The success of UNSCOM has resulted, in large part, from its orientation toward simple and practical procedures, and its ability to innovate. UNSCOM has demonstrated a remarkable ability to solve technical and information problems; to operate within severe restrictions on time, personnel and equipment; to work in difficult conditions; to integrate expertise and resources from UN member states and from IAEA; and to deal with unexpected challenges directly, decisively and judiciously. One of

UNSCOM's most useful innovations has been the systematic application of parallel monitoring and verification techniques, not merely to gather more data, but to achieve and exploit synergy.

VERIFICATION SYNERGIES

Verification synergies have been defined as "combinative effects arising between verification methods and techniques, between agreements or regimes, between implementing mechanisms and forums, between organizations and agencies within a country, between countries party to an agreement, and various combinations of these items" (McFate et al., 1993, iii). Informally, synergy is achieved when data from one source is used to increase the information content of data from another source, making verification more effective, or less costly.

Synergies across monitoring techniques have been exploited extensively by UNSCOM. A typical strategy is to begin with a monitoring technique that is cheap and can assess a large number of cases, but may not be particularly accurate. Then a more expensive but more accurate technique is used to follow up on each anomaly, or "potential violation site," identified previously. Of course, there may be many subsequent steps, and very complex conditional response sequences, as used, for example, in chemical identification procedures, are sometimes of value.

The existence of the BMVC has facilitated a large-scale program to "cue" on-site inspections using aerial surveillance. Among UNSCOM's aerial assets are high-altitude surveillance aircraft (over 250 missions by the end of 1995), conventional aircraft, and helicopters. Helicopters for rapid transport of inspection teams to potential violation sites make feasible no-notice inspections following up on aerial imagery. Another essential component is the BMVC's photographic development laboratory, which can process and interpret aerial photographs in short order. These elements have proven crucial to the success of many inspections.

In fact, the organization and operation of the Baghdad Monitoring and Verification Center itself illustrates UNSCOM's "layered" approach. With staff of about 100, the BMVC is the in-country headquarters for on-site inspection teams, and the central collection point for data from *in situ* remote monitoring equipment, overhead imagery, and so on. In fact, the BMVC can automatically "fuse" images transmitted from remote cameras with data from other sources.

In only a few years, UNSCOM's package of verification techniques expanded from on-site inspections to the long list shown in table 11.1. But what the table does not show are the simultaneous and sequential synergies among the techniques, a few of which have been suggested above. Even the BMVC's integration of facilities and accommodation for inspectors and support personnel from all inspection disciplines represents another form of synergy, one that may be more difficult to measure but that is valuable nonetheless. As Zlauvinen (1997, 6) puts it, "No one of these elements on its own would suffice to provide confidence in the system. But together they constitute the most comprehensive international monitoring system ever established in the sphere of arms control."

Harmonization is an idea related to synergy that also came to be important to UNSCOM, and may be equally important for future arms control. Under a policy of harmonization, priority is given to maximizing comparability and consistency across functions and procedures, even when they are unrelated in purpose and methodology. Examples include common standards and norms for equipment, common units of measurement and commonly accessible records. UNSCOM has harmonized across inspection disciplines by using common maps and codes, and by maintaining multipurpose facilities (for example, photographic laboratories) and equipment (for example, helicopters). When information gath-

Table 11.1: Monitoring and Verification Methodologies in Iraq, 1995

Methodology	*Sources and Varieties*
1. Satellite Imagery	NTM and commercial
2. High-Altitude Aerial Imagery	UNSCOM U-2 Reconnaissance
3. Medium Altitude Aerial Imagery	AN-30 (Russia) (currently on hold)
4. Helicopter Aerial Imagery	UNSCOM C53 heilicopters (Germany)
5. On-site Inspections	Many cued by other methodologies
6. Environmental monitoring	Air, soil and water sampling
7. IAEA Safeguards	NPT mandate
8. Ground Penetrating Radar	Bell helicopters
9. Radiation detectors	Multipurpose
10. Remote sensors in situ	Cameras, sniffers, etc.
11. Collateral analysis	Literature search
12. Human information	Travelers, defectors, etc.

ered for one purpose can be used for another, monitoring effectiveness is enhanced. Harmonization aims to facilitate such multiple uses.

LESSONS FROM UNSCOM'S EXPERIENCE IN IRAQ

The United Nations Special Commission has demonstrated that the United Nations can meet one of the prerequisites for imposing behavioral constraints on a sovereign state. This capability may be crucial in the prevention of future humanitarian and environmental disasters. Moreover, UNSCOM's operations in Iraq have generated important new ideas, such as verification synergies and harmonization, to improve arms control. UNSCOM has integrated these ideas and applied them in practice on a large scale.

Another valuable set of lessons from UNSCOM's Iraq experience is evident in its procedures for on-site inspections, a fundamental component of any arms-monitoring system. UNSCOM has given careful attention to its techniques for assembling, organizing, equipping, briefing and debriefing on-site inspection teams. It has also been attentive to the "strategy" of on-site inspections, and the implications of inspection objectives for team composition, organization and equipment. Based on the problems faced by UNSCOM and the solutions it adopted, Kilgour and Cleminson (1996) suggest the development of a theory to explain how inspection purposes and team size might evolve through the phases of an inspection program. Similarly, Duncan and Johnson (1996) applied principles developed by UNSCOM to possible verification of the Biological and Toxin Weapons Convention. UNSCOM's practical experience with different models for on-site inspection team compositions, objectives, procedures and time frames may prove invaluable in many arms-control arenas.

Early in UNSCOM's mandate, it became clear that a "forensic" approach was unavoidable. In fact, many of UNSCOM's greatest successes involved a focus on the assessment of physical evidence, often trace evidence. For instance, Zlauvinen (1997, 6) details a number of forensic studies to evaluate Iraq's records of the destruction of missile engines. These include material analysis of remnants for traces of the products of missile engine firing (to establish that they were missile parts), computer reconstruction of destroyed missile components to determine whether engine remnants without identifiable serial numbers represent additional engines or parts of engines already counted, and test explosions to assess whether critical components could have been removed from engines prior to destruction.

The forensic analysis of documents detailing Iraq's actions to destroy weapons of mass destruction and the means to deliver them was also part of another UNSCOM success. Along with the dramatic revelations of Hussein Kamel (the son-in-law of Saddam Hussein, who had been in charge of various weapons programs) in 1995, UNSCOM's determined attempts to correlate biological-growth medium purchases with actual inventories led to the discovery of Iraq's secret biological weapons program (Wedgwood, 1996). Zlauvinen (1997, 5) calls this episode "one of the most effective investigations of arms control history."

The Secretary-General of the United Nations called the implementation of United Nations Security Council Resolutions 687, 707 and 715 a "verification laboratory" for the testing of verification methods, procedures and techniques (United Nations, 1995). The importance of UNSCOM's innovations for future arms control is difficult to overemphasize.

The experience of UNSCOM points to the desirability of enhancing the technical capability of the UN in verification for possible future missions, when the many of the lessons of UNSCOM would be valuable. Proposals have even been made for a permanent UN verification capability, unit or agency. Such a body could be used to monitor a range of disarmament activities, whether imposed by the Security Council, mandated by treaty or conducted unilaterally by a nation wishing to have its positive initiatives verified objectively. A detailed study and proposal has been made by Dorn (1990A, 1990B).

UNSCOM's successes do not imply that the United Nations has developed the capacity to impose order on sovereign states. The regime upheld by UNSCOM in Iraq was always an imposed institution and was never fully accepted by Iraq. As discussed above, imposed institutions can endure only when backed by the realistic potential for punishment in cases of violation. UNSCOM's role was to monitor behavior to identify violations; responsibility for responding to violations fell to the Security Council.

In 1997–98, an escalating series of crises indicated that the will of the UN to enforce the Security Council resolutions on Iraq is flagging. In April and May 1997, a dispute arose about the right of UNSCOM to inspect security-related facilities. In October and November 1997, Iraq refused on-site inspection teams that included U.S. citizens, and UNSCOM withdrew all its inspectors from Iraq briefly. In January and

February 1998, the issue of inspection of presidential sites was not resolved until UN Secretary-General Kofi Annan intervened. In August 1998, Iraq began to refuse "spot" inspections, surprise on-site inspections following up on data from other sources, often remote cameras (Crossette, 1998). While UNSCOM may have succeeded beyond reasonable expectations, the overall success of the United Nations in its efforts to impose rules on Iraq became open to serious doubt. Human history contains few examples of the successful imposition of behavioral norms on sovereign governments. To impose rules requires the ability to enforce them, and enforcement presupposes not only the resources, technology and expertise to detect violations of those rules, but also the will and capacity to respond appropriately to such violations. In this context, the United Nations Special Commission in Iraq has made a positive contribution by demonstrating how monitoring and assessment can be carried out effectively and efficiently. But monitoring is not enough, and the United Nations will need to address serious deficiencies in violation response if it is to have the capacity to impose order on recalcitrant states, or within states in which governments have broken down.

ACKNOWLEDGMENTS

The author gratefully acknowledges the assistance of the Department of Foreign Affairs and International Trade, Canada, in the early stages of this research. Research support was provided by the Laurier Centre for Military Strategic and Disarmament Studies and the Social Sciences and Humanities Research Council of Canada.
This chapter is a substantially revised version of Kilgour (1997).

REFERENCES

Axelrod, Robert. 1984. *The Evolution of Cooperation.* New York: Basic Books.
Crossette, Barbara. 1998. "Iraq Increasingly Defiant on Arms Inspections." *New York Times,* August 13.
Crossette, Barbara. 1996. "Iraq Isn't Doing So Well at Hide and Seek." *New York Times,* June 16, 4–16.
Dorn, A. Walter. 1990(A). "UN Should Verify Treaties." *Bulletin of the Atomic Scientists,* July-August, 12–13.

Dorn, A. Walter. 1990(B). "The Case for a United Nations Verification Agency: Disarmament Under Effective International Control." Working Paper 26, Canadian Institute for International Peace and Security, Ottawa.

Duncan, Annabelle and Kenneth G. Johnson. 1996. "Strengthening the Biological Weapons Convention—Lessons from the United Nations Special Commission on Iraq." Department of National Defence, Canada.

Kilgour, D. Marc. and Ronald C. Cleminson. 1996. "Arms Control Verification Synergies: Theory and Applications in the United Nations Context," in *Probabilistic Safety Assessment and Management,* ed. D. Cacciabue and I. A. Papazoglou, 210–216. London: Springer.

Kilgour, D. Marc. 1997. "Establishing the Rules: The United Nations Experience in Iraq," in *Proceedings of the Interdisciplinary Conference: The Evolution of World Order: Building a Foundation for Peace in the Third Millennium,* Toronto, Ontario, June 6–8, 58–63.

Loehman, Edna T. and D. Marc Kilgour, eds. 1998. *Designing Institutions for Environmental and Resource Management.* Cheltenham, Eng.: Edward Elgar Publishers.

McFate, Patricia B., Sidney N. Graybeal, George Lindsey, and D. Marc Kilgour. 1993. "Constraining Proliferation: The Contribution of Verification Synergies." Arms Control Verification Studies No. 5, Foreign Affairs and International Trade Canada, Ottawa.

North, Douglas C. 1991. "Institutions." *Journal of Economic Perspectives* 5, 1, 97–112.

United Nations. 1995. "Verification in All its Aspects, Including the Role of the United Nations in the Field of Verification." Report of the Secretary General, UN Document A/50/377.

Wedgwood, Ruth. 1996. "Keep Rooting Out Saddam Hussein's Arsenal." *International Herald Tribune,* June 21, 8.

Zlauvinen, Gustavo. 1997. "Meeting the Multilateral Proliferation Challenge Through United Nations Actions," in *Cyberspace and Outer Space: Transitional Challenges for Multilateral Verification in the 21st Century,* ed. J. Marshall Beier and Steven Mataija, 1–7. Centre for International and Security Studies, York University, Toronto, Canada.

Chapter 12

The Creation of an Independent and Effective International Criminal Court

Fergus Watt

*Executive Director,
World Federalists of Canada1*

The Rome Statute of the International Criminal Court was the result of a three-year process of UN preparatory negotiations, leading to the five-week diplomatic conference in Rome. From June 15 to July 17, 1998, diplomats from over 150 states gathered in Rome, Italy, for the final phase of negotiations to create a permanent International Criminal Court. A coalition of over 800 non-governmental organizations (NGOs) also gathered there to track the negotiations, lobby intensively and relay information to their constituencies around the world. This paper offers a brief account of these negotiations, as well as analysis of the dynamics that shaped outcomes regarding some of the political issues of concern to the NGO community.

Following an eleventh-hour drama during which amendments proposed by the United States and India were both defeated, a treaty text was adopted amid much celebration and emotion. At the signing ceremony the next day, UN Secretary-General Kofi Annan said:

> By adopting this Statute, participants in the Conference have overcome many legal and political problems, which kept this question on the United Nations agenda almost throughout the Organization's history. . . . The establishment of the Court is a gift of hope to future generations, and a giant step forward in the march towards universal human rights and the rule of law. It is an achievement which, only a few years ago, nobody would have thought possible.

Completion of the Rome Statute for an International Criminal Court adds meaning and substance to the world's commemoration, in 1998, of the fiftieth anniversary of the Universal Declaration of Human Rights. The Court, which will be established once 60 governments have submitted their instruments of ratification, will give the world a powerful new tool to punish individuals who are guilty of committing genocide, war crimes and crimes against humanity.

Heading into the Rome Diplomatic Conference there was much cause for concern regarding the outcome. Over 1,300 square brackets remained in a complex, 172-page draft of the Statute. Would the international community succeed in creating an ICC that is not subject to interference from political organs, like the UN Security Council? Would the crimes under the Court's jurisdiction be adequately defined? Would the Court's Prosecutor have the capacity and authority to act independently, in a manner that maintains the confidence of the world's states and people? Would the Court be empowered to effectively assert its jurisdiction when these most serious crimes of concern to the international community are alleged to have occurred?

In principle, creation of a Criminal Court strengthens the UN's capacity to maintain international peace and security. Whereas the UN typically punishes an entire state for the crimes of a few, an ICC will hold individuals, including national political and military leaders, accountable for violations of some of the worst offenses under international law.

Rather than respond to acts of genocide occasionally and after the fact, creation of a permanent International Criminal Court will allow the UN's application of humanitarian law to become much more consistent and reliable. A permanent Court will also allow for greater efficiency and cost-savings. And the existence of the Court will serve a preventive function by deterring other potential criminals.

In the aftermath of war, criminal prosecution of leading individuals can help defuse the animosities and mistrust among formerly warring communities. By individualizing guilt, entire groups are not held responsible for genocide or other humanitarian crimes, thus contributing to social and political healing and reconstruction. Furthermore, the existence of an ICC will help erode the outdated notion that the world is little more than a collection of nation-states. It is an important step, conceptually and politically, from state-centered thinking to a framework in which the individual has rights and responsibilities under international law.

With all this going for it, there is little wonder that the negotiations to create a permanent ICC attracted the attention of a global NGO constituency. It was worldwide revulsion following reports of genocide and ethnic cleansing in Rwanda and the former Yugoslavia that led to the creation of the Ad Hoc Tribunals to try war criminals from those states. Popular interest in a permanent Criminal Court contributed to a positive outcome at the ICC negotiations. Continued citizen interest and involvement will be essential to the establishment and operation of the Court.

Whereas the Ad Hoc Tribunals are created in resolutions of the UN Security Council, the ICC is to be established by treaty. Nevertheless, the structure of a permanent Court draws heavily on the model established by the Tribunals.

The Court will consist of a Presidency, Trial and Appeals Chambers, and a Registry or secretariat. An independent Prosecutor will assume responsibility for investigation of complaints. Like the Judges of the Court, the Prosecutor will be elected, by secret ballot, by an absolute majority of states parties to the Statute.

Eighteen Judges will be selected from a pool of nominees (each state being able to propose the names of two nominees). They will be selected for a nine-year, non-renewable term on the basis of their criminal trial experience and knowledge of international law. In electing Judges, states are asked to keep in mind the need to represent on the Court all the principal legal systems of the world. The Judges will elect from among their number a President, two Vice-Presidents and two alternate Vice-Presidents.

At the UN Preparatory Committee meetings, the elaboration of numerous draft options on many fundamental issues revealed substantial political differences of view on the scope and purpose of the ICC. For example, some Arab states and other members of the Non-Aligned Movement did not want an effective ICC. They were wary in particular of the capacity of an ICC to intrude upon their sovereign prerogatives by asserting jurisdiction over crimes committed in the course of internal conflict, and therefore sought to water down the treaty at every turn. Additionally, some powerful states supported creation of an ICC, but wanted a minimal Court, a sort of permanent version of the Ad Hoc Tribunals, that would be activated at the discretion of the UN Security Council.

However, the key to the success of the ICC negotiations was an alliance of middle-power governments (the "Like-minded") and the international coalition of citizen-based nongovernmental organizations (NGOs). The Like-minded and NGOs were able to move world public opinion in favor of a strong Court, and marginalize the big powers that were opposed to the treaty. Although some unfortunate compromises were made along the way, the views of the Like-minded prevailed in most instances.

The contours of debate over some of these broader political issues, and the manner in which they were resolved, are summarized below.

THE COURT'S JURISDICTION

The Statute for an International Criminal Court includes genocide, crimes against humanity, war crimes and aggression as crimes under the Court's jurisdiction.

AGGRESSION

Although aggression was among the crimes prosecuted at Nuremberg, its eventual inclusion in the jurisdiction of a permanent Court was thought unlikely. At the Rome Conference, many states offered support in principle for inclusion of the crime of aggression. However, there were serious disagreements over its definition and the proper role of the Security Council in determining whether an act of aggression has been committed. (The crime of aggression under international law has never been adequately defined. A 1974 UN resolution comes closest to doing so, but is still far too vague and ambiguous.) As a compromise, the Statute provides that the Court will exercise jurisdiction over aggression once an amendment is adopted that resolves those outstanding issues.

The debate over whether to include aggression demonstrates the limits of the political will to develop a criminal jurisdiction within international law (and, conversely, the future potential for the Criminal Court system). It seems that the international community is not prepared at this juncture in history to establish a Court that could help deter acts of aggression and curtail war, but only the means to limit the worst excesses of war.

Some states argued for the inclusion within the Statute of other "treaty crimes," such as apartheid, drug trafficking, terrorism and endangering the safety of UN personnel. However, a majority of states, not wanting to extend already difficult negotiations, opposed inclusion of these crimes. As a compromise, a provision of the Rome Conference's Final Act calls specifically for an ICC Review Conference to "consider the crimes of terrorism and drug crimes with a view to arriving at an acceptable definition and their inclusion in the list of crimes within the jurisdiction of the Court."

Once the ICC is established and has proved its usefulness, amendments to the Statute may very well broaden the range of crimes within its jurisdiction.

EXERCISE OF JURISDICTION

One of the most Court-limiting compromises agreed in Rome is found in an article entitled "Pre-conditions to the exercise of jurisdiction." This concerns the extent of the Court's jurisdiction over non-state parties. The treaty provides that, absent Security Council referral, the Court can only take a case when either the territorial state or the state of the suspect's nationality has accepted the Court's jurisdiction. This compromise language is narrower than an initial proposal by Germany for "universal jurisdiction" which would have permitted the Court to prosecute any suspect for any core crime, whether or not the suspect's state of nationality had accepted the Court's jurisdiction. Germany had argued the case for universal jurisdiction on the grounds that the three core crimes are universally recognized (that is, almost all states are party to the treaties prohibiting these crimes). A subsequent proposal by South Korea would have permitted the Court to exercise jurisdiction if one or more of the following four categories of states has accepted the Court's jurisdiction: the state of the suspect's nationality, the state where the crime was committed, the state of the victim's nationality or the state with custody over the suspect.

The South Korea language was widely supported up until the final two days of the Rome Conference. The final compromise is more expansive than a U.S. proposal, which would have limited jurisdiction over non-state parties to cases in which the state of nationality of the perpetrator has given consent. Nevertheless, some observers wonder what was gained in the bargain by Philippe Kirsch, the Canadian who chaired the Committee of the Whole and brokered most agreements that found their way into the final version of the Statute. Most of the states opposed to the South Korea language proved ultimately to be among those who either abstained in the final vote or (like the United States) opposed. These are states that are not likely to participate in the treaty in its early years. The loss in particular of the Court's ability to prosecute when the custodial state is a party to the treaty is particularly regrettable. The territorial state and the state of the suspect's nationality will often be one and the same. All of this means that, in the Court's early years, many crimes may go untried. Until there is widespread support for the Court and participation in the treaty, the world will see an ICC whose jurisdiction is asserted occasionally and inconsistently.

RELATIONSHIP TO SECURITY COUNCIL

The Statute allows the Security Council to refer to the Court Prosecutor situations for investigation that come to its attention. This is, of course, reasonable and was agreed to without difficulty.

More controversial were the efforts of most permanent members of the UN Security Council (with the exception of the United Kingdom, a late convert to the "Like-minded") to secure agreement on provisions allowing the Council too much scope to influence the work of the Court. The United States. and other permanent members wanted the ability to prevent the Court from commencing a prosecution "arising from a situation which is being dealt with by the Security Council as a threat to or breach of the peace, or an act of aggression under Chapter VII of the UN Charter, unless the Security Council otherwise decides." This would have limited the independence and impartiality of the Court by allowing permanent members of the Security Council, individually, the ability to shield their nationals from prosecution, simply by placing a situation on the Council's agenda. This would have led to a two-tier justice system and exacerbated the already inequitable power relationships at the UN.

Instead, a compromise, which was proposed by Singapore in 1997 and not substantially changed in Rome, allows the Security Council to defer an ICC investigation or prosecution for renewable 12-month periods. To do so would require more than just a motion by one member to place an item on the Council's agenda; the Council would need to take an affirmative decision (which requires agreement by a three-fifths majority of Council members including all five permanent members). This will probably succeed in preventing permanent members from using their position on the UN Security Council to obstruct ICC investigations or prosecutions.

INDEPENDENT PROSECUTOR

The evolution of the negotiations on the powers of the ICC Prosecutor speaks most directly to the role of NGOs and the Like-minded in advancing conditions needed to ensure that the new Court would be independent and effective.

The draft of the ICC Statute that emerged in 1994 from the UN's International Law Commission (ILC) did not call for a "Proprio Moto" Prosecutor, that is, a Prosecutor able to initiate investigations or prosecutions on his/her own initiative. The ILC draft called for an ICC Prosecutor who would initiate investigations only after receiving a complaint from a state party to the ICC treaty or a referral from the Security Council.

However, experience at the UN Human Rights Commission and other forums offer ample evidence that states are reluctant to complain about violations of humanitarian law by other states. Similarly, the UN Security Council is often unable and/or unwilling to take action even when the evidence of atrocities is clearly documented. Many NGOs, as well as many delegations, argued that the Prosecutor should be empowered to independently initiate investigations and prosecutions, on the basis of information provided by individuals (such as citizens' organizations or relatives of victims) as well as states. The call for an independent Prosecutor became one of the most prominent benchmarks for an effective ICC.

Opponents argued (unsuccessfully) that this proposal may give rise to a rogue Prosecutor; that he/she might initiate investigations or prosecutions for political or otherwise unfounded reasons; or that an independent Prosecutor would lead to a huge backlog of cases in a Court designed only to address the most serious crimes of concern to the international community.

The final treaty gives the Prosecutor the power to initiate proceedings on his/her own initiative (not having to depend on Security Council referrals or state complaints). This authority is checked by a requirement that the Prosecutor obtain approval by a pre-trial chamber of the Court at an early stage in the proceedings.

A long-term partnership between civil society, which can report violations, and the institution of the ICC Prosecutor is virtually built into the Rome Statute. This is among the reasons why the ICC will continue to garner widespread support from NGOs and civil society. Indeed, continued NGO support will be essential if the Court is to succeed. In the immediate future, NGOs will need to maintain their support for the Court if the campaign for ratifications and entry into force is to prove successful.

The ICC Statute sustained some bruising and still retains ambiguities following the difficult negotiations and compromises at the 1998 Rome Diplomatic Conference. Once the Court is established it will require that states parties select determined and forward-thinking judges and officers in order for the institution to succeed.

The idea of an international court that would provide a forum in which individuals could be held accountable for their crimes under international law represents a very significant evolutionary development for humanity. By strengthening the world's international criminal jurisdiction, the international community helps build the means to provide that the application of humanitarian norms becomes more a matter of law, order and due process, and less a matter of diplomacy.

The ICC heralds a historic step in civilizing human relations. It can, and should, succeed.

NOTE

1. World Federalists of Canada (WFC) serves as the administering agency for the Canadian Network for an International Criminal Court, which includes over 150 organizations and individuals.

Chapter 13

The United Nations in the Twenty-First Century: A Vision for an Evolving World Order

A. Walter Dorn

Cornell University

INTRODUCTION

How should we organize ourselves, as a human race, as a human family, at the highest level of governance—that is, on the level of nations, on the global level? How can we move towards a better world, with greater peace and justice, in which we would like to live in the twenty-first century and beyond? These are the grand issues I attempt to address in this chapter.

LESSONS OF THE TWENTIETH CENTURY

There are many lessons that we can learn from the successes and failures, the gains and the follies of the present century as we step into the next

one. The twentieth century has witnessed two world wars and unprecedented destruction; it is our moral, even sacred duty to make sure that no
such global horrors happen again. The gradual evolution of world order
and international institutions must serve as the basis of our hope and our
vision.

Immediately after the First World War, the leading nations of the
world, led by President Woodrow Wilson of the United States, decided
that there needed to be new rules to help prevent nations from going to
war and that there needed to be a forum in which to discuss all matters of
international importance and to take collective action to maintain peace.
So the League of Nations was created in 1920. President Wilson wanted
America to be the progressive leader of the League, but that was not to be.
The great treaty debate of 1919–20 in the U.S. Senate showed very clearly
the difference between broad-minded internationalism and narrow-
minded nationalism. A band of conservative and crafty Republican senators prevented the United States from joining the League. The
isolationists asked why America should be concerned if the European or
Asian powers fight. The United States had, they argued, two oceans to
fully protect it from harm. (The attack on Pearl Harbor certainly proved
this theory to be erroneous.) Some senators, working for partisan gain
and unwilling to directly confront the League ideal, called for amendments and reservations to the League Covenant, something that would
have required the renegotiation of the entire treaty, which was clearly
impossible. President Wilson made an unsuccessful last-ditch effort to
"go to Caesar" (his term for the American people) but suffered a stroke
during the grueling cross-country tour. In one of his final speeches of the
voyage, he predicted that unless there was a concerted effort to support
the League, another war, of greater intensity, fought with more powerful
weapons—ones that would make the World War I weapons look like
"toys," he said—would once again consume the youth of the world.

Since there was no leadership from America and little dedication to
the ideals of the League on the part of the major European powers (who
were mostly colonial powers), and since Japan was bent on its aggran-
dizement, the League was unable to halt the slide to World War II that
occurred in the 1930s. As Wilson foresaw, a greater war fell upon
humankind. As he also predicted, a new attempt was made to renew and
rebuild international organization in the wake of this terrible destruction.

Near the end of the Second World War, U.S. President Franklin Roosevelt, who had supported Wilson in his fight for the League of Nations
some 25 years earlier, was able to put into place a stronger, greater orga-

nization, the United Nations, with the United States playing the leading role after the war. The Senate, realizing its former mistake, voted overwhelmingly in a bipartisan fashion and without reservations for U.S. membership in the UN.

However, in recent decades conservative elements in the U.S. Congress have once again raised their "America-first" attitude and turned a cold shoulder to the UN, refusing even to pay America's dues in full or on time. They made it clear that America would act for her own ends, not necessarily according to international law. This unilateralism of the 1980s and the isolationism of the 1920s, in fact, are two sides of the same coin. Both come from an unfortunate, narrow and self-centered attitude that is very unhealthy, not only for international order but also for the United States itself.

As fate would have it, while the United States under Reagan was turning against the UN, the Soviet Union under Gorbachev became a strong proponent of the international organization. It was because of Gorbachev's enlightened attitude that the Cold War came to a close in the second half of the 1980s and that the UN could settle many conflicts.

The West greeted the new Soviet approach to the UN after Gorbachev's arrival with skepticism. The superpower policies virtually reversed themselves from the 1950s to the 1980s. Concepts that the United States had advocated in the 1950s and 1960s, such as a UN disarmament organization and a stronger UN Secretariat, were being boldly championed by Gorbachev's Russia and coldly rejected by Reagan's America. While the United States did not actively seek to undermine the UN, and thus allowed it to realize a remarkable number of achievements, it did not seek the UN's enhancement either. For over ten years, the UN has been struggling against financial hardships imposed largely by the United States.

At the end of the Cold War, the leading nations, particularly the United States, missed many opportunities to build a stronger UN and to create a foundation for peace in the coming century. The West talked of preventive diplomacy but did nothing to strengthen the UN machinery for such creative initiatives. As the UN's sphere of responsibility increased, it didn't expand the structure of the United Nations or give its Secretary-General more resources. Furthermore, the United States certainly didn't help the East bloc nations, especially Gorbachev's Russia, with the kind of generosity that it had helped the defeated powers after the Second World War (for example, with the Marshall Plan). The "new world order," a phrase used by President Bush, was just the same old world order except that instead of two superpowers there was now only one. Granted, the end of the Cold War made many things possible, but it still left many things undone and new challenges unmet. To summarize our brief sweep through history in this century: After the First World War, we made progress by creating the League of Nations. After the Second World War, we made a further step by establishing the United Nations. But after the end of the Cold War, which consumed as much resources and finances as each of the previous two world wars (of course, over a time period about ten times longer), we simply relied on the institutions we had, without strengthening them. In short, there was a lack of forward-looking international leadership. Historians may well look back on this period as a time of missed opportunities.

The great people of the past, like George Washington, were those who built nations and national law and order, and the great persons of the future will be those who build international institutions and international law and order. However, very few such leaders have stepped forward— Mikhail Gorbachev being the most recent example. Progressive individuals and nations must now forge ties to move ahead on reforms without having to wait for the sole remaining superpower to take the lead.

A VISION FOR THE FUTURE

A person's vision of future progress depends a great deal on how far he or she is willing to look ahead. Many people, especially government representatives, reject good proposals because they cannot be implemented today. But if we dare to look beyond our present mandates, beyond our terms of office and even beyond our own lifetimes, there are new vistas to explore. The road to world peace and order may be long (perhaps endless!) and arduous, but progress is achieved with modest steps. With a long-term vision, we can, at least, examine the direction in which we want to go and the steps to be taken. Here, we aim for a world of greater peace, harmony and justice. The United Nations, in spite of all its shortcomings and limitations, is still the best avenue for progress towards such a world.

Let us explore the future in three steps: the short term (5 years), the medium term (25 years) and the long term (50 years and beyond). Table 13.1 summarizes the current status of the UN system and the envisioned developments. These ideas for UN reform, many of them originally proposed by others, are placed into a chronological framework that gives some idea of how far down the line their implementation might be. Obviously the more far-reaching proposals will take longer to become reality

Table 13.1: Reforming the UN System: Proposals and Predictions

Current Status (1999)

General Assembly (GA): 185 member states; majority voting

Security Council (SC): 15 member states; 5 permanent (with veto)

Secretariat (Sec): approx. 10,000 international civil servants headed by the UN Secretary-General (SG)

International Court of Justice (ICJ): 15 judges; only states have standing

New International Bodies (IOs): World Trade Organization (WTO), Global Environment Facility (GEF), Organization for the Prohibition of Chemical Weapons (OPCW), Comprehensive (Nuclear) Test Ban Treaty Organization, International Criminal Tribunals (Yugoslavia and Rwanda)

Military: ad hoc national contingents in peace-keeping forces

Next 5 Years

GA: membership increases to 190 (e.g., Switzerland, East Timor)

SC: membership increases to 20–22 through Charter amendment (Germany/EU, Japan & 3–5 developing countries, e.g., India, Brazil, South Africa and/or rotating seats; no new veto rights); more refined sanction system ("Smart sanctions")

Sec: SG develops early warning systems; plays more prominent role in preventive diplomacy

Legal: Establishment (after sufficient ratifications) of an International Criminal Court

Military: peace-keeping standby forces (nationally based)

Next 25 Years

GA: membership decreases to 180 (e.g., unification of Koreas)

SC: French and German seats merge into powerful European Union seat (retaining the veto); new seats to Far Eastern nations; rules guiding use of veto and enforcement provisions (including advisory opinion and review of SC decisions by the ICJ)

Sec: revamped election procedure for SG; global open skies agreement with agency under SG reporting to SC; greatly improved early warning systems

ICJ: compulsory jurisdiction nearly universal

Legal: new treaties emphasize responsibilities of individuals in addition to that of

Table 13.1 (continued)

states; expansion of International Criminal Court; verification of the ban on secret
treaties (Art. 102)

Financial: non-governmental sources of revenue accepted

IOs: reorganization and amalgamation (e.g., of IVOs)

Military: standing peace-keeping forces (nucleus under direct UN employment)

Next 50 Years

GA: weighted voting

Parliamentary Assembly (PA): new body composed of parliamentarians (elected
directly or sent from their parliaments) complements already existing UN bodies

SC: membership increases

Military: standing peace-keeping and peace-enforcement units

---

and progress must be evolutionary. I concentrate on the principal organs
of the UN: the General Assembly, the Security Council, the Economic
and Social Council, the International Court of Justice and the Secretariat.

THE GENERAL ASSEMBLY

The General Assembly is currently composed of 185 member states. The
dream of universal membership, which the League never attained, has
very nearly been achieved. I believe that within 5 or 10 years the few
important non-members (including Switzerland and the Taiwanese
Republic of China and several new states such as East Timor) will
become members. This will increase the membership to an all-time high
of 190. After national reunifications within the next 25 years (for example, possibly the Koreas, Chinas and certain of the former Soviet
republics) we will come down to 180 or so. Over 50 years, with regional
unifications, the number may fall even further.

The voting in the General Assembly is currently by majority (two-
thirds majority on questions of substance). In the current system, San
Marino, the United States and China have equal votes. Adding a weighted
voting system (perhaps incorporating the important factors of population
and financial contribution to the UN) will provide a more balanced
approach. A vote on a given resolution could be considered in two fashions: by the regular majority approach and by the weighted majority
approach. If both criteria were satisfied, then the resolution could be given

more importance, even the force of law. To adopt this new approach to General Assembly voting would likely, but not necessarily, require Charter amendment. In any case, it may be many years before it is seriously considered.

THE SECURITY COUNCIL

The Security Council is arguably the most powerful body in the world today. Under the UN Charter, it has "primary responsibility for the maintenance of international peace and security" and it has the power to impose its decisions by force through sanctions or military measures (i.e., under Chapter VII of the Charter).

The most important victors of World War II, who were also the principal authors of the UN Charter, gave themselves permanent seats on the Council. These five permanent members (the P5—China,[1] France, Russia, the United Kingdom and the United States) also gained a "veto" right, which allows each of them to prevent a resolution from being adopted even when it is approved by all the rest.

The ten non-permanent members are elected by the General Assembly on a rotating/regional basis for two years. Since the permanent seats were created to reflect "the reality of power in the international community," many have asked why have there been no changes in the permanent members as power has shifted over the decades. Countries like Germany and Japan, who now contribute in a major way to the world's economy and security, would like permanent seats. At present, Japan contributes the most financially to the UN; it beats the United States because that country is so much in arrears.

For several years, there has been a push to reform the Security Council. I would dare to predict that within five years, Germany and Japan will be added to the Council. Since the developing world already complains about the "over-representation" of the developed world in the Council, it is likely that new seats will also be given to developing countries, either by country or region. Since a Council of more than 20 or 25 members is generally considered too unwieldy for rapid action, the number of seats given to developing countries as a whole or to some of the most important ones (Brazil and South Africa, for instance) would not be more than 3 to 5. Given the general discontentment with the use of the veto, it is unlikely that any of the new permanent members will be given the veto right.

In a quarter century, there will be even greater pressure for reform of the Council. If European integration continues, despite the obstacles and delays, then it is conceivable that the French, British and potential German seats will be merged into a powerful European Union seat, which might begin to exert as much influence as the United States currently does. New permanent seats could be given to Far East nations or groupings (for example, ASEAN), since this area of the world will become more powerful economically and politically.

The veto is an inherently undemocratic instrument. It absolutely prevents action from being taken against the most powerful states or their allies. While it is unlikely that even in a quarter century it could be abolished, one could hope that its use will be constitutionally restricted. For instance, on the question of electing a Secretary-General, one could fairly ask that the veto be prohibited. If veto rights are not constitutionally curbed, one could hope that the Security Council itself would give itself guidelines for the use of the veto. The abuse of the veto was painfully apparent during the Cold War: over a hundred Soviet vetoes were cast before the first American one. It is in peaceful times such as these that we must prepare for difficult times and take measures to prevent future abuses of this power.

At present the Security Council is a law unto itself. It can interpret the UN Charter in its own way, even if its interpretation is at odds with other organs of the UN, the majority of member states and a reasonable interpretation of the Charter. There should be a means for judicial review of its decisions. If the Council acts in a clearly unconstitutional manner, one or more nations should be able to bring the issue before the International Court of Justice. The executive branches of most democratic nations permit judicial review of their actions and there is no reason why this should not be the same for international bodies (such as the Security Council), which draw their moral authority from the rule of law.

THE INTERNATIONAL COURT OF JUSTICE (ICJ) AND LEGAL ISSUES

At present only states can bring cases before the Court. It is envisioned that sometime in the next 10 years, this provision will be loosened to allow international bodies to do so. Within 25 years, the ICJ (or a new court) should be able to take cases concerning the interpretation of international law upon request from commercial and non-governmental bodies. Since most armed conflicts are now of an internal character, there is a need for an internationally authoritative judicial body to which parties to a conflict could turn for a legal settlement. There may be many instances in which such a court would not find itself with jurisdiction, but there could be important instances where it could pass judgement.

The ICJ Statute (Article 36) provides that nations may obligate themselves to present themselves before the Court whenever they are so requested by one or more nations who have made a similar declaration. Such "compulsory jurisdiction" is currently accepted by some 59 states. It can be hoped that this number will increase as a means to elevate and expand the standards of international law and accountability. Perhaps we can aim for 100 countries by 2010.

A smaller step, to be taken over the next five years, would be to give the UN Secretary-General the ability to ask for "advisory opinions" from the Court. The previous Secretary-General, Boutros Boutros-Ghali, saw this as a means to mildly "threaten" nations that were unwilling to negotiate a dispute. Even the most powerful nations do not wish to be seen as acting contrary to international law and would be wary that they might lose in a court of law. Thus, they would be more receptive to reach agreement.

The Security Council has established two International Criminal Tribunals, for the former Yugoslavia and for Rwanda. These are important because they are the first to be created since the Nuremberg trials in which individuals are subject to arrest and prosecution. In a sense they are even more fair than the World War II trials, since individuals on both sides of the conflicts are subject to arrest and prosecution. In addition, monitoring of atrocities was being conducted in the former Yugoslavia even as the tribunal was in session. The next step is the creation of an International Criminal Court, upon entry into force of the 1997 Rome Statute, that would activate when there are substantive allegations of crimes against humanity (see chapter 12).

Several important principles and practices are also beginning to emerge. There must be more accountability of national leaders as individuals. Instead of punishing a nation for violations of international law, we must as far as possible identify and punish those in power who made the decisions to violate those laws. In addition, international law should increasingly be supported and enforced by national law enforcement agencies. National parliaments could make selected international treaties part of national law with specific penalties for their violation (as was required, for example, by the Chemical Weapons Convention). Also treaties must contain provisions for international verification and binding mechanisms for dispute settlement to confirm compliance objectively and to make their implementation more fair. This may make the texts of treaties longer and more complicated, but also will make them harder to violate.

One important provision of the UN Charter that is constantly being violated is Article 102, which states that all international agreements should be registered with the UN and published by it. This provision dates back to the first of Wilson's Fourteen Points ("open covenants of peace openly arrived at") and the similar provision in the League Covenant. Many nations maintain "secret" treaties that they do not reveal even to their own publics. There is at present no body that monitors which treaties are not being registered with the UN. The existence of many secret agreements is acknowledged by governments and their titles are often known (for example, many defense treaties), but their contents have never been published. The UN should have a "watchdog" function to make sure that nations are not circumventing this important Charter provision and that transparency in international relations is maintained.

The verification of multilateral arms control and disarmament treaties is a function now routinely given to international organizations. For example, the International Atomic Energy Agency verifies non-diversion of nuclear materials under the 1968 Non-Proliferation Treaty. The newly created Organization for the Prohibition of Chemical Weapons (OPCW) monitors compliance with the 1993 Chemical Weapons Convention, and the Comprehensive Test Ban Treaty Organization (CTBTO) is to monitor compliance with the comprehensive ban on nuclear explosions. What does not now exist is an international organization that can carry out ad hoc verification of unilateral disarmament measures (such as those carried out by Gorbachev in the late 1980s, for example) and bilateral measures upon the request of the involved states. It is desirable to create a disarmament verification organization or unit under the UN to carry out these functions. This has the potential to do for disarmament what peace-keeping has done for conflict resolution: introduce a stabilizing new international actor as a monitor or even supervisor of agreements and measures.

Similarly, the current approach to sanctions monitoring is very ad hoc and generally ineffective. The UN has imposed mandatory and recommendatory sanctions in about a dozen cases, but all of them were violated to some extent. The UN has no system or resident expertise to keep track of prohibited arms flows; it depends on reports from nation states and ad hoc and usually ineffective monitoring arrangements. For instance, large convoys bringing goods, including weapons, into Serbia at the Macedonia border went unreported. The United States decided unilaterally to stop reporting on naval shipments of armaments to Bosnians. It is time that the UN Secretariat develop at least rudimentary forms of sanctions-monitoring expertise. This might possibly be done in conjunction with an arms monitoring and verification unit.

SECRETARY-GENERAL/SECRETARIAT

Of the five principal organs of the UN, the one that has grown the most in power and prestige since the creation of the organization in 1945 is the office of the Secretary-General at the head of the UN Secretariat. Through the creative leadership of the Secretaries-General, particularly Dag Hammarskjold and U Thant, new roles were given to that office, including peace-keeping and good-offices functions. The Charter did not provide for such roles, but the Secretary-General proved to be an indispensable actor and, as the most senior "international civil servant," these roles came naturally.

Of all the organs and actors, the Secretary General most clearly speaks for the global interest, beyond the narrow national interest. The General Assembly mainly represents the developing world, which holds the large majority of its seats. The Security Council is dominated by the most powerful nations, which have permanent seats. The Court is limited to the issues on which it can speak: only those relating to international law. The Secretary-General has become the closest thing we have to the "voice" of the world's conscience on the wide range of political, economic and humanitarian issues.

The Charter states that the Secretary-General is the "chief administrative officer," and that he or she is to perform the functions entrusted to him by the other organs. The one area where the Charter explicitly gives the Secretary-General a significant independent role is for warning. Article 99 states that "the Secretary-General may bring to the attention of the Security Council any matter which in his opinion may threaten the maintenance of international peace and security." But, ironically, because of a lack of means and political boldness, such warning has rarely been done by the Secretary-General. Article 99 has been invoked explicitly only three times. Usually the Secretary-General has become involved only after conflicts have escalated into armed clashes and are well known to the world.

A major thrust should now be made in conflict prevention, which means strengthening the capacity for early warning and rapid reaction. There has been recent progress in both areas, with the creation of a

Humanitarian Early Warning System (HEWS) and a Rapidly Deployable Military Headquarters (RDMHQ), but much more attention and resources should be given to these efforts.

For effective early warning, the UN needs to improve two things: access to information and the capacity to analyze it. Access involves, first of all, the ability to observe and inspect areas where there is a potential for conflict and to talk with the parties. Currently, national sovereignty dictates that UN fact-finding missions require the consent of the host state, something that is often not forthcoming. While the major powers have reconnaissance satellites, which operate above the boundaries of national sovereignty and which can observe all countries of the world, the UN has no such system. A major priority should be to obtain regular access to useful information possessed by member states, such as satellite imagery. There are not, at present, any agreements for the automatic transfer of information to the UN and only vague responsibilities are recognized by member states. These responsibilities should be formalized in one or more information-sharing agreements to help the UN better anticipate conflicts.

An even greater step forward would be for member states to develop a treaty that permitted the UN to conduct inspections on an "any time, any where" basis. Creating more openness is the key to early warning. One component could be to establish a "global open skies" system, which would allow the UN to overfly any desired sites on short (perhaps 12 hour) notice. This would, for instance, allow the UN to spot preparations for surprise attacks. While this is not a guarantee of conflict prevention, it makes the risk of exposure of preparations for attack much greater and hence it is a deterrent to armed conflict.

A greater capacity for analysis is necessary within the Secretariat, including the capacity for scenario-building of conflict escalation and prospective responses. It is therefore proposed that the UN develop an Information, Analysis and Research branch under the Secretary-General to carry out in-depth work, that is beyond the capacity of the current departments and could be of use to them also.

The UN Secretariat is currently understaffed and under-resourced. Subject to U.S. pressure, the number of staff (currently about 10,000 under the Secretary-General) will be cut further. The UN's regular budget, being held at zero growth, is a small fraction (less than 0.5 percent) of the world's military expenditure. The world needs to shift its priorities. An increase in UN staff and resources is needed. After the Cold War, the workload of the UN Secretariat jumped significantly but more staff and resources were denied, leading to a decline in morale. If the UN is to meet the major global challenges of peace and security, environment and development, it will be necessary to at least double the staff and resources at the UN and its agencies over the next 25 years.

MILITARY

Of all the UN reform issues, the question of creating UN armed forces is probably the most controversial. It also is the cardinal question of the twenty-first century: whether (and how) to place military force under international authority. In 1945, if you had asked San Francisco delegates to identify the primary difference between the new UN and the old League, the most frequent response would undoubtedly have been that the UN will have its own fighting forces. Under Article 43 of the Charter, nations are supposed to make such forces available to the Council and to sign agreements with the UN on the nature of these forces. However, as the Cold War quickly paralyzed the Council, no such agreements were ever developed. Even now, after the Cold War, the necessary unity of will and vision is not present. The UN is not yet ready to collectively organize and control military forces that might be engaged in war fighting. Military enforcement will have to remain in the hands of members states for at least a few decades, though the Security Council must remain the sole forum to authorize military enforcement actions. At present we will have to continue to rely on existing military organizations (such as NATO in the former Yugoslavia) and ad hoc coalitions (such as the U.S.-led coalition in the 1991 Gulf War) for military enforcement. In the long run (over 50 years), it will become possible to create an international force to operate under strict guidelines and rules of engagement, but the international maturity and will is not now present.

Peace-keeping tasks are a different matter altogether. The UN should now boost its current arrangements for standby peace-keeping forces. Some nations (such as Scandinavian countries) have units ready to assume peace-keeping duties on short notice on request of the UN Secretary-General—but still subject to final national consent. More nations should make such commitments with the fewest possible conditions, in order to strengthen the capacity of the Secretary-General for rapid reaction. Even more desirable would be the establishment of a standing peace-keeping force recruited on an individual basis. The use of national military contingents has many drawbacks: units rarely train together before they reach the field, the standards between contingents are wide ranging, as are their capabilities, equipment and attitudes. Most importantly, peace-keepers in the field feel a dual allegiance: to their own countries and to the UN. At times, this leads to problems, such as a lack of discipline and unwillingness to follow orders from the Secretary-General. An individually recruited force, even if it is only a vanguard force, would overcome many of these problems. The soon-to-be-established Rapidly Deployable Military Headquarters is an important initiative in this direction. It will need an information/intelligence unit for its many tasks, including early warning. If funding can be obtained, the UN could, within the next ten years, start to build its own peace-keeping units of civilians as well as military personnel to be ready on short notice for deployment to the field.

GENERAL PRINCIPLES

All actions of the UN should be guided by the following principles: impartiality, proportionality, automaticity, legitimacy and accountability. These principles are the same ones that we have come to demand (though not always obtain) of our national civil services and our domestic law enforcement agencies. Favoritism should be discouraged and an even-handed approach taken (impartiality). The punishment of a crime should be proportional to the severity of the crime (proportionality). Responses should come with minimum delay (automaticity) and the bodies dealing with these matters should have the proper legislative mandate (legitimacy), and be held responsible to a higher body or the larger international community (accountability). It is especially important to hold the Security Council, the UN's most powerful body, to these principles. One often has the feeling that its responses are driven by favoritism (or national interests) of the major powers rather than impartiality. The application of mandatory sanctions on Libya for its refusal to hand over alleged terrorists (in the Lockerbie bombing) is a case in point. It can be questioned whether the application of sanctions was impartial and proportionate, since many nations have refused to yield suspected criminals to accusing nations (Canada, for instance, has often refused to deport such persons to the United States) and no such sanctions regime was applied. Its legitimacy might have been tested before the ICJ, but the Court found that Libya could not bring Great Britain and the United States, which were unwilling, to judgement, under the compulsory jurisdiction clause. And finally, although the Security Council reports once a year to the General Assembly and is mandated to act on behalf of all member states, its reports are not substantive and do not provide justifications of its actions. The body must be reminded of its accountability to the international community. In the future, it would be wise to codify these basic principles in a major document.

TOWARD A GREATER VISION

For this exercise, we have to look far into the future, to the second half of the twenty-first century. Thinking beyond 2050 involves a great stretch of the imagination but, for that reason, it's also the most interesting (and controversial!). I envision that the structure of international organization will increasingly resemble that of national organization. I believe this trend is desirable and will help secure peace and good governance. It must happen in an evolutionary fashion over a period of decades and apply only to clearly delineated areas of international responsibility, which will grow over time.

Modern governments have three universally accepted branches: the executive (which includes the foreign affairs department and the military), the legislative (parliamentary bodies such as the U.S. Congress, the Japanese Diet or the Canadian House of Commons), and the judiciary (the courts, usually headed by a Supreme Court). See figure 1A (top part).

Figure 1.
The Structure of World Organizations
A. Current and B. Proposed

A. Current Organization (second generation, uses the first-generation Leage of Nations model)

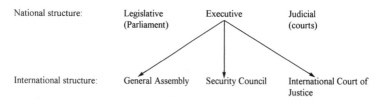

B. Future Organization (third generation, proposed model)

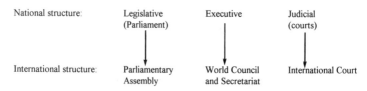

The international counterparts to these already exist in rudimentary form, as illustrated in the lower half of figure 1A. The UN Secretariat functions, to some extent, as an executive body with limited decision-making powers. The Security Council is partly an executive and partly a legislative body. The General Assembly is mostly a legislative body, through its resolutions are only recommendatory upon nations. The judiciary is, of course, represented by the International Court of Justice (located in The Hague) but at present the Court can only hear cases with the consent of the disputants, who must be states.

In the current system (figure 1A), it is the executive branches of the national governments that send representatives to the General Assembly and the Security Council and place their officials in the senior ranks of the Secretariat. Since it is the General Assembly that elects judges to the ICJ, one can also say that it is the executive branches that also control the composition of the ICJ.

In the distant future, I envision that there will be direct links between the main branches of national governments and their international counterparts. This will help to ensure checks and balances at the international level. This will reduce the power of the executive bodies of national governments and strengthen the legislative and judicial bodies, giving them more influence over international problems, which are the real challenges of the future.

Specifically, I envision, as shown in figure 1B, that the legislative branches of nations will elect representatives drawn from their own ranks directly to an international parliamentary assembly. National executive branches will send representatives to an executive council and the legal bodies in nation-states will be the source of judges to the international courts. A modified approach is to follow more closely the European Union model. There the European Parliament members are directly elected by constituents and the decisions of national courts can in certain areas be overturned in European courts. In the very long term this may be a desirable model, but it is hard to see how such a "global government" could be made to function fairly and effectively even in 50 years. As long as there are undemocratic national regimes it will be hard to envision free and fair votes for an international parliament.

National governments hold the predominance of economic, political and military power in the world today. This narrow concentration of power in nation states, as opposed to municipal and global organizations, is illustrated by the solid curve in figure 2. I believe that a more even distribution of power would be better, with local and global organizations gaining power at the expense of the nation state. World peace and world

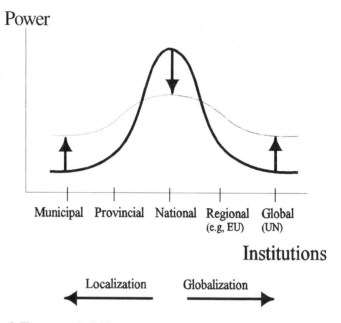

Figure 2. The current (solid line) and desired (dotted line) distribution of power in the world among governmental institutions. What is deemed necessary is an increase in the power of both international and municipal governance at the expense of national governments (i.e., national sovereignty), as shown by the arrows. The diagram also illustrates how localization and regionalization can take place at the same time.

order would increase as would the capacity of people to govern themselves locally. This way of thinking shows that globalization and localization can occur simultaneously and need not be competing factors. For instance, international laws can be developed to increase the power of local government and to protect local cultures.

CONCLUSION

The UN has been in existence for over 50 years. I have proposed a vision for its second half-century and beyond. Perhaps I am dreaming when I think that major changes can come about, but I do not think so. I have used the yardstick of the past to measure the future. If we make as much progress in the next hundred years as in the past hundred, I think my predictions will not have gone far enough.

Of course, progress is never linear. Things may have to get worse before they get better and for every two steps forward we may have to take one step backwards. But I believe that human beings have the resourcefulness, the strength and the capacity to strengthen the rules and the standards of international behavior, and to improve the institutions that govern them. We should aim to have the same strength of law and order on the international level that we have come to expect on the national level. To avoid the bloodshed that has been a characteristic of this century, we have to expand international organizations to meet the greatest challenge of the next century: creating peace on Earth. At the same time, we have to create a greater awareness of the blessings of peace, on the individual, national and international levels.

For the first time in human history, at the dawn of the new millennium we can think seriously about and plan actively for world peace. Through the centuries, the European powers were so often at war; now they are developing a European Union that makes war between them impossible. For centuries the colonial and imperial powers (for example, France and Great Britain in Europe; others in Asia) fought "hot wars" with each other; in this century the capitalist and communist states fought a Cold War. With the end of the Cold War, we no longer have global power blocs menacing one another. There remain many threats to the peace, no doubt, but we now have, for the first time in a thousand years, the opportunity to create a peaceful world, to establish sufficient harmony so that wars between nations, and eventually within nations, become obsolete.

There will always be tensions and some conflicts among nations, as long as there is conflict among individuals and in our societies. But these conflicts need not become reasons to mobilize armies, fight wars and kill human beings. Instead we should mobilize the tools of peace, of united nations and of the United Nations.

We can now dream of a world so interdependent, so close and so respectful that major wars can become a things of the past. It may take more than one century. It may take two or even three. But I have the fundamental faith that the capacity for peace now exists in seed form. The institutions we have now can form a basis for a strong, harmonious, and peaceful world order.

NOTE

1. In 1971 the Peoples Republic of China replaced the Republic of China (Taiwan) in the Chinese seat on the Security Council.

Part II

Cultural and Spiritual Approaches

Developing a Culture of Peace

Chapter 14

The Evolution of Diplomacy: Coordinating Tracks I and II

Cynthia J. Chataway[1]
Dept of Psychology, York University

In 1981, Davidson and Montville wrote a defining article that made the distinction between official or Track I Diplomacy and Track II Diplomacy. At the time, they defined Track II as the many non-official interactions between members of groups or nations in conflict (sometimes facilitated or catalyzed by unofficial people outside the conflict) that develop strategies, influence public opinion, and organize human and material resources to help resolve the conflict. Since then, that non-official track has been differentiated into Tracks II-IX by Diamond and MacDonald (1996) who have coined the term "multi-track diplomacy." Track II diplomacy now designates, more specifically, those efforts by skilled conflict resolution practitioners to facilitate dialogue, analysis and joint problem-solving between members of societies in conflict. In a recent series of interviews with distinguished retired American diplomats, randomly selected from the American Academy of Diplomacy, a wide range of opinions regarding Track II diplomacy were expressed; from outright hostility and resentment, to bemused tolerance, to openness and appreciation (Chataway, 1996). These 26 interviews were too few to draw definitive conclusions, but it appeared that the more recently the interviewees had left active service, the more open they were to accessing and appreciating Track II diplomacy.

In this chapter I will examine one possible contradiction and one misconception that appeared repeatedly in these interviews. My goal is to clarify the complementary roles and strengths of Tracks I and II in order to contribute to successful collaboration between them. At this point in history we have an opportunity to explore and design the mechanisms by which each can most effectively contribute to the advancement of peace in situations of protracted intersocietal or interethnic conflict.

A BROAD CONCEPTION OF DIPLOMACY

Interviewees frequently expressed broad conceptions of modern diplomacy as a process that benefits from a variety of official and non-official sources. "You have to recognize all the people who are travelling as a form of diplomacy. Find a way to keep yourself informed," said one interviewee.[2] In part, this attitude is fuelled by a concern that, as a result of massive cuts to diplomatic budgets, "diplomatic readiness" must be accomplished in new ways. "The U.S. Foreign Service is disappearing" and "We're set for a blooming crisis, perilously close to not performing standard functions," these diplomats said. A re-evaluation of the role of Track II diplomacy has allowed some of these interviewees to describe themselves as having "joined the enemy," and to reconsider the role of private citizens throughout history. For instance, one mused, "I'd wager that there has never been an international agreement on conflict between states where there hasn't been a combination of official and unofficial [efforts]." Concurrently, official diplomacy is changing its face, focusing more on civil-society building, trade, and the development of international agreements and normative standards. Peace talks themselves "now include issues never before included like cooperative exchanges, research institutes, social services, cultural exchange. These used to be the work of Track II," said an interviewee.

Likewise, Track II practitioners are conceiving of the process of diplomacy quite broadly, and advocating a place for their work within a complex mix of diplomatic efforts. For instance, Saunders (1996), a former diplomat who has since retired and become a Track II practitioner, writes that "[t]here are some things that only governments can do, such as negotiate binding agreements; there are others that only citizens outside government can do, such as change human relationships" (Saunders, 1996, 421). Other Track II practitioners concur, saying Track II "[w]orkshops are not intended as a substitute for official diplomacy, but as a complement" (Babbitt, and d'Estree, 1996, 521). "Private initiatives offer considerable advantages in protracted conflicts, or in the pre-negotiation phase of a conflict, [enough] to warrant adding them to the list of mediation attempts in any conflict in international relations" (Hare, 1992, 62). "I do not propose that interactive problem solving—or any other form of unofficial diplomacy—can substitute for official diplomacy or that it can operate independent of the constellation of historical forces and national interests that are themselves shaped by domestic and international political processes. I am convinced however, that this approach can make a significant contribution to conflict resolution and that it should be seen as an integral part of a larger diplomatic process, rather than as a sideshow to the real work of diplomacy" (Kelman, 1996, 502).

WHAT IS TRACK II GOOD FOR?

The potential contributions of Track II to this complex mix were somewhat unclear to many of these former diplomats. Somewhat tentatively, most suggested that Track II can contribute to good relations between states or societies through communication at a deeper level, with greater accuracy, and can reach people who otherwise would not be involved or heard from. However, to others these efforts were just a nuisance. "I can't imagine this is something one would want to encourage," said one diplomat. But perceived contributions of Track II ranged considerably, from collecting and analyzing information in a sort of think-tank environment, to delving deeply into the historical grievances and hatreds on each side.

Perhaps because of this ambiguity regarding the goals of citizen or Track II diplomats, concern was most frequently expressed about the involvement of these potential "meddlers" while official negotiations are going on. There was concern that Track II practitioners might raise unrealistic expectations, contribute to misunderstandings regarding the government's negotiating position, or create greater resistance to negotiations. Most interviewees felt that if citizen diplomats are involved during official negotiations at all, they should stick closely to the needs and limitations of the negotiators, because "The press misunderstands unofficial talks as official. [You] have to be very careful."

Without exception, these interviewees stated that it is the job of the official negotiators to "cut a deal" on specific issues, in contrast to citizen diplomats, who should "not try to negotiate specifics." The role of official negotiator, which entails ultimate responsibility for the agreement that is signed, may not even allow for the adoption of formulations that have been developed through non-official channels. "At most, non-officials should be involved in relationship-building and generating agreement around broad principles and frameworks on difficult issues, which might serve as a starting point for negotiations," one diplomat explained. Across the interviewees, there was consensus that Track II practitioners should stay away from attempts to be directly involved in official efforts.

WHO BRINGS HOME THE "HOLY GRAIL?"

While all stressed that only official diplomats can generate formal agreements and that Track II practitioners should not be trying to duplicate this function, when it came to evaluating Track II work, several interviewees said they wanted to see examples of how Track II had pushed people to agreement, or had had a "direct impact on solving a problem." "I have heard of all the unofficial work in the Transcaucuses, and it hasn't pushed people to agreement," said one interviewee. "These people rarely come up with the Holy Grail, an agreement," said another. Although without exception these former diplomats stated that it is inappropriate for citizen diplomats to be directly involved in formal negotiations, the value of citizen diplomacy was repeatedly measured by the extent to which this direct link could be documented. This contradiction may be evidence of a latent hope that citizen intervention will help diplomats in the difficult task of hammering out an agreement. Or, these criticisms of Track II may be one way in which diplomats are protecting themselves from the threat of citizen diplomacy, by highlighting the abilities of Track I and the inabilities of Track II. Of course, not all interviewees exhibited this contradiction between prescribed roles and evaluative criteria for Track II. Some were consistent throughout their interview that direct input is an unrealistic expectation. "I can't point to where it has resulted in agreement, but it helps the ferment," said one diplomat. "Unofficial work is not susceptible to solution, but generally not counterproductive," said another.

The Oslo Peace Process, which resulted in the Declaration of Principles, the first comprehensive Israeli-Palestinian peace agreement in an almost 100-year old conflict (Makovsky, 1996), seems to have contributed to the ambiguity regarding what can be expected of Track II. People have not been clear that this "Norway Channel" was distinctly different from Track II dialogues, which are closely facilitated by trained process-facilitators. The Oslo process involved off-record, secret meetings, set up but not chaired by the Institute for Applied Social Science (FAFO) in Norway, with the support of the Norwegian Foreign Ministry. The FAFO director, Terje Larsen, remained outside the room in which the Israeli and Palestinian participants had their discussions. Larsen and others contributed to the process by providing for the participant's meals and lodging in an attractive environment to which they would wish to return, and cajoling them when their resolve to continue waned. This was clearly the role that was needed by the participants at this moment in the overall peace process.

The Oslo process seemed, for many of the officials involved in the Middle East negotiations (including the chief Israeli negotiator), to emerge out of obscurity with a concretely formulated Declaration of Principles (DOP) that was then officially adopted, allowing the official Middle East Peace Process to move forward. However, from very early on in the process, the Oslo participants were selected by officials at very high levels on both sides, and these participants took direction from their official leadership, placing phone calls to consult with their leadership during the final stages of drafting of the DOP (Makovsky, 1996). Thus, participants at Oslo did not have the benefit of skilled facilitation or the liberty to range broadly in their conversations without the pressure of accountability—both defining features of Track II diplomacy.

The importance of confidentiality for effective dialogue is one of the reasons that there are few public examples available of Track II diplomacy. However, recent publications by the United States Institute of Peace (Smock, 1998) and Fisher (1997) give some detail regarding dialogues that have been facilitated around conflicts in the Transcaucasus, Cyprus, Northern Ireland, the Middle East, Tajikistan and elsewhere, by university professors and other non-official conflict resolution practitioners from nonprofit organizations.

NEGOTIATING THE RELATIONSHIP
BETWEEN TRACKS I AND II

If Track II diplomacy were able to deliver official agreements, there would be grounds for the concern, that was expressed by some of these diplomats, that this non-official approach might replace official diplomacy. The high profile of some recent Track II initiatives and the way citizen diplomats have been perceived to take undue credit, has not helped to generate an openness or to reduce the sense of threat from Track II. For instance, one diplomat said, "Officials feel really ticked when they work on a complicated issue for years and an unofficial comes in saying they can solve it. [It] makes officials look incompetent [and] feel resentment." Others said, "That they will supplant diplomacy is ridiculous," and ". . . it is not likely that we will move to secular decision making." Track II practitioners were frequently mentioned with suspicion and resentment for projecting a sense of superiority, as though they are practicing a kind of "diplomacy by immaculate conception." One diplomat said, "[You] have to be careful about citizens' claims, made for their own selfish aims."

If the roles of Tracks I and II are perceived as clearly different from each other, with complementary contributions to make to international diplomacy, then a hierarchical ordering or replacement of one by the other is not necessary. However, if one assumes that only one role is needed to meet the goals of international diplomacy, then the statements of some of these interviewees, laden with the sense that citizens diplomats or others are intent on replacing diplomacy, make sense.

As implied by the contrasting names—Track I and Track II—these efforts operate in different forums, gaining their strengths from the advantages of their respective contexts. Free from the need to produce formal agreements, participants in a non-official forum have the time and liberty to engage in the slow process of trust building, to begin to understand the conflict from the other's perspective, and to delve into the complex patterns of action and counteraction that keep a conflict in place over decades. On the other hand, the public accountability of official diplomacy means that peace agreements carry the authority necessary to deliver the resources for implementation.

Both in context and contribution, Tracks I and II are complementary. Official diplomacy has to "handle many issues at once," and to "serve many masters with equal integrity." Nonofficial diplomacy, on the other hand, has the liberty to focus on a single issue, if necessary, over a considerable length of time. "[We] want them to operate as a whole, not placing public dialogue or government dialogue in a superior position. Need them to function together. . . . A conceptualization of the whole would result in some saying they can't do this so why don't you try," suggested one diplomat.

In negotiating this collaboration, the dilemmas are numerous. While "it's not useful to have people working against the government," it is helpful to have people "tell you where you are going wrong." While feedback and direction from officials ensures that Track II work will be relevant, freedom to think outside the constraints of official policy allows for the development of creative new ideas. One diplomat articulated another dilemma: "Track I has little time, has to act fast, and can only take in what is immediately relevant and useful. Track II often does not know when this is, or what exactly is needed, or how to frame it. Different Track I people seem to want different kinds of input also. It is hard for Track II to know what to say to whom when." Another gave advice: "Their [Track II] energies need to be channeled to be more useful, but the initiative has to come from Track II. Track I can't seek them out, direct them, play favorites, or else it becomes an official process." Even as the complementarity of these roles becomes clearer, achieving the right distance and balance between them will be an ongoing challenge.

BIBLIOGRAPHY

Babbitt, E. and T. d'Estree. 1996. "Case Study: An Israeli-Palestinian Women's Workshop: Application of the Interactive Problem-Solving Approach," in *Managing Global Chaos,* ed. C. Crocker & R. Hampson with P. Aal, 521–532. Washington, D.C.: U.S. Institute of Peace.

Chataway, C. 1996. *How Policy Makers Perceive Interactive Conflict Resolution.* Commissioned presentation to the Committee on International Conflict Resolution, National Research Council, Washington, DC.

———. 1998. "Track II Diplomacy: From a Track I Perspective." *Negotiation Journal 14* (4), July, 239–255.

Davidson, W. and J. Montville. 1981–82. "Foreign Policy According to Freud." *Foreign Policy* 45, 145–157.

Hare, P. 1992. "Informal Mediation by Private Individuals," in *Mediation in International Relations,* ed. J. Bercovitch & J. Rubin, 52–63. New York: St. Martin's Press.

Kelman, H. 1996. "The Interactive Problem-Solving Approach," in *Managing Global Chaos,* ed. C. Crocker and R. Hampson with P. Aal, 501–520. Washington, D.C.: U.S. Institute of Peace.

Makovsky, D. 1996. *Making Peace with the PLO.* Boulder, CO: Westview Press.

Saunders, H. 1996. "Prenegotiation and Circum-negotiation: Arenas of the Peace
    Process," in *Managing Global Chaos,* ed. C. Crocker and R. Hampson
    with P. Aal, 419–432. Washington, D.C.: U.S. Institute of Peace.

NOTES

1. Correspondence on this chapter can be addressed to Chataway at email chat-away@yorku.ca or 416–736–2100 ext. 20940.
2. Occasional quotes from the interviewees will be inserted into the text to give the flavor of what was said, while maintaining the anonymity that was guaranteed. Detailed reporting and analysis of the interview transcripts can be found in Chataway (1998).

Chapter 15

Quality of Life and a Culture of Peace

Shirley Farlinger
Voice of Women for Peace, Toronto

In 1992, the UN Educational, Scientific and Cultural Organization (UNESCO) launched an initiative called a Culture of Peace. In 1995, the largest gathering of governmental and grass-roots groups in the history of the world occurred when 30,000 women met in Beijing to address the world's problems and to continue the UN Decade for Women begun in Nairobi in 1985. In 1996 the Independent Commission on Population and Quality of Life issued its final report after five years of work. Each of these bodies has issued an important list of recommendations. There is some overlap but also many ways in which the three womens' plans for action fit very well together.

I give a quick summary of the three reports and then look at what is happening to them now. My apologies to the thousands of people who labored over the wording that I am now going to compress mercilessly!

A CULTURE OF PEACE

The Culture of Peace program addresses the problems of war-torn countries searching for ways to restore peace and social justice. UNESCO in its report describes poverty, overpopulation, environmental degradation and massive migrations as spin offs from war.

The Culture of Peace program calls for non-violent relations among states, individuals, groups, other governments and citizens, as well as between humans and the environment. It sees cultural diversity as an opportunity for appreciation and cooperation using the avenues of education, science, culture and communication, the mandate of UNESCO.

Looking at the experience of countries, the report finds that reconciliation is best accomplished by a process of working together on a superordinate shared goal chosen by the people involved. The work starts with those affected by a real war: the soldiers, the leaders, the governments and the population.

In 1994 in El Salvador, which was coming out of civil war, UNESCO decided to begin by supporting poor women using the radio. Programs were broadcast on 24 radio stations covering topics such as the legal rights of women, violence against women, the sharing of domestic work and the need to raise women's self-esteem. Music and entertainment lightened up the programs.

In a historic decision of 110 non-governmental groups and 1,500 trained peace promoters working in 51 places, a national dialogue was begun on what would build a Culture of Peace after so much war and terror in El Salvador. One event was a Peace Festival held on the anniversary of the signing of those peace accords.

In El Salvador they discovered that a Culture of Peace includes a process of national participation and consensus, emphasizing sustainability. It includes the training and deploying of local peace promoters and requires continuous evaluation and renewal. The evidence of success was the national adherence to the peace accords and the cease-fires, disarmament of both sides, demobilization of soldiers with guarantees of security, jobs for former combatants and legal and institutional reforms to eliminate the causes of war. This also meant changing the education system and the media. They found that people in the related fields of health, women's rights and human rights were good material for peace promoters.

The next countries to use the Culture of Peace program were Mozambique, Burundi, the Philippines and Somalia. A story comes out of Somalia. A young woman wanted to test her suitor so she asked him two questions: What is the best mat to sleep soundly on and what is the best shield to protect camels from looters? It seems the correct answer to both was "peace." Women in a Culture of Peace see men as cowards if they continue with war but as heroes if they succeed in making peace.

Women are key to promoting a Culture of Peace but academics can be vital too. The Canterbury Centre for Conflict Analysis at the University of Kent has been facilitating a dialogue on Moldova for two years to prevent violent conflict.

So far only small countries have taken up the initiative. However, the report states that "a Culture of Peace cannot be sustained in one country while the world retains the cult of war and violence." One of the problems, of course, is money. Individual countries are helping to fund Culture of Peace programs. We are beginning to understand that war is far too expensive, not only in economic costs but in human, societal and environmental costs as well.

CARING FOR THE FUTURE: REPORT OF THE INDEPENDENT COMMISSION ON POPULATION AND QUALITY OF LIFE

As we contemplate sharing our spinning blue home planet with six billion people it is tempting to lecture the world on birth control. However, as the report says, "we do not solve population problems by tackling population alone." The growth rate of global population has declined in the past five years to 1.54 percent per year, and female literacy and empowerment have been crucial. The report advocates listening to women's voices because "women are at the center of population policy and societal activities."

The quality of life and even the survival of humankind requires a transition to a new type of development, an eco-development whose guiding principles are equity, sharing, sustainability and human security in the broadest sense.

These are the highlights from 34 pages of recommendations:

1. Demilitarize society. "A state profiting from war cannot argue convincingly for peace." Enable the UN Security Council to address socioeconomic security (or establish a UN Economic Security Council, as advocated by Stephen Lewis, Canada's former Ambassador to the UN and Deputy Director of UNICEF).

2. Universalize the four UN Quality of Life conventions: the Convention on the Elimination of Discrimination against Women (CEDAW), the Convention on the Rights of the Child (CRC), the International Covenant on Economic, Social and Cultural Rights (ICESCR) and the International Covenant on Civil and Political Rights (ICCPR). These four need to be ratified by more countries, put into effect, and monitored for progress.

3. Set indicators and standards for Quality of Life goals, such as proper food, housing, health and education, and set schedules for accomplishing these goals. Instead of being published as averages, indicators should be disaggregated to provide information to highlight various groups, especially women and the poorest sector.

4. Appoint a Quality of Life ombudsman, who is independent of government, to prepare a regular Quality of Life audit.

5. Reform the UN System of Accounts and set up parallel accounts to reflect environmental costs, depreciation of natural capital and unpaid home and volunteer work.

6. Address environmental problems by phasing out the burning of fossil fuels (I would add nuclear fuels), funding renewables such as solar, geothermal and biomass, and adopting conservation measures.

7. Invite the participation of indigenous people, grass-roots groups and other affected citizens to formulate policy on water, fish, forests and on social policy such as education, public health, housing and urban renewal.

8. Ensure that Quality of Life and population problems are major issues at the top level of governments.

9. Ensure that governments support micro-credit groups, decentralize resources to poor people, and advance novel solutions to unemployment problems locally and globally.

10. Train teachers to respond to the needs of society, especially the 1.5 billion illiterates, who are mostly women. The decade 2001–2010 has been declared the Decade for Universal Basic Education. As in Nicaragua, "Each one teach one" can work.

11. Warn countries to reject the structural adjustment programs of the World Bank and International Monetary Fund, which are adversely affecting women. Institute a new social contract whereby sovereignty rests with the people and where there is commitment to improve the Quality of Life.

12. Support voluntary family planning and reproductive rights with the goal of health care for all. This includes safe birthing, prevention and treatment of sexually transmitted diseases, sex education, contraception and personal reproductive freedom and responsibility.
13. Help women build even more solidarity and raise the awareness of men in order to reduce their resistance to the empowerment of women and women's entry into politics and decision making.

Then the report looks at funding to accomplish all of this. Funding on the scale of the Manhattan Project is needed, the report says. To quote: "The financial markets ought to play a key role. And the private sector must be induced to finance the recommendations in this report." The report also recommends that "an international charge should be made on all transactions in global financial markets with a new authority to administer the funds."

You can imagine how pleased I was to see this in the report when we had just published Alex Michalos's book, *Good Taxes: The Case for Taxing Foreign Currency Exchange and Other Financial Transactions.* Money could actually become the root of all good.

PLATFORM FOR ACTION AND THE BEIJING DECLARATION

The 30,000 who attended the Fourth World UN Conference on Women came from every part of the globe. They were acquainted with the Nairobi Document, "Strategies for the Advancement of Women to the Year 2000," and its themes of equality, peace and development. They also knew how little had been accomplished for women in the intervening ten years. So it was time for action and they drew up a Platform for Action.

All of the topics in the Platform reflect the urgency for gender analysis: poverty, education, health, violence, armed conflict, the economy, decision making, human rights, the use of power and the effect of the media. This means that every policy should be examined for its impact on women and altered in consultation with women or by women to prevent the adoption of unfair or disastrous policies. Each section of the document lists specific actions needed in (1) international organizations such as the UN, (2) local governments, and (3) grass-roots or non-governmental bodies.

Mindful that there are one billion people living in dire poverty, most of them women and children, the Platform begins with a discussion of women and poverty. "Macroeconomic policies need rethinking," states the Platform. This rethinking includes debt-forgiveness strategies; mobilization of universities, NGOs and women's groups to recognize that social development is primarily the responsibility of governments; and revision of laws and practices for women's access to economic resources and credit.

Next, the Platform calls for universal primary education by 2015. Lack of education affects family planning, health measures and income from employment. Early pregnancies should not preclude higher education.

Health is seen as necessary for women's empowerment. Men also need education to respect women's self-determination and to accept equal responsibility for sexual behavior. The structural adjustment programs are adversely affecting women's health. Incapacity and mental disorders are rooted in stress, overwork, marginalization, powerlessness, substance abuse and violence.

The issue of violence against women is finally coming out from behind kitchen doors in every country. Violence and the fear of it and harassment constrains women's education, activities and organizing. To change this there needs to be special training for lawyers, judges, the police and the media. Part of the violence picture is the trafficking in women and children, prostitution, drugs and other crimes. Assistance is needed for the UN Special Rapporteur of the Commission on Human Rights. Now that rape in war has been recognized as a war crime, there are added legal ways to address that shocking form of violence against women. Also, women and children are 80 percent of the victims of war and most of the 25 million refugees under UN care.

It is no wonder, then, that the Platform urges working actively towards "general and complete disarmament under strict and effective international control." This has been an impossible dream, an unreachable goal. Why has such demilitarization been so elusive? The Platform offers a response. It is essential for peace and security that there be equal access and full participation of women in the power structures and their full involvement in all efforts at prevention and resolution of conflicts. Research on peace, conflict resolution and conversion from military to civilian production has already been done, but needs to continue and to be put into practice.

On the economic side, the costs of war have been gargantuan. Even with the end of the Cold War and the collapse of the Warsaw Treaty Organization, the world spends about U.S.$800 billion a year on arms and arms deployment, a theft from those in need. The cost of removing the 100 million land mines awaiting the unwary child or farmer in 64 countries is immeasurable. A major step, led by Canada, was to adopt a convention to abolish such weapons.

Getting back to the Platform for Action, and putting aside the huge costs of war, women are still disadvantaged in financial, monetary and commercial civil policies. There are legal and traditional barriers to women's access to land, technology, education and paying jobs. The UN System of Accounts ignores the input of volunteer time, including household work. What is not measured cannot be planned.

All of this leads to the next issue of women and power. Women are now only 10 percent of elected politicians in so-called democracies in the world and the number has been declining. However, there are bright spots: the UN Secretary-General called for equal representation at the upper levels of the UN by the year 2000 and Bangladesh has legislated 30 percent of seats in its parliament for women. Equality would strengthen democracy, justice, peace and development, the Platform contends. The talents of women are not being utilized. So we must build solidarity and men must begin to mentor women in their careers.

The institutions for the advancement of women need to be strengthened and seen not as a threat but an advantage to men as well. The conventions on human rights and the rights of the child can be used to prevent horrors such as female infanticide, harmful child labor, the sale of children and their organs, child prostitution and pornography, sexual abuse, genital mutilation, rape, incest and sex tourism. The discrimination against girls in education, in the allocation of food and in household duties must end. Women need to be empowered and to learn about their legal rights.

How many of us have ever heard of these three UN documents? The role of the media has been to divert us from the issues or to present them in an "infotainment" way. This keeps us from acting and suits the status quo very well. That has to change. The Internet may provide a boost for women; we'll see.

The last area to cover in the Platform for Action is perhaps the most important—women and the environment. In some ways, women are the canaries in the mine—the group at the bottom of the environment degradation chain. They haul water for the family when the well runs dry, they nurse the children when dysentery strikes, they lack fuel for cooking when forests are denuded, they get cancer from the use of chemicals, they are displaced and made poorer by our unsustainable patterns of consumption and production. Yet women remain "largely absent at all levels of policy formulation and decision-making in natural resource and environmental management and conservation despite the recent rapid growth and visibility of women's NGOs working on these issues." "Women's experiences and contributions to an ecologically sound environment must be central to the agenda for the twenty-first century."

Recommended actions include attention to indigenous knowledge, national legislation consistent with the Rio Summit and the Convention on Biological Diversity, the incorporation of gender analysis in the Commission on Sustainable Development, the Global Environment Facility and other UN bodies, and work at all levels to promote sustainable and affordable energy sources, such as wind, solar and biomass. Congruent with this is the need to educate women in science and to encourage, rather than discourage, the advocacy role of women's groups, sometimes denigrated as "special interest groups."

Women have been at the wrong end of the stick for too long. They need to be consulted and listened to before polluting businesses and disastrous urban designs are put in place. Research and gender-sensitive data are especially needed on the effects of drought, global warming, toxics and pesticide residues, desertification, poor water quality, radioactive waste, and armed conflict and its consequences, which are often environmental.

The Platform urges women "to use their purchasing power to promote the production of environmentally safe products and encourage investment in environmentally sound and productive agriculture, fisheries, commercial and industrial activities and technologies." We have just begun to use the immense power of the purse.

IMPEDIMENTS TO ACTION ON THE THREE DOCUMENTS

That is my view of the highlights of these three reports. I want to say how thankful I am as a woman that those three documents were born. I say "born" because I know the labor pains that go into these undertakings. The thoughts and ideas of millions of women have been contributed. These women want to see these documents move from words to live action. Whether progress will be made depends on various factors.

First, a strong United Nations is essential. Unfortunately there is a concerted effort to downsize the UN in the name of efficiency but actually more in the cause of U.S. hegemony. The United States is withholding its legally required funding until the UN is "reformed." In 1996 the UN staff was cut by 10 percent and this year it will be cut further. Newton Bowles reports that in 1996 the U.S. share of peace-keeping expenses was less that 1/4 of 1 percent of the annual U.S. military budget. The UN and all its special funds and programs, such as UNICEF, the UN Environment Program and the World Health Organization, require U.S.$4.6 billion a year to cover food distribution, care for 25 million refugees, addresses agriculture concerns, children's needs, population, the environment, land mine clearance and so on, while the world wastes $778 billion on military expenditures. The UN contributes $3.2 billion a year to the economy of New York City alone. And how many people are we talking about? In the UN Secretariat and 28 other UN organizations there are 53,333 employees. Three times as many people work for McDonalds.

On the positive side there are now 185 states in the UN and most of them are deeply committed to the work of the UN and its agencies. Secretary-General, Kofi Annan, brings long experience at the UN and has already begun reforms. Also, there has been an enormous increase in the number of non-governmental organizations working with the UN. The former Secretary-General urged more involvement of the NGOs, but if this is not supported by UN staff then this energy will be lost.

Second, the implementation of the three documents requires sovereign governments willing to act in response to their citizens even when this contradicts current "free-market" principles. The most discouraging factor today is the globalization of the market system, bordering on financial dictatorship. The World Trade Organization, the Asian Pacific Economic Council, the several free-trade deals and the proposed Multilateral Agreement on Investment being pushed by Canada at the Organization for Economic Cooperation and Development (OECD), will destroy the proposals made in these three documents. The instantaneous free flow of capital chasing the highest returns without regard to labor, health, safety or environmental concerns, much less gender equity, is killing people and the planet. Governments are encouraging foreign investment with export-processing zones and lower or no taxes on corporations or high income earners. There is a race to the bottom as companies compete for the lowest wages by moving offshore or downsizing staff. The more unemployed people there are—and Canada's rate is twice that of the United States—the more willing the unemployed are to put up with appalling working conditions. This affects women more than men.

Government debt has soared; there are those who see this as a deliberate policy to discredit and disempower governments. That governments took no action to borrow money at lower interest rates from their own banks to reduce their interest payments and that they are now advocating lower taxes makes one think that they missed something at the grade one mathematics level. Social programs are cut more than military spending, indicating the close connection between business and militarization. Government policies have increased the poverty of the underclass and the rape of the environment, and free trade has even been of benefit to drug running. Only strong governmental regulations, like good traffic rules, can protect the environment and human and democratic rights.

The large government debts of many countries are used as an excuse for cutting services and employment. The United States is in a unique position here. Unlike most countries, the U.S. overseas debt is written in its own currency. So it is able to depreciate the value of that debt by depreciating the value of the U.S. dollar. Under the structural adjustment programs, as the currency of a country is devalued the national debt increases, but in the United States the debt decreases. This U.S. prescription is not available to any other country because no other country can write its foreign debt in its own currency.[1] In addition, U.S. industries are protected by the Buy America Act, the Multifiber Arrangement and special safeguard provisions to prevent damage to local industry, not exactly "free trade" and not allowed to other countries.

The media, along with most academics, have been either an enthusiastic promoter of the free-market system and the globalization of trade or have repeated the mantra, "there's nothing we can do about it." Meanwhile, business groups in North America can and do direct money to economic think tanks, to election campaigns of politicians, to buy media control, to alter or influence school curricula, and to lobby continuously. These are not impartial interest groups. They are destroying the democratic system and creating social structures where the rich live in locked, gated communities and the poor, many of them our brightest young people, lose hope.

WHAT CAN WE DO?

Can civil society succeed in spite of these problems?

At the grass-roots level there has never been, in all of history, so much activity. The NGOs who attended all the UN Summits, at Rio, Vienna, Copenhagen, Cairo, Istanbul and Beijing, are still active. It was extremely hopeful when people almost spontaneously protested the nuclear bomb tests of France in the South Pacific. In France and Germany we now see massive protests against racist government policies. What a change from the 1930s! In Russia people are on the streets protesting the catastrophic drop in their quality of life following the "success" of the Cold War in bankrupting the Soviet Union. In Belgrade thousands protested daily the results of elections until faults were admitted. In Ontario, Canada, massive protests have been organized against the policies of the Conservative provincial government. The trick of politicians campaigning on one set of policies and putting a different set into practice after the election is not going to work.

There are two ways to deal with protests: one is to set up a process of dialogue and mediation, the other is to stamp it out with riot police or the army. The second seems more decisive, less wimpy, but it offers no clues for good answers. Removing funding, reducing people's leisure time and disposable income will help to kill interest groups but it won't solve the problems.

People are searching for non-violent ways to act. The grass roots are learning to boycott. Since Canada now makes delicious wine it was not hard to boycott French wines, but recently students networked internationally to boycott PepsiCo and get the company out of Burma. Using the Internet they succeeded!

The idea of social investment is catching on. Other initiatives are the LETS (Local Economic Trading System), which allows money to stay in the community and gives people a job and the necessities of life, and Community Assisted Agriculture, which provides organic, chemical-free food with the taste of justice. I'm sure you know of many more examples seldom marked by the media.

As a writer, I sometimes sympathize with the work of reporters. They are suddenly faced with an urgent matter in a foreign country with a multiplicity of languages, a time constraint of instant relay, no historical background or thoughtful analysis and the job of describing it all in 60 minutes!

For instance, was the war in Chechnya an independence movement? An Islamic revolution? A war to control oil and gas? A resurgence of old injustices? A replay of history? A role for the unemployed Russian army? A problem for NATO or the Blue Helmets? Another example of male aggression? A gross violation of human rights that we chose to ignore? We still don't know.

Finally, I have a challenge for everyone involved in the study of a new world order and interested in building peace in the next millennium.

Let's begin by allowing that all grass-roots movements, even the protests, have a message we ought to heed. Let's assume that these people are not out on the street for the fresh air, that they gain nothing material and often stand to lose something, maybe their jobs, by their actions. (Interest groups with a vested interest, such as the rich Business Council on National Issues in Canada, should be discounted.)

Let's assume that the labor movement and the work of unions are important for the quality of life of all working people as they were in the past.

Let's assume that the environment movement is actually trying to make the planet habitable far into the future; that saving endangered animals is the vanguard of saving endangered humans.

Let's assume that the word "peace" is a valuable, credible word; that peaceniks help all of us by explaining the human and environmental costs of global miltarization; that a Culture of Peace would bring maximum benefits at minimum cost.

Let's start from a position of being in favor of what women are saying or might say if given the chance to speak up. Let's go even further and suggest women speakers at our conferences, pay their way to attend, publish their research and books, mentor and network with them. We've tried male politicians, male CEOs, male Gods, male economists and male advisors. Isn't it time to seek out female wisdom for the next millennium? Mother Earth is waiting.

BIBLIOGRAPHY

Adams, David, ed. 1995. *UNESCO and a Culture of Peace: Promoting a Global Movement.* UNESCO Culture of Peace Programme.

Farlinger, Shirley. 1995. *A Million for Peace: The Story of the Peacemaking Fund of the United Church of Canada.* United Church Publishing House.

Michalos, Alex C. 1997. *Good Taxes: The Case for Taxing Foreign Currency Exchange and Other Financial Transactions.* Toronto: Dundurn Press/Science for Peace.

Permanent People's Tribunal. 1996. *Chernobyl: Environmental, Health and Human Rights Implications.* Vienna, Austria.

1995. *Platform for Action and the Beijing Declaration.* Fourth World Conference on Women, Beijing, China, September 4–15, 1995.

1996. *Caring for the Future: The Report of the Independent Commission on Population and Quality of Life.* Oxford University Press.

1996. *Take Action for Equality, Development and Peace. A Canadian Follow-up Guide to Beijing '95.* Canadian Beijing Facilitating Committee.
1997. *Economic Reform.* Toronto: Comer Publications.

NOTE

1. From an article by Malcolm Fraser, former Prime Minister of Australia, in *The Australian*, October 10, 1996

Chapter 16

UNESCO Declarations and Appeals

Compiled by the Editor
A. Walter Dorn, Cornell University

THE SAN SALVADOR APPEAL

Editor's note: The first year of the new millennium is the "International Year for the Culture of Peace." The United Nations Educational, Scientific and Cultural Organization (UNESCO) has been a leader in the development of the "Culture of Peace" concept. UNESCO has fostered and adopted several significant statements, declarations and appeals which are reproduced below with permission.

In 1993, as UNESCO was preparing to launch the "Culture of Peace" program, the Director-General of the Organization, Federico Mayor, made an inspiring global appeal for activities that could set an example for building of such a Culture of Peace in the world. The appeal was made in San Salvador, the capital of the Republic of El Salvador, on April 28, 1993.

I hereby appeal to all Heads of State and Government, to Ministers and senior officials responsible for Culture, Education and

Development, to Mayors of cities, towns and villages, to thinkers, scientists and teachers—above all, perhaps to the men and women whose work in teaching makes them the chief moulders of our conduct—to all those who take on responsibilities in the running of civil society, to members of religious communities, to parents and to the young of the whole world:

To promote the apprenticeship and practice of the Culture of Peace, both in the formal and non-formal education process and in all the activities of daily life;

To build and strengthen democracy, a political system resting upon the exercise of freedom of expression, upon participation and upon peaceful civic relations for negotiation, concerted action and the equitable settlement of the conflicts that arise in any human and social relationship;

To strive towards a form of human development which, with the collaboration of the entire population, has proper regard for the social capabilities and the intellectual, moral and physical potential of all members of society;

To give pride of place to cultural contacts, exchanges and creativity, at national and international levels, as a means of encouraging recognition of and respect for *others* and the ways in which they differ from oneself;

To strengthen international co-operation to remove the socio-economic causes of armed conflicts and wars, thereby permitting the building of a better world for humankind as a whole.

In 1994, on the initiative of its Executive Board, UNESCO is to initiate a programme of action on the Culture of Peace at the world level. Its viability and relevance will depend upon the determination of all the peoples of the world and, more specifically, of those to whom this appeal is directed. If we all work together we shall at last be able to build a world of peace.

YAMOUSSOUKRO DECLARATION
ON PEACE IN THE MINDS OF MEN

Adopted by the participants of the International Congress on Peace in the Minds of Men held in Yamoussoukro, Côte d'Ivoire, June 26–July 1, 1989.

Peace is reverence for life.

Peace is the most precious possession of humanity.

Peace is more than the end of armed conflict.

Peace is a mode of behaviour.

Peace is a deep-rooted commitment to the principles of liberty, justice, equality and solidarity among all human beings.

Peace is also a harmonious partnership of humankind with the environment.

Today, on the eve of the twenty-first century, peace is within our reach.

***

The International Congress on Peace in the Minds of Men, held on the initiative of UNESCO in Yamoussoukro in the heart of Africa, the cradle of humanity and yet a land of suffering and unequal development, brought together from the five continents men and women who dedicate themselves to the cause of peace.

The growing interdependence between nations and the increasing awareness of common security are signs of hope.

Disarmament measures helping to lessen tensions have been announced and already taken by some countries. Progress is being made in the peaceful settlement of international disputes. There is wider recognition of the international machinery for the protection of human rights.

But the Congress also noted the persistence of various armed conflicts throughout the world. There are also other conflictual situations: apartheid in South Africa; non-respect for national integrity; racism, intolerance and discrimination, particularly against women; and above all economic pressures in all their forms. In addition, the Congress noted the emergence of new, non-military threats to peace. These new threats include: unemployment; drugs; lack of development; Third-World debt, resulting in particular from the imbalance between the industrialized countries and the developing countries together with the difficulties encountered by the countries of the Third World in turning their resources to account; and, finally, man-induced environmental degradation, such as the deterioration of natural resources, climatic changes, desertification, the destruction of the ozone layer and pollution, endangering all forms of life on Earth. The Congress has endeavoured to generate awareness of these problems.

Humans cannot work for a future they cannot imagine. Therefore, the task of this Congress has been to devise visions in which all can have faith.

Humanity can only secure its future through a form of co-operation that: respects the rule of law, takes account of pluralism, ensures greater justice in international economic exchanges and is based on the participation of all civil society in the construction of peace. The Congress affirms the right of individuals and societies to a quality environment as a factor essential to peace.

Additionally, new technologies are now available to serve humankind. But their efficient use is dependent on peace—both in their being used for peaceful purposes and in the need for a peaceful world to maximize their beneficial results.

Finally, the Congress recognizes that violence is not biologically determined and that humans are not predestined to be violent in their behaviour.

**

The pursuit of peace is an exhilarating adventure. The Congress therefore proposes a new programme that makes practical and effective provision for new visions and approaches in co-operation, education, science, culture and communication, taking into account the cultural traditions of the different parts of the world. These measures are to be implemented in co-operation with international organizations and institutions, including the United Nations University, the University for Peace in Costa Rica and the Fondation international Houphouët-Boigny pour la recherche de la paix in Yamoussoukro.

UNESCO by virtue of its Constitution is engaged in the cause of peace. Peace is likewise the calling of Yamoussoukro. The Congress is a confirmation of the hopes of humankind.

PROGRAMME FOR PEACE

The Congress invites States, intergovernmental and non-governmental organizations, the scientific, educational and cultural communities of the world, and all individuals to:

    (a) help construct a new vision of peace by developing a peace culture based on the universal values of respect for life, liberty, justice, solidarity, tolerance, human rights and equality between women and men;

(b) strengthen awareness of the common destiny of humanity so as to further the implementation of common policies ensuring justice in the relations between human beings and a harmonious partnership of humankind with nature;

(c) include peace and human rights components as a permanent feature in all education programmes;

(d) encourage concerted action at the international level to manage and protect the environment

and to ensure that activities carried out under the authority or control of any one State neither impair the quality of the environment of other States nor harm the biosphere.

The Congress recommends that UNESCO make the fullest possible contribution to all peace programmes. It recommends in particular that the following proposals be examined:

1. The endorsement of the Seville Statement on Violence (1986) —first stage in an important process of reflection tending to refute the myth that organized human violence is biologically determined. This Statement should be disseminated in as many languages as possible together with appropriate explanatory material. The process of reflection should be pursued through the convening of an interdisciplinary seminar to study the cultural and social origins of violence.

2. The promotion of education and research in the field of peace. This activity should be conducted using an interdisciplinary approach and should be aimed at studying the inter-relationship between peace, human rights, disarmament, development and the environment.

3. The further development of the UNESCO-UNEP International Environmental Education Programme, in co-operation with Member States, in particular to implement the International Strategy for Action in the Field of Environmental Education and Training for the 1990s. This should incorporate fully the new vision of peace.

4. Study of the establishment with the United Nations University of an international institute of peace and human rights education, particularly aimed at training future cadres through a system of exchanges, teaching and internships.

5. The compilation of texts from all cultures, highlighting the common lessons they yield on the themes of peace, tolerance and fraternity.

6. The development of measures for the enhanced application of existing and potential United Nations—and, in particular, UNESCO—international instruments relating to human rights, peace, the environment and development and those encouraging recourse to legal remedies, dialogue, mediation and the peaceful settlement of disputes.

STATEMENT ON WOMEN'S CONTRIBUTION TO A CULTURE OF PEACE

Adopted by the Fourth World Conference on Women held in Beijing, China, September 4-15, 1995.

On the eve of the twenty-first century, a dynamic movement towards a culture of peace derives inspiration and hope from women's visions and actions.

It is important to draw strength from cultural diversity and redefine the concept of security so that it encompasses ecological, economic, social, cultural and personal security. To replace unequal gender relations with authentic and practical equality between women and men is imperative in order to allow for true participatory democracies.

Ours is still an armed and warring planet. In the first half of this decade alone, more than 90 conflagrations of various kinds have taken a vast toll of human life, impeded social and economic development and depleted the world's resources. Women continue to experience systematic violations of their human rights and to be largely excluded from decision-making. In situations of war and military occupation, women are to an alarming degree the victims and targets of atrocities and aggression.

To combat war as the ultimate expression of the culture of violence, we must address issues such as violence against women in the home, acts and reflexes of aggression and intolerance in everyday life, the banalization of violence in the media, the implicit glorification of war in the teaching of history, trafficking in arms and in drugs, recourse to terrorism and the denial of fundamental human rights and democratic freedoms.

A culture of peace requires that we confront the violence of economic and social deprivation. Poverty and social injustices such as exclusion and discrimination weigh particularly heavily on women. Redressing the flagrant asymmetries of wealth and opportunity within and between countries is indispensible to addressing the root causes of violence in the world.

Equality, development and peace are inextricably linked. There can be no lasting peace without development, and no sustainable development without full equality between men and women.

The new millennium must mark a new beginning. We must dedicate ourselves to averting violence at all levels, to exploring alternatives to violent conflict and to forging attitudes of tolerance and active concern towards others. Human society has the capacity to manage conflict so that it becomes part of a dynamic of positive change. Always provided it involves the full participation of women, action to remedy a pervasive culture of violence is not beyond the capacity of the people and governments of the world.

Efforts to move towards a culture of peace must be founded in education; as stated in UNESCO's Constitution: since wars begin in the minds of men, it is in the minds of men that the defences of peace must be constructed.

Girls and women constitute a large majority of the world's educationally excluded and unreached. Ensuring equality of educational access and opportunity between the sexes is a prerequisite for achieving the changes of attitudes and mind-sets on which a culture of peace depends.

Equality in education is the key to meeting other requirements for a culture of peace. These include: full respect for the human rights of women; the release and utilisation of women's creative potential in all aspects of life; power sharing and equal participation in decision-making by women and men; the reorientation of social and economic policies to equalise opportunities and new and more equitable patterns of gender relations—presupposing a radical reform of social structures and processes.

Women's capacity for leadership must be utilised to the full and to the benefit of all in order to progress towards a culture of peace. Their historically limited participation in governance has led to a distortion of concepts and a narrowing of processes. In such areas as conflict prevention, the promotion of cross-cultural dialogue and the redressing of socio-economic injustice, women can be the source of innovative and much needed approaches to peace-building.

Women bring to the cause of peace among people and nations distinctive experiences, competence, and perspectives. Women's role in giving and sustaining life has provided them with skills and insights essential to peaceful human relations and social development. Women subscribe less readily than men to the myth of the efficacy of violence, and they can bring a new breadth, quality and balance of vision to a joint effort of moving from a culture of war towards a culture of peace.

To this end, we the undersigned, commit ourselves to:

support national and international efforts to ensure equal access to all forms of learning opportunities, with a view to women's empowerment and access to decision-making;

promote relevant quality education that imparts knowledge of the human rights of men and women, skills of non-violent conflict resolution, respect for the natural environment, intercultural understanding and awareness of global interdependence, which are essential constituents of a culture of peace;

encourage new approaches to development that take account of women's priorities and perspectives;

oppose the misuse of religion, cultural and traditional practices for discriminatory purposes; seek to reduce the direct and indirect impact of the culture of war on women—in the form of physical and sexual violence or the neglect of social services for excessive military expenditure;

increase women's freedom of expression and involvement in the media as well as the use of gender-sensitive language and images;

promote knowledge and respect for international normative instruments concerning the human rights of girls and women and ensure widespread dissemination in order to further the well-being of all, men and women, including the most vulnerable groups of societies;

support governmental and intergovernmental structures as well as women's associations and NGOs committed to the development of a culture of peace based on equality between women and men.

We, the signatories, appeal to women and men of goodwill and of diverse cultural backgrounds, religious beliefs, ethnic and social origins to join us in a global endeavour to build, in solidarity and compassion, a culture of peace in the domestic realm and in the public sphere.

Only together, women and men in parity and partnership, can we overcome obstacles and inertia, silence and frustration and ensure the insight, political will, creative thinking and concrete actions needed for a global transition from the culture of violence to a culture of peace.

DECLARATION ON THE ROLE OF RELIGION IN THE PROMOTION OF A CULTURE OF PEACE

We, participants in the meeting, "The Contribution by Religions to the Culture of Peace," organized by UNESCO and the Centre UNESCO de Catalunya, which took place in Barcelona from 12 to 18 December, 1994,

Deeply concerned with the present situation of the world, such as increasing armed conflicts and violence, poverty, social injustice, and structures of oppression;

Recognizing that religion is important in human life;

Declare:

OUR WORLD

1. We live in a world in which isolation is no longer possible. We live in a time of unprecedented mobility of peoples and inter-mingling of cultures. We are all interdependent and share an inescapable responsibility for the well-being of the entire world.

2. We face a crisis which could bring about the suicide of the human species or bring us a new awakening and a new hope. We believe that peace is possible. We know that religion is not the sole remedy for all the ills of humanity, but it has an indispensable role to play in this most critical time.

3. We are aware of the world's cultural and religious diversity. Each culture represents a universe in itself and yet it is not closed. Cultures give religions their language, and religions offer ultimate meaning to each culture. Unless we recognize pluralism and

respect diversity, no peace is possible. We strive for the harmony which is at the very core of peace.

4. We understand that culture is a way of seeing the world and living in it. It also means the cultivation of those values and forms of life which reflect the world-views of each culture. Therefore neither the meaning of peace nor of religion can be reduced to a single and rigid concept, just as the range of human experience cannot be conveyed by a single language.

5. For some cultures, religion is a way of life, permeating every human activity. For others it represents the highest aspirations of human existence. In still others, religions are institutions that claim to carry a message of salvation.

6. Religions have contributed to the peace of the world, but they have also led to division, hatred, and war. Religious people have too often betrayed the high ideals they themselves have preached. We feel obliged to call for sincere acts of repentance and mutual forgiveness, both personally and collectively, to one another, to humanity in general, and to Earth and all living beings.

PEACE

7. Peace implies that love, compassion, human dignity, and justice are fully preserved.

8. Peace entails that we understand that we are all interdependent and related to one another. We are all individually and collectively responsible for the common good, including the well-being of future generations.

9. Peace demands that we respect Earth and all forms of life, especially human life. Our ethical awareness requires setting limits to technology. We should direct our efforts towards eliminating consumerism and improving the quality of life.

10. Peace is a journey—a never ending process.

COMMITMENT

11. We must be at peace with ourselves; we strive to achieve inner peace through personal reflection and spiritual growth, and to cultivate a spirituality which manifests itself in action.

12. We commit ourselves to support and strengthen the home and family as the nursery of peace. In homes and families, communities, nations, and the world:

13. We commit ourselves to resolve or transform conflicts without using violence, and to prevent them through education and the pursuit of justice.

14. We commit ourselves to work towards a reduction in the scandalous economic differences between human groups and other forms of violence and threats to peace, such as waste of resources, extreme poverty, racism, all types of terrorism, lack of caring, corruption, and crime.

15. We commit ourselves to overcome all forms of discrimination, colonialism, exploitation, and domination and to promote institutions based on shared responsibility and participation. Human rights, including religious freedom and the rights of minorities, must be respected.

16. We commit ourselves to assure a truly humane education for all. We emphasize education for peace, freedom, and human rights, and religious education to promote openness and tolerance.

17. We commit ourselves to a civil society which respects environmental and social justice. This process begins locally and continues to national and trans-national levels.

18. We commit ourselves to work towards a world without weapons and to dismantle the industry of war.

RELIGIOUS RESPONSIBILITY

19. Our communities of faith have a responsibility to encourage conduct imbued with wisdom, compassion, sharing, charity, solidarity, and love; inspiring one and all to choose the path of freedom and responsibility. Religions must be a source of helpful energy.

20. We will remain mindful that our religions must not identify themselves with political, economic, or social powers, so as to remain free to work for justice and peace. We will not forget that confessional political regimes may do serious harm to religious values as well as to society. We should distinguish fanaticism from religious zeal.

21. We will favor peace by countering the tendencies of indi-

viduals and communities to assume or even to teach that they are inherently superior to others. We recognize and praise the non-violent peacemakers. We disown killing in the name of religion.

22. We will promote dialogue and harmony between and within religions, recognizing and respecting the search for truth and wisdom that is outside our religion, We will establish dialogue with all, striving for a sincere fellowship on our earthly pilgrimage.

APPEAL

23. Grounded in our faith, we will build a culture of peace based on non-violence, tolerance, dialogue, mutual understanding, and justice. We call upon the institutions of our civil society, the United Nations System, governments, governmental and non-governmental organizations, corporations, and the mass media, to strengthen their commitments to peace and to listen to the cries of the victims and the dispossessed. We call upon the different religious and cultural traditions to join hands together in this effort, and to cooperate with us in spreading the message of peace.

Further information on the UNESCO "Culture of Peace" program can be obtained from:
UNESCO
Culture of Peace Programme
7, Place de Fontenoy
75352 PARIS 07 SP FRANCE
«www.unesco.org/cpp/»

Chapter 17

Building Peace through a New Ethics: An Educational Task

Guy Bourgeault
*Faculté des sciences de l'éducation,
Université de Montréal
President, Québec Press Council*

SPIRITUALITY AND THE EVOLUTION OF WORLD ORDER

I will discuss, speaking as a citizen of Québec, for sure, and hence of Canada, and at the same time, through this local belonging and citizenship, as a citizen of our common Planet Earth. Also I speak as an atheist, nevertheless conscious of the Judeo-Christian tradition I have inherited and constantly try to reinterpret in non-religious and properly atheist terms. Finally, I speak as one who was and still is involved, in Canada and at the international level, in UNESCO affairs and in its commitment toward building peace in the hearts and minds of men and women.

I will share with you some personal thoughts that have progressively emerged from a very ordinary and common and daily experience. For many years, almost every evening, at 11, as if I was obeying to the command of an obligatory religious ritual, I have sat in front of my TV set—facing the world—looking and listening to what seems to be from day to day more and more dramatic. Flashes and stories of war and violence are offered every day to our eyes and, sometimes, to our hearts and minds.

A few years ago, I felt quite suddenly that this daily experience was more painful, more stressful. I nevertheless refused to give it up. Why?

I find unacceptable the absurd horror that TV news and newspapers steadily report, of terrifying wars, catastrophes, rapes, and so on. I have believed for a long time in the progress of human consciousness and willingness at work despite all the contradictory signs. Our common action, I thought, was condemned to so many contradictions, but finally oriented toward establishing through development liberty, equality, fraternity—and peace. I had to face the evidence that war and injustice and violence in their many forms were the reality; and that peace and justice were mere desire or common aspiration and, although unattainable, a permanent ongoing task.

Referring to this personal—though probably very common—background, I will divide my presentation in three parts:

1. peace as always unachieved . . . and as unachievable;
2. the necessary renewal of what I call an Ethics of Peace, an Ethics for Peace or an Ethics toward Peace;
3. a few major orientations of building peace through the promotion of a new ethics as an urgent educational task.

PEACE

Peace has always been and still is a utopia: the reality of nowhere, the unattainable reference of our hopes and myths inventing it at the beginning of time or at the end of history. Origin or achievement. Peace as the unattainable horizon of our hopes, the Homeland we never enter, but which offers the common goal and hence a direction—and sense, and meaning—for our lifelong participation in the March or Adventure of Humankind.

Peace is also and nevertheless a most concrete and daily task, and an individual and collective responsibility. We build peace or we oppose and contribute to war in all our thoughts, and even our ways of thinking, deciding and acting.

In 1945, after what is commonly called World War II—although war has been a pervasive reality since then—and, after the horrors of Nazi camps and of Hiroshima, the creation of the UN System was viewed as both the result and the means of a common will to establish peace on solid grounds and preserve it.

As stated in the Founding Act of UNESCO, as war begins in minds and hearts of men, it is in their minds and hearts we must build the foundations and the defenses of peace, that is, an Ethics for Peace.

But peace, like liberty, equality and human solidarity, the three colors of the French and American Revolutions and flags, is an unattainable goal and a daily realization, and a very concrete task. In order to illustrate this, I will refer to the Judeo-Christian or Western tradition: to the myth of the Long March in the desert toward the Promised Land—the land of justice and peace and love, where constantly flow the milk and honey of our endless happiness. At the very last moment of his life, Moses, the leader of the Exodus from slavery toward freedom, had a last look at the horizon where he could see the goal, the Promised Land. Nobody has ever entered in; nobody can enter in the land that always appears farther when we think we are getting close.

The whole people, with Moses, had to realize that the justice and peace of the goal were and are indeed the reality and the task of the March. In the solidarity of the common March, there is at least partial experience of freedom, justice and peace—never fully achieved.

ETHICS FOR PEACE

This leads us to the second part: peace is fundamentally an ethical concept.

Harmony and peace are not even given in nature. I will only evoke here storms, typhoons, floods, earthquakes and volcanic eruptions.

Nor are harmony and peace given in human personal or collective experience. And here I will recall the Darwinian theory of an evolution based on the struggle for life, to which we may oppose the accommodation theory of Kinji Imanishi. Competition and war on the one hand, adjustment and adaptation on the other. In history, these two dynamics worked in turn and sometimes in combination. We made war to enlarge territory by annexing the land of the inhabitants being hounded; we conquered lands that were supposedly new; and we exploited the resources without taking into account the will and the fate of the original residents. But why am I speaking of this as if it were all in the past? To this day, tribal struggles and civil wars tear up so many countries; world competitions between the stronger international companies turn to commercial wars and eradication of the weaker companies in the same old unchanged dynamics.

Disharmony, war and competition are parts of our personal and collective experience, concrete conditions of our existence.

Paradoxically, we have built our ethical approaches and principles and our moral or even legal codes as if we were living on a planet and in societies where harmony and peace, and justice, and freedom were the reality.

A more realistic and maybe more efficient ethics should (1) take into account war, injustice, inequalities and exploitation. Let's think for one moment of the fantastic economic worldwide competition in which worldwide war is a much more pregnant and concrete reality up to now than the so-called worldwide web, and which will probably be one of the instruments of the worldwide web, and then (2) propose, with a vision of the utopia of the Promised Land, ways and means of dealing with division, contradiction and conflict.

The best is sometimes the enemy and an obstacle to the simply good, a good that quite often consists itself in achieving something that is less bad.

I do think we have to build a realistic ethics, but also learn to celebrate what we experience and live in accomplishing our task and in the midst of our fight, that is, pieces of justice and peace.

PEACE AND ETHICS: AN EDUCATIONAL TASK

In order to develop, or at least contribute to developing, a new ethical competence, education has a most important role to play. Education has in all societies a moral role and mission: socialization through moralization and conformity. I refer to the French philosopher and psychologist, but also educator, Francis Imbert. Could education contribute also to the development of an ethical competence or capacity through critical thinking, autonomy and lucid commitment? More is needed here than exhortation. A new approach to knowledge building—which is at the core of education—that is, to teaching and learning, is needed, learning to think both with an audacious freedom and with the full consciousness of the interdependences through time and space that call for shared and true responsibility.

I will only suggest here a few potential orientations for action, a few hints.

In order to contribute to the development of an ethical competence—and that means in order to educate, ethical capacity being considered as defining human beings—education should:

1. take into account, in teaching and in learning, uncertainty, that is, the consciousness of the finitude and partiality of all knowledge, even of scientific knowledge; and the consequent openness to new approaches and new knowledge coming from others. This happens if and when we do not try to defend our knowledge and to combat, to compete with others, but really want to learn and act in order to learn, because learning requires this openness;
2. take into account the complexity of the reality by developing complex instead of linear thinking, embracing instead of only and always dividing opinions and understanding;
3. promote and develop critical thinking, that is, the capacity to analyze, to establish links with the past and with the present realities; to anticipate; to look under the surface of things and to build a new knowledge taking into account its impacts and consequences in advance;
4. promote also autonomy and solidarity in knowledge building and commitment in linking individual and collective knowledge, desires and rights, and local and planetary approaches—"think globally and act locally";
5. prepare and help to develop the needed capacities for deliberation and discussion in pluralistic societies.

CONCLUSION

Finally, ethics for peace demands profound changes. We must learn to think in a systemic manner, no longer according to the cross-sectional elements we are accustomed to, and to act in solidarity, while respecting the differentiation of tasks and responsibilities. The cross-sectional approach has permitted the development of scientific knowledge up until now. But if we want to go further, we have to take into account the complexity in order to continue the scientific development, among other objectives. We must also learn of the limitations: limitations of resources imposed by ecological demands, that is, the necessity of a prudent use of the resources available. There are limitations also of our knowledge and even of our ways and approaches to it. And we must learn conviviality: between us humans, breaking through so many barriers between countries and disciplines and expertises; between us and other living beings and between the environment and nature. We must finally learn shared and differentiated responsibility in view of concerted action, of synergy.

These views are similar, I believe, to those Daisaku Ikéda has already indicated in his book entitled *The Environmental Problem and Buddhism* (1992), in which he has made explicit some of the orientations that should be at the heart of an ethics of and for our time.

I feel that it is through education that an ethic of responsibility could be developed that will permit us to face the issues of today and tomorrow.

Today and tomorrow, like yesterday, peace will indeed have to be promoted in a world divided by conflicts and competition and contradiction. We will not be allowed to avoid being a party in and to those divisions and conflicts. Education should therefore not prepare us to live in peace, but to fight for peace, to move toward peace.

Spiritual Dimensions

Chapter 18

World Order: Verbalized or Operational Concept? (A Christian Commentary)

Edward W. Scott
former Archbishop of the Anglican Church of Canada

In the Judeo-Christian view, world order is seen as the "will of the creator" —a goal that Christians affirm and are called upon to seek. Existence is not an accident but a creation—the result of an action of a creator. Creation involves the "cosmos" —all that exists—and it is seen as being "good." The whole of creation is seen as being interrelated and interdependent, with human beings seen as being in the image of the creator because they possess self-consciousness, rational capabilities, emotional capabilities and volitional (decision making) capabilities. They are seen as being "in nature" —not "over nature" but in nature as decision makers whose decisions affect all aspects of creation.

The human reality is that all too easily values or goals are verbalized, given lip service, but not really sought—they are not operational values. The challenge confronting not only those who call themselves Christian but the whole of humankind is that of making the values we so easily verbalize into operational values—values that in fact influence and shape the actual decisions we take.

Until this challenge is confronted, world order will remain as a hope or a dream—a very important one, but, notwithstanding, a mental concept rather than a reality.

The process of changing "world order" from a dream or hope into reality requires both changes in individual persons—changes in you and me—and also changes in corporate or systemic relationships in every area of life—political, economic, social—and in virtually every discipline.

Because we live in a world of expanding knowledge, changes in outlook and in action are essential. These changes need to be related to and take into account the new knowledge that becomes available to us. This new knowledge needs to be integrated in our individual and corporate being. This is a demanding and lifelong process, which needs to be taken seriously. Persons and society are not static but "becoming"; whether the direction of the becoming is toward world order or toward chaos depends upon a wide range of factors, including our personal decision making. Each of us needs to address the question, "Are our individual and corporate decisions helping the human community move towards world order or towards chaos?" In asking this question we need to seek to analyze and understand more deeply, rather than to take the all too easy road of looking for someone or some system to blame.

Chapter 19

A Christian Statement of Faith on "Peace in a Nuclear Age"

The United Church of Canada
(Adopted by the 33rd General Council of August 1990)

Editor's note: This statement embodies the Christian aspiration to a better, more peaceful world. In true Christian fashion, it contains references to scripture (the Bible), a confession of wrongs committed and a commitment to action.

THE CONTEXT

We live in a world rich in resources and diversity. In this world we are dependent on each other and on the environment. This world is threatened.

We live in a world of violence. There is a growing disparity between rich and poor. There is a power disparity between women and men, between Native and non-Native, and between marginalized and the privileged. People are treated as expendable commodities. Military spending robs the poor and wastes resources. War and nuclear weapons are constant threats to survival. Human activity is destroying the global environment.

We live in a world of fear. We fear for the future of our children and our children's children. We sense the despair of youth caused by the continuing arms race. We fear the violence that maintains the systems of domination and oppression. We experience a world of mistrust, loneliness and lack of community.

We also live with signs of hope: in the spirit-filled lives of peacemakers; in the covenant community, living and speaking God's love; in other communities sharing similar aims. We are encouraged by the witness of the poor and all new voices for peace. We see hope in the willingness to continue the struggle.

BIBLICAL AND THEOLOGICAL FOUNDATIONS

In the beginning God created the heavens and the Earth . . . and God created humans; in the image of God were they created . . . and God saw all that had been made, and it was very good. (Gen. 1:1, 27, 31)

We believe the Scriptures witness to the creation of the world by God who intends that creation reflect the fundamental harmony we have come to call *shalom*. The *shalom* community is one of wholeness, peacefulness, harmony and justice for all creation.

God made us in God's image, to live in covenant with the creator and all other creatures. Compassionate and just, God renews the covenant in faithful love again and again.

We lament that the creation is lost in fear and conflict. God calls us to be peacemakers, to heal the world in wholeness. We are not alone, God is with us.

[Jesus] is the image of the unseen God and the first-born of all creation for in him were created all things in heaven and on Earth. (Col. 1:15–16)

We believe God's nature and intention break into our world in

Jesus of Nazareth, who both embraces our humanity and proclaims the redemption of our brokenness.

Jesus is central to our understanding of peace: reconciling, forgiving and manifesting human life with fullness. Jesus frees us from oppression, fear and conflict.

We remember Jesus' teaching, to love our enemies, to care for 'the least of my sisters and brothers,' to pray and forgive. We remember Jesus' understanding of his ministry:

The Spirit of the Lord has been given to me, for he has anointed me. He has sent me to bring the good news to the poor, to proclaim liberty to captives, and to the blind new sight, to set the downtrodden free, to proclaim the Lord's year of favor. (Luke 4:18–19)

Jesus called to account the powerful of the day and lived a new relationship with the powerless and the poor. We remember, particularly, his willingness to die in unconditional love for those who rejected him. Jesus calls us to be sisters and brothers.

The Advocate, the Holy Spirit, whom the Father will send in my name, will teach you everything and remind you of all I have said to you. Peace I bequeath to you, my own peace I give you—a peace the world cannot give—this is my gift to you. (John 14:26–27)

We believe the Scriptures witness to the ongoing work of the Spirit, who urges and empowers us to be peacemakers in our image of the Prince of Peace, and to work faithfully, using our many and varied gifts. The Spirit is gentle and kind, compassionate and caring, searching and acting; calling us to be open to the whole human family; to act justly, love tenderly and walk humbly with our God. Sustaining and nurturing, the Spirit guides and directs if we listen. As the transforming power of God's love and justice, the Spirit works through us to effect change in the world.

We are called to be the Body of Christ, to bring forth *shalom* in the global community, where all are neighbors, loved by God. As stewards and gardeners, we are called to care for others, to resist systems of destruction, to relinquish power that rules over others and embrace power that enables. And, together with the Spirit, we are to work towards the healing and reconciliation of the world.

God shall judge between the nations, and shall decide for many peoples;
and they shall beat their swords into plowshares, and their spears into
pruning hooks; nation shall not lift up sword against nation, neither shall
they learn war any more. (Isaiah 2:4)

CONFESSION

We confess that we are part of a world culture that has broken
God's covenant:

- we allow the proliferation of nuclear and other weapons
  at great social cost;
- we abuse the environment and overuse the Earth's
  resources;
- we, in our greed, permit the growing gap between the rich
  and the poor, and the crippling burden of world debt. We
  tolerate mass starvation, homelessness and other misery;
- we stereotype other political systems, races, cultures and
  religions;
- we, as citizens, abdicate our responsibilities to others.

We confess that as Canadians we share in this brokenness:

- our treatment of Native peoples is intolerable;
- our refugee policy is unjust; Our economy depends, in
  some measure, on the manufacture of arms and their
  sale, even to developing countries and repressive
  regimes;
- our contributions to foreign aid are being reduced and our
  social services are being eroded;
- our social attitudes and our condonation of personal and
  family violence have reinforced an ethic of domination
  which allows for hierarchies, authoritarianism, and the
  undue use of force to maintain order.

We confess as people of The United Church of Canada that:

- we often lose the vision of *shalom,* despairing and allowing
  fear to motivate or paralyze us;

- we tolerate a theology which reflects the dominant culture of our time;
- we are not always willing to act respectfully toward children or to be in loving community with them;
- we continue to exercise 'power over' others—even within the Church;
- we are frequently unwilling to truly listen to those whose views differ from our own;
- we fail to rely on the grace of God through prayer.

COMMITMENTS

We the church are called to grow in faith, seeking a truer vision of God; *shalom*. In partnership with God and creation and the power of the Holy Spirit we act out God's peacemaking call in worship, reflection, education and action. In the *shalom* community we relate with trust, risking vulnerability; we are called to love our enemies.

We the church commit ourselves to the *shalom* community, living by the strengths and insights of those we have made powerless, such as the poor, children, women and Native people.

We the church commit ourselves to stand boldly against the powers and principalities of war, militarization, violence, injustice, greed, ignorance, world debt and exploitation of people and resources.

We denounce false beliefs and myths. We name the evils and sins of the church, our culture, and the present powers and principalities that govern our lives.

We commit ourselves personally and corporately to a simpler life. We commit ourselves to work towards a world in which wealth and resources are shared equitably.

We commit ourselves to economic conversion: reducing and transforming the arms industry and eliminating its profit motive; standing in solidarity with those who would lose jobs; protecting the rights of persons to reject participation in war or war preparation. We commit ourselves to common security and the adoption of non-threatening policies of defense.

We commit ourselves to learn and teach our children non-violent conflict resolution skills.

We, the church, commit ourselves to peacemaking.

Chapter 20

Pursuing Opportunities for Shalom in the World: A Jewish View

Martin I. Lockshin
York University, Toronto, Ontario

INTRODUCTION

The Jewish religion and the Jewish nation arose, as described in the Bible, some three thousand years ago. Judaism became firmly established as the result of an act of war, the conquest of the land of Canaan, which then came to be known as the land of Israel. For a little more than the first thousand years of Jewish history, Judaism was centered in that land of Israel. Jews dealt with invasions of their land by numerous enemies, including Assyrians, Babylonians, Egyptians, Greeks and Romans. At times the Jews of antiquity fought off their invaders militarily and at times they tried to come to terms of peace with them. Issues of war and peace have remained central in the Jewish agenda ever since.

For almost the last two thousand years, Jews have lived a diaspora existence, as landless minorities scattered in various countries where they were at best tolerated but often expelled, persecuted or worse. Modern Jewish attitudes to war and peace are certainly a function, at least to some extent, of the Jewish experience of being victims and scapegoats.

Since the middle of the twentieth century, the Jewish experience has been undergoing some very radical changes. After the terrible horrors of the Second World War—when 6 million diaspora Jews were systematically murdered as part of the Nazi war effort—a Jewish state once again arose in the land of Israel. For the first time in almost two thousand years, Jews re-entered the world of national politics, and questions of war and peace again came to be central to all Jewish thinking. No modern discussion of Jewish attitudes to war and peace can ignore the events of this century. But it would seem foolish to try to analyze Jewish attitudes to war and peace without a careful study of the classic works of Jewish religious thought, the Bible and classical rabbinic literature.

There are only some 12 or 13 million Jews in the world today. Of those, only a minority think of themselves as being "religious." Many Jews today understand their identity in terms of nationalism, ethnicity or culture. So the Jewish "religion" is practiced today by a rather small number of people. Still, the Jewish religion has had a powerful impact on the Western world. It is the oldest monotheistic religion, and the other two great monotheistic religions of the West—Christianity and Islam—found their roots, or at least some of their roots, in Judaism. So an analysis of Jewish religious attitudes could shed light also on the roots of much of Western thinking about the issue of peace.

PEACE: GOD'S TASK OR OUR TASK?

Classical Jewish religious texts often center around the question that believers of all faiths grapple with: how should we properly delineate the role played by humans in this world and the role played by God (however we might conceive of God)? Generally, religious people postulate that there are some things that human beings simply cannot accomplish on their own and turn to God to ask for help. Is peace in that category? Can we seriously expect that people will put aside their differences and establish world peace without the intervention or assistance of a higher almighty force? Do we reasonably feel that we should *work* toward peace or should we *pray* to God for peace?

The religious Jew tends to turn to classical texts from the Bible or from rabbinic literature for guidance on such questions. There we discover that the Hebrew Bible ascribes crucial peacemaking roles to God. God promises to "establish *shalom* [peace] in the land; you will lie down untroubled by anyone" (Leviticus 26:6). God will "establish true *shalom* in this place" (Jeremiah 14:13) and "will bless you with *shalom*" (Numbers 6:26). God, for the prophet, is responsible for everything in this world: "forming light, creating darkness, making *shalom* and creating misfortune" (Isaiah 45:7).

But the quest for shalom is not left for God alone to take care of. In many biblical verses, we humans are charged to work hard for the cause of shalom and are praised when we do so. The most famous verse is the Psalmist's exhortation that instructs us to "shun evil and do good, seek *shalom* and pursue it" (Psalms 34:15).

Biblical scholars, though, tell us that the issue is not that simple. The word "shalom" in the Hebrew Bible can tolerate quite a large number of meanings. It comes from a Semitic root that in Hebrew usually means "whole" or "perfect." This is the same Semitic root, "s-l-m" , that in Arabic refers to resignation or submission of one's self, yielding the words Moslem and Islam, referring to those who practice submission to God, and the word "salaam" , the Arabic word for peace. Scholars of biblical Hebrew often argue about how many of the 237 instances in which "shalom" appears in the Bible are really references to what we would call "peace." Perhaps, scholars argue, when Isaiah is describing God in the verse cited above, it is as the source of "weal and woe,"[1] not as the cause of "peace." Perhaps the "shalom" that human beings are charged by the Bible to seek and pursue should be understood as the similar but not identical terms of "amity" or "integrity."[2]

While the meaning of "shalom" may be unclear in biblical Hebrew,[3] it becomes clear in later classical rabbinic Hebrew, from around 2,000 years ago. In the Hebrew of the Mishnah and Talmuds and the other great rabbinic classics, "shalom" unequivocally means "peace," although it can mean either peace between nations or between individual human beings. Furthermore, in rabbinic Judaism shalom is virtually an unrivalled value.

THE VALUE OF SHALOM IN RABBINIC JUDAISM

"God," the rabbis teach, "has found no vessel more fitting to contain blessing than *shalom*" (Mishnah '*Uqtsin* 3:11). Shalom is described as one of God's gifts to this world (Bereshit Raba 6:5). Rabban Simon ben

Gamliel, the great first-century rabbi, teaches that "the world is preserved by three things: by truth, by judgement, and by peace" (Mishnah *Avot* 1:18). The Jerusalem Talmud, elaborating on his comment, argues that those three items are inseparable, and ultimately are mutually dependent (*Megillah* 3:6, folio 74b).

Some of the rabbinic teachings about shalom are surprising and controversial. Peace, we are taught, is such a crucial value, that one may lie if the lie will help establish peace. One rabbinic opinion says that such lying is not only permissible; it is even a mitzvah, a meritorious deed. Even God, according to rabbinic tradition, was willing to stretch the truth in order to increase peace between human beings (Babylonian Talmud *Yevamot* 65b). The paradigmatic peace-maker of rabbinic legend was Moses' brother, Aaron, who is reputed to have appeased antagonists in feuds by telling each one of them that the other antagonist was contrite and repentant even when there was no basis in fact to such statements (*Avot de-Rabbi Natan*, version a, chapter 12).

Not only do the rabbis claim that peace is more important than truthfulness, they also argue that peace is more powerful than true religiosity. Rabbinic exegesis was troubled by a very difficult verse in the Bible, Hosea 4:17, which might be seen as meaning "Ephraim [that is, the Jewish people] is united in addiction to idols—let him be!" Why, ask the rabbis, would the Bible say "let him be!" if Ephraim is guilty of the sin of idolatry? Rabbinic tradition answers that since the verse suggests that the entire people is *united* as one in this pursuit—the pursuit of idolatry!—the people will not be punished. "Peace," according to Rabbi Judah the Prince, "is so great that even if Israel worships idols, as long as they are at peace, God, so to speak, says, "I cannot punish them, because they are in a state of peace" (Bereshit Rabba 38:6).

One should not imagine for a moment that the classical rabbis feel that lying and idolatry are insignificant misdemeanors. These two sins are considered to be extremely grave ones in rabbinic Judaism. When the rabbis teach, then, that peace is more important or forceful than truthfulness or monotheism, they are making a very powerful statement.

PURSUING SHALOM EVEN WHEN IT SEEMS INAPPROPRIATE

On one occasion, according to rabbinic interpretation, Moses even defied God for the sake of peace. Bemidbar Rabba (19) tells the story of the war between the Israelites, led by Moses, and the Amorites, led by King

Sihon. God, the rabbis note, had given unambiguous instructions to
Moses:

> Up! Start out and cross the wadi Arnon! See I give into your power
> Sihon the Amorite, king of Heshbon and his land. Begin the occupa-
> tion, engage him in battle. This day I begin to put the dread and the
> fear of you upon the peoples everywhere under the heaven. . . .
> (Deuteronomy 2:24–25)

Moses' instructions are clear: attack the Amorites, engage them in war.
But the rabbis note that that is *not* what Moses did. Instead of following instructions, Moses, as the Bible tells us,

> sent messengers to Sihon, king of the Amorites saying, "Let me pass
> through your country. We will not turn off into field or vine-
> yards. . . . We will follow the king's highway until we have crossed
> through your territory." (Numbers 21:21–22)

Moses decided (according to this rabbinic reading) to ignore God's specific instructions. He figured that since the Israelites had no dispute with
the Amorites, the reasonable thing to do was to offer them terms of peace
and cooperation, not engage them in war.

The rabbis explain that Moses was acting properly when he ignored
or modified God's instructions, because Moses was actually fulfilling a
different (and apparently more important) divine command. He was
implementing the program of action later described by the Psalmist,
"seek *shalom* and pursue it."

That same rabbinic text goes on to explain the way in which the
command to pursue peace differs from most of the other laws in the Bible.
Most of the commands of the Bible are casuistic in style ("If . . .
then . . ."), implying that they apply only in a specific set of circumstances. Even many of the ethical laws of the Bible are dependent on a
specific situation. We are commanded that *if* we see our enemy's donkey
struggling while carrying a heavy burden, *then* we must help our enemy
deal with the problem (Exodus 23:5). But, the rabbis note most reasonably, there is no imperative in the Bible that we expend our energies
searching for struggling donkeys. The Bible commands us that *if* we are
gathering the olives or grapes from our trees or vines, *then* we should
leave some of them behind for the poor, for the foreigner, for the orphan
and for the widow to come and pick (Deuteronomy 24:20–21). But again

the rabbis note that such a commandment would apply not to all people but only to landowners.

But shalom is different. The Bible commands us to seek peace and to pursue opportunities of making peace in this world. Concerning the other commandments, "if the situation arises, then you are commanded to fulfil the decree. But concerning peace, 'seek it' when it is close to you, and 'pursue it' when it is somewhere else."

WHY DID THE RABBIS VALUE SHALOM SO HIGHLY?

Pursuing peace is not the only tradition of Judaism. Both the Bible and rabbinic Judaism suggest that some wars are not only permissible but even obligatory—the fulfilling of God's will. But the thrust of rabbinic Judaism is clearly in the direction of peace. Why?

Occasionally one hears the argument that historical changes in the Jewish condition were responsible for the rabbinic emphasis on peace. The rabbis of the Mishnah and Talmud, according to this argument, lived either in the Diaspora or else in the land of Israel when it was under Roman occupation. Theirs was a period of Jewish powerlessness, when Jews had few opportunities of pursuing a military option. This cynical reading of history argues that Jews pursued peace only when they were the victims of aggression and persecution, and that once the Jews had the power to create armies, they did so. Often the proponents of that approach argue that modern Judaism will be pacifist only if it is divorced from nationalism, and that peace is impossible in the Jewish state of Israel.

I feel that that claim is a terrible distortion of Jewish intellectual history. The argument that only powerless, persecuted people are attracted to peace is, first and foremost, based on a very low assessment of human nature and human possibilities. I believe that human beings, even when they have other alternatives, can and do pursue peace. And I feel that a careful examination of Jewish texts will show that that was the case with Judaism.

SHALOM AND MESSIANISM

We find that the most famous and moving Jewish texts about peace come from biblical times, from the days of the Jewish monarchy, from the days of Jewish power. Some 2,700 years ago, the first Temple stood in Jerusalem and the Jews were sovereign in their own land. A Jewish monarchy had been in place for some three hundred uninterrupted years of rule. In that period, two prophets share with us their vision of "the days to come," when all the nations of the world will flock to Jerusalem to learn about God and to receive instruction. The prophets continue:

> They will beat their swords into plowshares
> And their spears into pruning hooks:
> Nation shall not lift up sword against nation
> They shall never again know war.

As mentioned, this prophecy appears twice in the Bible, in the words of two prophets (Isaiah 2:2–4 and Micah 2:1–5). In the less well known version, in Micah, the text finishes with a comment that is difficult to translate with certainty. It may mean "All peoples shall walk in the name of their gods, and we [the Jews] shall walk in the name of our God for ever and ever." Whatever the precise translation is, one thing is certain: the prophet Micah is prophesying about a perfected world, which for him means that true peace has arrived, but that does *not* mean that all peoples of the world have adopted the same religion. Peace, for the prophet Micah, means that all peoples cooperate, even if they disagree on other fundamentals.

Ever since the days of Micah and Isaiah, Jews have written about peace as the ultimate messianic goal. In the twelfth century, the greatest Jewish philosopher, Moses Maimonides, wrote that Jews have always dreamed of a messianic era, not because of a desire to see a Jewish world order established, but because it will be a period in which tyranny will cease, all nations will leave each other alone and people will be able to pursue spiritual advancement. Maimonides loved to quote an old rabbinic line that read, "The only difference between the present and the messianic era is that political oppression will then cease" (Mishneh Torah, *Teshuvah* 9).

For Jews, messianism has some implications of a spiritual nature, but the ultimate test of whether a messiah is truly the messiah is the test of peace. Judaism sees a messiah who claims to redeem humanity but does not bring peace to the world as a basic contradiction in terms. Peace is the most important gift that God will send us through a messiah. Jews always took literally the words of the prophet who describes "How welcome on the mountain are the footsteps of the herald announcing *shalom,* heralding good fortune . . ." (Isaiah 52:7) and who calls the messiah the "prince of *shalom*" (Isaiah 9:5). A world without peace, according to Judaism, is, by definition, an unredeemed world.[4]

IMITATING GOD, THE SOURCE OF SHALOM

Still Jews do not usually assume that the messianic tasks are the work of God alone. It is our human responsibility to try to work toward messianic goals on our own. Perhaps this concept is connected to the general religious principle espoused by Judaism (and most other religions) that one of the highest forms of religious activity is *imitatio dei,* imitating God's actions in the world, striving to be merciful and caring just as God is. Religious Jews most certainly do *pray* to God for peace. In the Priestly Benediction, what might well be the oldest,[5] and the shortest, Jewish prayer (only 15 words long in Hebrew), the priests invoke God's blessings on the people. The crescendo is the request that "God grant you peace." That prayer still plays a central role in Jewish liturgy, as does the Amidah prayer (recited by the religious Jew at least three times a day), which also closes by praising God "for giving us a Torah [that is, "teachings"] of life, lovingkindness, uprightness, blessedness, mercy, love and *shalom.*" Still, religious Jews realize well that they too must work hard together with God for the cause of peace.

JUDAISM AND LIBERALISM

The teachings of Judaism about peace have had a strong effect on many Jews—both religious and non-religious—who have dedicated their lives to fighting against injustice, militarism and tyranny. Jews, as it is well known, have often been present in liberal peace-seeking movements beyond what one would, statistically speaking, expect. To my mind, the fact that recent Israeli governments have been making steps toward peace should also be seen in part as a result of traditional Jewish teachings. Few countries in the world would pursue peace when that peace has *not* yet led to perceptibly increased security.

The biblical prophets predicted more than 2,500 years ago that the Jews who were scattered around the world in the Diaspora would once again be gathered into their homeland in the land of Israel. Their vision was *not* that that reborn state would be in a near constant state of war.

Part of their prophecies have come true. Let us hope and pray that Israeli leaders will continue to pursue shalom and take chances for the sake of this crucial value in order to fulfil the fullness of this prophetic vision.

Peace is such a crucial value to Jewish tradition that the classical rabbis even claim that "shalom" is one of God's names. Seeking shalom therefore means seeking God. God, for rabbinic Jews, is not sought solely by sitting in synagogue or by studying texts.

Rabbi Simon ben Elazar says:

> If people sit at home and are silent, how can they be considered to be pursuing peace? . . . Rather, people should leave their homes and travel through the world and pursue peace . . . as it is written, "Seek peace and pursue it." Seek it close by and pursue it even if it is far away. (*Avot de-Rabbi Natan,* 12)

CONCLUSION

The Jewish vision of peace and world order is one in which nations and individuals alike can live in harmony and without bloodshed. It involves tolerance, good neighborliness and, for the Jews and others, additional opportunities to pursue spiritual goals and to live according to God's will. The messianic vision that claims that "the wolf shall dwell with the lamb and the leopard lie down with the kid" (Isaiah 11:6) was probably understood by most Jews over the years metaphorically. Jews hardly expected such gigantic changes in the laws of the world in the perfected messianic world. But Jews always took literally and very seriously the promise that the new post-messianic world would be one where "the lowly shall inherit the land and delight in abundant *shalom*" (Psalms 37:11).

The question which opens this essay is how to achieve peace. Is it given by God or the result of human effort? Based on the Jewish sources cited here it is safe to say that the Jewish answer is both. We must work for peace as well as pray for it.

NOTES

1. As the *Tanakh* translation of the Jewish Publication Society (Philadelphia, 1978) translates the verse in Isaiah 45:7.

2. Both suggestions may be found in the *Tanakh* translation of Psalms 34:15. The Revised Standard Version translates "peace."

3. The question of how many times "shalom" really means "peace" in the Bible may never be resolved and is probably not that important. Every biblical scholar will tell us that *sometimes* the word "shalom" signifies what we would call peace. At other times it can have a very wide range of meanings, including "completeness, "soundness," "welfare," "security," "prosperity," "tranquility," "contentment," "friendship" and more. (See, e.g, by F. Brown, S. R. Driver and C. A. Briggs , *A Hebrew and English Lexicon of the Old Testament* (reprint edition: Oxford, 1974), pp. 1022–1023.) The idea that the ancient Jews did not distinguish between "completeness," "welfare" and "peace," and used the same word to describe all of those concepts and more is, to my mind, a very inspiring message.

4. See the impassioned arguments of Rabbi Moses Nahmanides in the Barcelona Disputation of 1263 to prove that Judaism cannot recognize the idea of a messiah who has not brought world peace. The text may be found in *Kitve ha-Ramban,* ed. by Ch. Chavel, vol. 1 (Jerusalem, 1963).

5. Originating in Numbers 6:22–26.

Chapter 21

From Inner Peace to World Peace: A Buddhist Perspective

Yoichi Kawada

*Director, Institute of Oriental Philosophy
Soka Gakkai International*

THE FLAMES OF DELUSION

The purpose of this chapter is to offer a Buddhist perspective on the question of peace. I would like to discuss three dimensions of peace and the contributions a Buddhist understanding may make to their achievement. These are inner peace; peace in the community of humankind; and ecological peace or peace with Earth. First, we have to understand what the root causes of the absence and the presence of peace are.

In a sermon given by Shakyamuni, the founder of Buddhism, he conveyed his essential outlook on the nature and cause of suffering. On this occasion, Shakyamuni ascended a mountain summit together with his recently converted disciples. Gazing at the view below, Shakyamuni began to expound: "Indeed, this world is burning with many and various fires. There are fires of greed, fires of hatred, fires of foolishness, fires of infatuation and egoism, fires of decrepitude, sickness and death, fires of sorrow, lamentation, suffering and agony."

What he was trying to convey was his understanding that the phenomenal world that we inhabit is engulfed in the "fires" of suffering originating in deluded impulses. These fires of greed, hatred and ignorance, raging fiercely in the hearts of people, are the basic cause of the suffering of human existence. Therefore, Shakyamuni urges us first and foremost to come to a clear understanding of the root cause of suffering.

Here, the deluded impulse of "greed" indicates uncontrolled desire for, and attachment to, material comforts, for wealth, power or fame. Desires of this kind grow and multiply without cease, and since their fulfillment cannot bring true and lasting happiness, a person in their grip is condemned to endless torment and frustration.

The deluded impulse of "hatred" describes emotions such as resentment, rage and envy, that are triggered when our egocentric desires are not fulfilled. Unless controlled, these escalate into various forms of destruction and violence. Simply put, the deluded impulse of hatred is the violence that grows from an egocentric view of life.

"Ignorance" refers to willful ignorance of reality, or the true nature of life and the cosmos. Thus it is this deluded impulse that generates discord and rebellion against the principles that govern the functioning of the cosmos. The wisdom that illuminates and reveals the true nature of the cosmos is referred to as "enlightenment," while this kind of willful ignorance is referred to as " fundamental darkness" because it clouds and obscures the light by which we might see things in their true nature. Of all the deluded impulses, Buddhism considers ignorance the most fundamental.

Buddhism views these impulses—greed, hatred and ignorance—as poisons inherent in life; together they are sometimes referred to as the "three poisons." What Shakyamuni sought to teach his disciples in his sermon is that the flames of the three poisons and of all deluded impulses originate in, and spew forth from, the inner lives of individuals to engulf families, ethnic groups, nations and eventually the whole of humanity.

We see this in the world today, where the impact of uncontrolled greed goes far beyond the individual level; it creates economic disparities among racial and ethnic groups, and between countries on a global scale.

The avarice of the industrialized nations has deprived people in developing countries of the conditions by which their basic needs can be met. And the greed of the human race is undermining the right of other living beings to exist.

Violence is commonly found within families, in schools and in local communities. Deep hatreds that trace back to distant historical events give rise to intractable ethnic and racial conflicts. In some cases, such historical hatred is bound up with religious causes or identities, and finds expression in terror and random killing.

Willful ignorance of the true nature of existence signifies a state of rebellion against, and denial of, the basic principles of life and the cosmos. As such, it distorts all aspects of life, from individual lifestyles to family, ethnic and national values. In other words, this kind of willful ignorance can be found in all value systems, ways of life, and views of nature that put one into rebellious conflict with the very principles that support one's own existence, the principles that, ultimately, govern the functioning of the living cosmos.

By sharing his enlightened understanding with others, Shakyamuni sought to help people minimize the destructive effects of these deluded impulses and in fact to transform them into the impetus for happiness.

A TRANQUIL HEART

In India, the equivalent of "peace" is "shanti," which means the state of inner tranquillity. It also means the enlightened condition attained by Shakyamuni sometimes referred to as "nirvana." With respect to the state of inner peace, a Buddhist text describes this as follows: "Tranquillity of mind comes from having successfully transcended greed, hatred and ignorance." As this passage makes clear, the Buddhist approach to peace starts from the fundamental act of surmounting these deluded impulses or inner poisons. The state of having brought these impulses under control, however, is not a static and private inner peace. Rather, it is limitlessly dynamic, expansive and evolutionary in its nature.

The thirteenth-century Japanese Buddhist Nichiren expressed this with the following image: "Burning the firewood of deluded impulses, we behold the flame of enlightened wisdom." In other words, through spiritual practice the energy inherent in our deluded impulses can be transformed in its entirety into the illuminating "flame" of enlightened wisdom. Thus, the three poisons can be subdued so that they no longer produce confusion and disruption; they can no longer drive us to act in a bizarre and destructive manner. It is for this reason that this transcendence of deluded impulses is known as inner tranquillity.

In the state of tranquillity, the light of enlightened wisdom shines brilliantly, unblocked and unhindered by the clouds of deluded impulses.

If one surveys the Buddha's teachings, from the earliest scriptures through the subsequent Mahayana tradition, one can see that the core of Shakyamuni's enlightenment was his awakening to the "law of dependent origination." This concept has been expressed in various ways and was developed in great depth and detail in Mahayana Buddhism; its essence is the interdependence of all living beings and indeed all phenomena. Dependent origination teaches us that all things occur and exist only through their interrelationship with all other phenomena and that this fabric of relatedness is of infinite extent both temporally and spatially. Herein lies the basis for the principle of mutually supportive coexistence of all beings so central to Buddhist thinking.

Each human being exists within the context of interrelationships that include other human beings, all living beings and the natural world. In other words, each person is sustained by the interdependent web of life. By awakening to this principle we are able to expand instinctive self-love into an altruistic love for others; we are able to nurture the spirit of tolerance and empathy for others.

The doctrine of dependent origination also provides a theoretical foundation for peace. In terms of concrete action, it manifests itself as the practice of compassion. In Buddhism, compassion indicates the practical ethic of always maintaining an empathetic involvement with others. It means sharing their sufferings and unhappiness, working alongside them to overcome the deluded impulses that are the root cause of suffering, transforming these into happiness, benefit and joy.

Ignorance is considered fundamental among these deluded impulses precisely because it blinds people to the reality of dependent origination, the unavoidable and all-encompassing interrelatedness within which we live. This ignorance gives rise to the greed that drives people to seek the fulfillment of their desires even at the cost of the suffering of others. It also leads to the kind of uncontrolled rage that seeks the destruction of a situation in which one's desires are frustrated. It is for this reason that the deluded impulse of ignorance is considered equivalent to a fundamental egocentrism. It is a blind and finally self-destructive egocentrism because it violently severs the strands of the web of life that supports one's own existence.

The state of mind of one who ceaselessly strives to transcend this fundamental egocentrism is that of inner peace and tranquillity. The heart of such a person is lit with the wisdom of dependent origination, and overflows with the spirit of compassion.

THE "FIVE DEFILEMENTS"

Buddhism's core contribution to peace is to be found in the struggle against the deluded impulses that, rooted in the depths of the inner life of the individual, cause so much suffering and destruction in the whole of human society. In Shakyamuni's Lotus Sutra, the destructive effects brought about by the deluded impulses are described as "defilements," and classified into five stages, from the innermost and most personal to that which stains an entire age or era. These are: defilements of desire, of thought, of the people, of life itself and of the age.

T'ien-t'ai, a Buddhist philosopher active in China in the sixth century, described the five defilements in the following manner: "The most fundamental of these five are the defilements of thought and of desire, which result in the defilements of the people and of life. These in turn give rise to the defilement of the age." "Defilement of desire" points to deluded impulses such as the three poisons themselves. "Defilement of thought" refers to excessive and unreasoning attachment to specific ideas or ideologies. According to T'ien-t'ai, the defilements of thought and desire are the most fundamental and, through their impact on individuals, bring chaos and disruption to families, nations and states. Passed on from one generation to another, these defilements give rise to the "defilement of life," instilling historical hatred and violence among different peoples, ethnic groups and nations. These defilements finally influence all people living in that era, resulting in the "defilement of the age."

Modern civilization increasingly exhibits the aspects of what Buddhism would term the "defilement of the age." Signs of this include rampant materialism, the ruthless domination and exploitation of nature, and unbridled consumption. Since the end of the Cold War, our world has been spared major outbreaks of conflict stemming from attachment to ideology, that is, defilement of thought. However, the kinds of conflicts that are flaring up are rooted in the irrational passions, such as extreme nationalism, that Buddhism would classify as "defilement of desire." These are considered even more deeply rooted in people's lives and therefore even more difficult to control.

In a world where deluded impulses cast the pall of their negative effects in the form of the five defilements described above, Buddhists have, I believe, a particular mission to contribute to the realization of peace on all planes. In other words, we should not be content with our inner peace of mind but should broaden our horizons and extend our endeavors to include abolition of war—that is, peace of the global human community—as well as peace with the natural world, through truly sustainable development and harmonious coexistence with the global ecosystem.

THE BODHISATTVA WAY IN THE MODERN WORLD

I would now like to elaborate on how the bodhisattva practice, compassionate action based on the Buddhist understanding of life, can contribute to the realization of peace in its three dimensions (inner, community and ecological peace).

First let us consider inner peace, or tranquillity of spirit and mind. In Buddhism, a bodhisattva is one who carries out altruistic acts and seeks to contribute to human society by fully manifesting the qualities of wisdom and compassion. A bodhisattva strives first to transform his or her own life; the locus for this struggle is the realities of human existence and the sustained effort to alleviate people's sufferings. In this way the bodhisattva strives to generate joy for both self and others.

The practice of the bodhisattva has been expressed in contemporary terms as "human revolution." The inner state of one striving for the realization of human revolution can be considered that of spiritual tranquillity; the state of inner peace expounded in Buddhism is a dynamic condition brimming with wisdom and compassion.

Soka Gakkai International (SGI), a Buddhist lay organization, exists to help facilitate people's practice of compassion in daily life by providing an environment of cooperation, spiritual sustenance and support. In this way, the SGI seeks to bring the practice of the bodhisattva to the contemporary world.

While the SGI pursues many diverse activities, the most fundamental of all are the discussion meetings held and rooted in local communities. In present-day society, where unrestrained egotism has brought profound disruptions to the human heart and where humanity is losing sight of the art of coexisting with nature, these small gatherings of people of all ages, races, interests and backgrounds offer a forum for rich and refreshing exchange. In a world afflicted by "social desertification," these meetings serve as a human oasis.

It is, after all, individual human beings who alone can work toward the realization of the grand goals of world peace and the prosperity of human society. As an organization, the SGI has consistently focused on people and on the movement for human revolution through the bodhisattva practice. As Buddhists, we strive to establish a condition of inner peace in daily life and, at the same time, to contribute to the realization of the peace of the world around us, by enabling each individual to develop his or her unique qualities to the very fullest.

Secondly, with regard to the dimension of social peace, or peace in the community of humankind, the SGI's cultural and educational activities support a variety of political and economic measures that are being proposed in various forums, seeking to move them toward implementation. These include the abolition of nuclear weapons and the reduction of economic disparity. As part of the SGI's ongoing efforts to promote public education regarding these and other global issues, we have mounted international exhibitions that have been seen by millions of citizens worldwide. Likewise, we have long been involved in efforts to provide concrete humanitarian support for the world's refugees and displaced persons.

With respect to these questions of security and development, Buddhism upholds the principle of non-violence and calls for a fundamental transformation in our way of life. At the individual level, this means a transformation from a way of life dominated by attachment to material desires to one more focused on spiritual and existential values. At the same time, it also means a compassionate way of life, of being ready to make those efforts required to ensure that the citizens of developing countries can have their basic needs fulfilled. In connection with human rights, we recognize the existence of the supreme life-condition—that of Buddhahood—in all people, and therefore insist that all members of the human family are without distinction capable of manifesting that condition of unlimited wisdom and compassion. Buddhism's unique contribution to the resolution of culturally based conflicts is related to the teaching of "dependent origination" cited above, and to the empathy and tolerance that issue from that cosmology.

As mentioned earlier, the law of dependent origination describes the insight that all things and phenomena are interdependent and all manifest the ordering principle of the cosmos, each in its own unique manner.

Since Buddhism views deluded impulses as those that prevent people from clearly seeing this reality, we feel that humankind will be best served when each religious tradition engages in its own characteristic struggle against the three poisons of hatred, avarice and ignorance, while cooperating toward the resolution of global issues. This is how Buddhism views the key concepts of cultural pluralism and religious tolerance.

Coming to the third dimension, "peace with the ecosystem," the Buddhist perspective on nature has always pointed to creative coexistence with nature. Shakyamuni's compassion was not limited to humankind but extended to all living things. The philosophical basis for sustainable development can be found in this kind of creative symbiosis with the rest of the natural world. Such a philosophical outlook will support the kind of lifestyle that is truly in harmony with the ecosystem. The SGI has supported afforestation projects in the Amazon and elsewhere. Local SGI organizations have been involved in a wide range of activities to protect the environment.

In resolving the global challenges confronting humanity, political, economic and scientific measures must be pursued together with a transformation of human consciousness. We should establish a lifestyle of conserving energy, recycling resources and pursuing spiritual values. Our overarching goal should be to cultivate a shared awareness of our common humanity and of solidarity with the living organism that is Earth. As we move toward that awareness, we must develop the wisdom to properly direct toward beneficial ends of the life sciences, including the burgeoning field of genetic engineering. In this, I feel that the outlook of the world's religious and ethical traditions can and must make an important contribution.

A Buddhist approach to peace, I believe, offers important common ground with other traditions. The cause of a truly comprehensive and lasting peace can most effectively be furthered by ceaselessly expanding circles of friendship and understanding through dialogue, exchange and cooperation.

Chapter 22

Creating Inner Peace: A Buddhist View

Daniel Vokey
*Theory and Policy Studies in Education,
Ontario Institute for Studies in Education
of the University of Toronto*

If the opposite to peace is aggression, then what is the root cause of aggression? This would seem to be an important question for anyone interested in building peace. In this chapter, I will summarize a Buddhist view of how aggression is rooted in duality, where *duality* refers to the human habit of interpreting experience in terms of a fundamental distinction between *self* and *other.* I will proceed by discussing two concepts central to Buddhism, *ego* and *Buddha-nature,* and conclude by describing how the practice of mindfulness-awareness meditation can promote peace by uncovering our innate wisdom and compassion.

Before going any further, I should acknowledge that Buddhism has crossed many geographical, political, linguistic and cultural boundaries during the course of its long history. In the process, it has developed a great variety of texts, practices and institutions. The "Buddhist view" I will present here is based principally on the teachings of the Vidyadhara the Venerable Chögyam Trungpa, Rinpoché, a meditation master and scholar in the Tibetan Vajrayāna Buddhist tradition.[1] I highly recommend that anyone interested in the Buddhist perspective I present consult Trungpa's texts for a more complete articulation of that view.[2]

EGO

According to Buddhism, the root cause of aggression is *ego*. Now, the ego of Buddhist psychology is not that of Freud or Jung. In Buddhism, "ego" refers to a collection of habitual tendencies and processes that together result in the distinction between *self* and *other*. In this Buddhist sense of the term, we all have strong egos because we all (with a few exceptions) are very attached to maintaining a sense of self—a sense that we exist separately from and independently of "the outside world." The flip side of this attachment to a sense of self is that we tend to respond to what we perceive as *other* according to a more or less "enlightened" self-interest. Buddhism observes that, generally speaking, we try to avoid pain and secure pleasure. We strive to make our lives as free of misfortune and as full of entertainment as possible. Consequently, if something appears pleasurable, or promises to confirm our sense of self, we tend to want to grasp and hold on to it. If something appears painful or unpleasant, or threatens our sense of self, we tend to attack it or push it away. If something appears to be neither potentially pleasurable nor painful, neither confirming nor threatening, we tend to ignore it. According to Buddhism, then, because of our self-attachment, our behavior is generally limited to variations upon these three themes of possessiveness, aggression and ignorance.[3]

It is important to note that the self-attachment to which Buddhism refers is prior to and somewhat independent of any particular ideas we might have about who we are. Even if we are intellectually convinced that our identities are socially constructed, we still tend to act *as if* we were each a single, permanent self. As one contemporary Buddhist teacher has observed:

> We all act as if we had lasting, separate, independent selves that it is
> our constant pre-occupation to protect and foster. It is an unthinking
> habit that most of us would normally be most unlikely to question

or explain. However, all our suffering is associated with this pre-occupation. All loss and gain, pleasure and pain arise because we identify so closely with this vague feeling of selfness that we have. We are so enormously involved with and attached to this "self" that we take it for granted. (Gyamtso, 1988, p. 20)

This might sound somewhat abstract, so let me suggest an example. According to Buddhism, all forms of grasping or possessiveness—such as greed, selfishness and envy—arise from a poverty mentality that *presupposes* a sense of self: it's *me* that doesn't have enough money, it's *me* that doesn't have enough time, or enough excitement in my life, or whatever I might feel that I lack. Buddhism refers to this as a poverty *mentality* because there is no necessary cause and effect relationship between how many resources we might have and how acquisitive or needy we might feel. As the story goes, Midas felt no richer for all his gold. Often, the more we have, the more we want. Buddhism warns that, so long as we experience the world in terms of the duality of self and other, we remain vulnerable to poverty mentality and so to greed, selfishness, envy and similar vices. Conversely, Buddhism claims that it is only when we personally realize the non-duality of self and other that we can manifest true generosity, patience, and compassion.

According to the Buddhist teachings, the habitual attachment to a sense of self represents an obstacle to *knowing* as well as to *doing* what is beneficial in any given circumstance. That is to say, even if we have the best of intentions, our actions are unlikely to be effective because we rarely perceive situations accurately. Most of the time, we react to our own projections instead. This notion of *projection* has become familiar with the popularization of Jungian psychology. The basic idea is that whatever we reject in ourselves we attribute to others. The Buddhist understanding of projection is similar while more radical in its claim that, because the dualism of self and other is only a fabrication of ego, we spend most of our time in a kind of dream state in which we cling to fantasies and struggle with enemies of our own construction.[4]

This may sound like a very pessimistic view of the human situation. However, it is not all bad news. Buddhism teaches that our constant struggle is actually unnecessary, that there is no need to maintain the distinction between self and other in order to relate accurately and effectively with our world. How is this possible?

BUDDHA-NATURE

Buddhism teaches that, if we take time to look closely at our experience, we will discover four things. One thing we will discover is that nothing is eternal. Thoughts come and go, emotions come and go, people come and go, nations come and go, even galaxies do not last forever. Sooner or later, everything changes. One consequence of this is that our struggles to maintain a safe and secure existence are futile: there is no such thing as happily-ever-after. As soon as we create a situation to our liking, it begins to dissolve. This is the truth of impermanence (*anitya*).

A second thing we will discover is that, contrary to our expectations, there is no solid, separate, continuous, independently existing self to be found in our experience. Instead, we will discover that our sense of continuity as subjects is an illusion, analogous to that produced by a movie projector. We know that each frame of a film is distinct, but they follow each other so quickly that we do not notice the gaps between them, and so perceive the movie as continuous. In the same way, our sense of self-continuity is based on missing—indeed, ignoring—the gaps in our experience. Although we implicitly believe that we are the thinker of our thoughts and the agent of our actions, no such independent entity as "the subject" has ever been found. This is the truth of egolessness (*anātman*).[5]

A third thing we will discover is that we are never completely free from anxiety or dissatisfaction. Precisely because we don't exist as solid, independent subjects, we can only maintain a sense of self through constant effort. For example, if you pay attention you will likely discover that you are holding a running conversation with yourself while you read this chapter. Buddhism suggests that internal dialogues are one of the ways in which ego maintains the illusion of a solid, independent self. Conversely, moments of relaxation can undermine our sense of self and result in feelings of panic. According to the Buddhist teachings, then, because we constantly struggle to maintain our sense of self, we will find that—even in the midst of our most pleasurable experiences—there is always a haunting sense of anxiety or uncertainty just below the surface. This is the truth of suffering (*duhkha*).

Fourth, and finally, there is the good news. If we stop struggling long enough, in the gaps between our thoughts we will discover an awareness that is completely unconditioned. It is unconditioned in the sense that it is not created or manufactured, but is always already there. It is unconditioned also in the sense that it is before thought, and so is free from all reference points, including the basic duality of self and other. Contrary to what we might believe, it is not the "self" that is aware; rather, all self-centered emotions and all thoughts of self arise within the space of unconditioned awareness. One traditional analogy for glimpsing this is the experience of being on an elephant and discovering that you are not riding the elephant so much as the elephant is carrying you!

Vajrayâna Buddhism teaches that this unconditioned awareness is our basic nature: It is what we most fundamentally are. Furthermore, it is inherently awake, intelligent and compassionate. It is called *Buddha-nature* because "buddha" is Sanskrit for "awake." Indeed, those who have woken up to their basic nature attest that all beings are nothing other than Buddha-nature. On this view, each one of us already has (or, more accurately, is) the insight to know and the energy to accomplish *without aggression* whatever any particular situation requires. According to Buddhism, it is only our habit of imposing the reference points of self and other that obscures this inherent clarity and compassion. Buddha-nature is thus traditionally compared to the Sun, and our self-centered thoughts and emotions to clouds: like the light and warmth of the Sun, wakefulness, intelligence, and compassion are always there, even when obscured by our confusion. Because there is no need to fabricate anything, then, the Buddhist spiritual path is essentially a process of uncovering this unconditioned awareness through learning to drop the habit of self-attachment.

MEDITATION

Dropping the habit of self-attachment is easy to talk about, but how do you actually do it? The principal means of travelling the Buddhist spiritual path is a form of sitting meditation known as mindfulness-awareness practice (*shamatha-vipashyanā*). Now, given that I have claimed that self-attachment is the root cause of possessiveness, aggression and ignorance, you might assume that the objective of meditation is to get rid of ego. As Trungpa presented it, however, the spiritual path is not about getting rid of anything. The practice of meditation should not be understood as a self-improvement program, or as any other project of manipulating our experience according to our preconceived notions about how things should be. The point of meditation is to learn to see things as they are instead of jumping into action based upon our projections. For one thing, learning to pay close attention to our experience enables us to judge for ourselves whether or not what Buddhism teaches is true. The Buddha himself insisted that his teachings should be tested against personal experience. Furthermore, and most importantly, if we are ever to let go of our need for self-confirmation, we must each *personally* realize how ego's struggles are futile, painful and unnecessary. Thus, rather than being another form of conflict presupposing dualistic preconceptions, meditation is a way to help us remember that we can afford to relax and make friends with who we are. It is this learning to pay attention in a non-judgemental way that allows the wisdom and compassion inherent in our basic nature to emerge from behind ego's confusion.

Like many other educational processes, the practice of sitting meditation begins by making things as simple as possible. In Trungpa's tradition, the technique involves three basic instructions. One, maintain an upright but relaxed posture. Two, place attention on the breath as it goes out, dropping that attention as breath dissolves into space, allowing the inbreath to happen naturally. Three, whenever thoughts or emotions arise, simply label them as "thinking," and then come back to the awareness of breathing.[6]

As already suggested, the effect of this practice is to cultivate a non-judgemental awareness of what arises in our mind, particularly our habitual patterns of thinking and feeling. From the Buddhist point of view, that thoughts and emotions arise in our minds is not a problem. The problem is that we usually become so caught up in those thoughts and emotions that we take them for reality. In such cases, it is like watching television or reading books and getting so caught up in the story lines that we forget that they are someone's creation. Consequently, the intent of meditation is neither to repress thoughts and emotions nor to entertain them, but to see their transitory nature. That non-judgemental awareness enables us to recognize how our possessiveness, aggression and ignorance arise in response to situations that we ourselves create out of our own dualistic conceptual processes.

An example may help: A man bumps into me as I walk down the street. Without thinking, I perceive it as an intrusion, an offense, a kind of threat. Anger arises. I glance at the person's clothes and manner, subconsciously labeling him a drunken oaf. I growl "Look out where you're going!" and march away indignantly. In this scenario, my aggressive behavior is a response not so much to being bumped as to the interpretation I impose on that encounter. And, of course, aggression breeds aggression: if the person I have growled at takes offense in the same automatic way, the bump could escalate into a shoving match or worse. Conversely, being aware of my anger as self-constructed allows me to see the situation more clearly and respond more appropriately. Perhaps the person bumped me because he is sick and needs help. Or perhaps I was bumped because I was not looking where I was going, and *I* am the one who should apologize.

CONCLUSION

I would like to conclude with a few caveats and qualifications. First, I should emphasize that Trungpa did not present the practice of meditation as a quick fix for world problems, nor as a way of eliminating what is irritating, embarrassing or inconvenient from our lives. Somewhat paradoxically, meditation is about making friends with who we actually are, rather than striving to live up to who we imagine ourselves to be or think we should become.[7] Cultivating friendliness to ourselves is one of the fundamental ways in which Buddhist meditation helps us unlearn aggressive habits, so preparing the ground for the emergence of wisdom and compassion.

Second, I should underline that there is more to the Buddhist path than just sitting meditation. For example, Trungpa taught that intellectual contemplation is a necessary complement to personal experience of nonduality. In his tradition, philosophical analysis and meditation practice are compared to the two wings of a bird: both are essential. In addition, many teachings and practices are presented on how to work with mindfulness and awareness in everyday life, and how to avoid harming others while trying to wake up. Trungpa taught that the understanding of our own suffering and the friendliness to ourselves that arises from meditation open naturally into a keen awareness of the suffering of others and a genuine desire to help them. Thus, as many have reported, working for the benefit of others is central to the spiritual path in Vajrayâna Buddhist traditions.[8]

Third, I should acknowledge that Buddhism in whatever form is not the only valid way of understanding and travelling the spiritual path that leads beyond fear and aggression. Trungpa himself very much encouraged inter-faith dialogue, and established an alternative training program in meditation for those who might not wish to become Buddhist.[9] One implication of this is that Buddhist traditions are not to be appropriated uncritically. In particular, I think Buddhism has much to learn from feminist critiques of the patriarchal biases that permeate virtually all cultures, and from other analyses of systemic oppression.[10] Similarly, I think there is room for learning on both sides in attempts to integrate Eastern and Western psychologies and their different views of personal development.[11] For example, I believe Kohlberg's theory of moral development will be radically incomplete until the personal transformations associated with realizing unconditioned awareness are explicitly acknowledged.[12] Conversely, Buddhist traditions could learn from cognitive developmental theories how to help people reach the point where Buddhist teachings on egolessness are accessible.

These qualifications notwithstanding, I believe that the practice of meditation, when guided by the teachings of a genuine spiritual tradition, is a form of peace building that we all should seriously consider. Buddhism observes that we are unable to be of genuine benefit to others until we acknowledge and address our own habitual patterns of possessiveness, aggression and ignorance. No one else can do this work for us. Buddhism thus teaches that, whatever else we might do in the name of peace, we must always begin by learning to live it ourselves.

BIBLIOGRAPHY

Chödrön, Pema. 1991. *The Wisdom of No Escape and the Path of Loving-Kindness.* Boston: Shambhala.

Gross, Rita M. 1993. *Buddhism after Patriarchy: A Feminist History, Analysis, and Reconstruction of Buddhism.* Albany: State University of New York Press.

Gyamtso, Tsultrim. 1988. *Progressive Stages of Meditation on Emptiness.* 2nd ed. Oxford: Longchen Foundation.

Kohlberg, Lawrence. 1985. "A Current Statement on Some Theoretical Issues", in *Lawrence Kohlberg: Consensus and Controversy,* ed. S. Modgil and C. Modgil, 485–546. Philadelphia: Falmer Press.

————, Charles Levine, and Alexandra Hewer. 1983. *Moral Stages: A Current Formulation and a Response to Critics.* New York: Karger.

Loy, David. 1988. *Nonduality: A Study in Comparative Philosophy.* New Haven: Yale University Press.

Rahula, Walpola. 1959. *What the Buddha Taught.* New York: Grove Press.

Trungpa, Chögyam. 1966. *Born in Tibet.* London: George Allen & Unwin.

————. 1973. *Cutting through Spiritual Materialism.* Boston: Shambhala.

————. 1975. *Glimpses of Abhidharma.* Boston: Shambhala.

————. 1976. *The Myth of Freedom and the Way of Meditation.* Boston: Shambhala.

————. 1988. *Shambhala: The Sacred Path of the Warrior.* Boston: Shambhala.

————. 1991. *The Heart of the Buddha.* Boston: Shambhala.

Walker, Susan, ed. 1987. *Speaking of Silence: Christians and Buddhists on the Contemplative Way.* New York: Paulist Press.

Wilber, Ken. 1985. *No Boundary: Eastern and Western Approaches to Personal Growth*. Boston: Shambhala.

Williams, Paul. 1989. *Mahâyâna Buddhism: The Doctrinal Foundations*. London: Routledge.

NOTES

1. Vidyadhara means "holder of the Crazy Wisdom lineage." Rinpoché, which literally means "precious one," is a Tibetan title given to respected teachers. Chögyam Trungpa was empowered to present both the Karma Kagyü and the Nyingma teachings, two of the four main lineages of Tibetan Buddhism.
2. Several of Trungpa's many publications are cited in my bibliography.
3. Pema Chödrön (1991) provides an excellent description both of our tendency to create personal territory and of how to use that tendency as part of contemplative practice.
4. For more on dualism as a form of projection, see Trungpa (1975), and Loy (1988, e.g., p. 279). Loy's book provides a systematic, detailed comparison of teachings on non-duality that, while focusing on Asian traditions, explores related themes in classical and contemporary Western philosophy.
5. See Loy (1988, pp. 18–37) for an excellent discussion of how experiencer, experiencing, and experienced are found to be inseparable.
6. The technique is simple, but meditation practice is not. The brief description I have provided here of mindfulness-awareness practice is not a substitute for meeting with a qualified instructor. Even after having received instruction in the technique, it is highly recommended that people practice meditation with the support of those experienced and trained in a genuine tradition.
7. I think it is fair to say that one of the chief obstacles faced by beginning practitioners is their preconceptions about what "good" meditation should be like, e.g., that it should be characterized by an absence of thoughts.
8. On this point, see Williams (1989, especially p. 198).
9. For transcripts of dialogues between members of different contemplative traditions sponsored by Trungpa and his organization, see Walker (1987). See Trungpa (1988) for a description of his more "secular" program of training in mindfulness-awareness meditation.
10. See, for example, Gross (1993).
11. For example, Wilber (1985).
12. On Kohlberg's theory, see Kohlberg, Levine, and Alexandra (1983); also Kohlberg (1985).

Chapter 23

Toward a "New World" Order: A Native Perspective

Gawitrha
Six Nations-Grand River Territory[1]

Being a person of Native heritage living in a European culture, I have had a good chance to observe the great differences between the two, and I feel there are a few things that should be said regarding the issues of peace and world order. For me there is one thing that has defined and molded Native American societies and that is their special relationship with the Earth. If this chapter accomplishes only one thing I hope it will be that at least some readers grasp the essence of this relationship. I am big on basics so I hope the reader forgives the simplicity of this presentation.

To begin with I will tell you something everyone knows—that a home is what we make it. It can be a place of security, warmth and love or it can be a place of fear, loathing and pain. Looking from the Native perspective, the Earth is our home but it is more than our home, it also functions as our Mother. Our Earth Mother has made things nice for us. There is everything here that we need. We come from her body. We draw our sustenance from her. In fact, we are made of Earth. We are walking, talking, thinking, moist pieces of Earth. About 150 years ago Chief Seattle mentioned something like that in a speech. He said "We are part of the Earth and it is part of us. The perfumed flowers are our sisters, the deer, the horse, the great eagle, these are our brothers. Every part of the Earth is sacred to my people. They love this Earth as the newborn loves its mother's heartbeat." And science has provided confirmation of this relationship by showing us that all life forms share the same simple DNA building blocks. So, the Earth is also us; us along with every other of our fellow creatures. We are all part of a large family.

I will offer an analogy. Let us compare our Earth to an inflated balloon. Let us say that both the Earth and the balloon are separate entities with definite boundaries. Now imagine squeezing the balloon so that a small portion of it protrudes. When you release your grip the protrusion will be absorbed back into the balloon—its parent structure. It should now become easy for you to imagine a tree, for example, as being a protrusion of Earth that will, when it dies, sink back into and become part of the Earth. Though humans do not have roots, they also can be thought of as protrusions of Earth that will, when their times come, sink back into and again become part of their parent entity, the Earth. In all these cases the "protrusions" cannot leave their parent entities as sustainable entities in their own right. This will give you some idea of why Native Americans thought it so odd that Europeans could imagine ownership of land.

Now, as I see it, there are two basic positions we humans can take relative to nature. Either we love and honor the Earth Mother by living within her "house rules" and respecting all our fellow creatures, or we deny our Mother/child, sibling/sibling relationships and live our lives alienated from nature. Those who choose alienation have a good excuse. They are merely the product of a very powerful Earth-alienating system. Their alienation from nature can be compared to the alienation process experienced by uprooted Native children forced into residential schools and taught to be ashamed of their own parents and all that their parents stood for.

Before the social acceptance of the private-property concept and the ensuing phenomenon called civilization, all humans lived in harmony, not, perhaps, with each other, but at least with the Earth. Social historian Michael Mann's studies have concluded that civilization is an abnormal phenomenon. "It involved the state and social stratification, both of which humans have spent most of their existence avoiding. The conditions under which, on very few occasions, civilization did develop, therefore, are those that made avoidance no longer possible."

Civilization serves to isolate and separate us from nature. Originally, this isolation was probably a reasonable price to pay for the increased life-chances offered by civilization, but now we can see that this isolated "protection" from nature has developed into a completely unwholesome alienation. It has now long been possible for civilized people to spend most of their lives in cities where they are totally surrounded by a man-made environment.

And Christianity, which once served as Western civilization's most important supporting structure, has also had an alienating influence on people. In the myth of the Creation and the "Fall," we find woman emerging as the villain. "In the bible narrative," according to Passionist monk Thomas Berry, "woman becomes the instrument for the entry of evil into the world and for the breakdown in human-divine relations." He deplores the fact that, for the Christian, the natural world is no longer the place for the meeting of the divine and the human. "A subtle aversion develops toward the natural world, a feeling that humans, in the depth of their beings, do not really belong to the earthly community of life, but to a heavenly community. We are presently in a state of exile from our true country. The natural world is little mentioned in the official prayers of the church." So it is easy to see why civilized people abuse the environment: they don't see themselves as part of the Earth.

And how do civilized societies treat those within their influence? Worthwhile history books tracing the course of Western civilization are filled with descriptions of almost constant warfare, oppression, massacres, theft and slavery. Millions of people, women and children included, were killed during the three European Inquisitions. Tribal societies were physically unable to defend themselves against the invasions of militant, resource-hungry states. Thirty to fifty million tribal people died as a result of the worldwide expansion of industrial civilization between 1780 and 1930. Tribal peoples and women together lost their free and equal status with the rise of civilization.

What took place during the colonization of the "New World" was simply murder and theft. There was no "just war." It was not a "discovery." It was not a case of *terre nullius*. It was the equivalent of a modern-day home robbery in which the residents are overpowered, robbed and assaulted in their own home. Colonial governments such as Canada and the United States have a vested interest in making sure that all the bloodstains are wiped clean from official history books. To further justify their larcenous acts they labeled their victims subhuman. No less a person than Immanuel Kant claimed that American Natives were "incapable of governing themselves" and were "destined for extermination."

So it is understandable that you might have never heard, for instance, that of the known foodstuffs, three-fifths originated in the "New World." Imagine an Italy without tomatoes, or a Hungary without paprika, or an Ireland without potatoes, or Russia without sunflowers. As for other areas of interest, electrification had to wait in the wings until wires could be insulated with "New World" rubber. And what of the superior "New World" cotton and the "New World" knowledge of dyes, which helped give birth to the industrial revolution? (Not that this was a good thing.) And what of asphalt? Or petroleum? Or the fact that the U.S. pharmacopoeia of 1820 listed over 200 Native medicines? A much more complete listing is included in Jack Weatherford's book *Indian Givers*. But the most important "New World" product for our purposes is the evolution of a particular government. This government was the world's first constitutional federation—which is noteworthy in itself—but this government was mandated to establish and maintain the Peace. There will be more about this Peace Federation further on.

Now some say that the present "democratic" capitalist system is the best of alternatives. I dispute that claim entirely. In just several hundred years it has destroyed many millions of people and created poverty and slavery for many millions more. It has gobbled up tomorrow's resources while poisoning our land, air and water. By what conceivable standards do they claim their system to be the "best"? In a general statement about property, Adam Smith, the "invisible hand" economy theorist, claims that "Wherever there is great property there is great inequality. For one very rich man there must be at least 500 poor and the affluence of the few supposes the indigence of the many. Civil government, so far as it is instituted for the security of property, is, in reality, instituted for the defense of the rich against the poor." Contrary to popular belief, Smith never really maintained that the exercise of self-interest led to the common good. He knew that "profit hunger" conflicted with public interest and that the search for profit and monopoly would not stop short of terrorization and crime.

Civilized society has always been patriarchal and hierarchical. Within it there is no room for democracy. For instance, many claim that Canada is a democracy, but John Nunziata knows different. He is the member of Parliament kicked out of the Liberal Party for not following party lines. He says that Canada is an elected dictatorship (as is the Catholic Church) run by six people, three of which are unelected. Such conditions have left the door wide open to intervention by powerful financial interests for who knows how long.

For the last 500 years nation-states have taken the place of the tattered Holy Roman Empire in running Western civilization. Now, so it seems, empire is making a reappearance, but not under the Catholic Church. This time it will be controlled by huge, unelected, unaccountable, clear-cutting, anti-Earth corporate powers. I would guess that this is the "world order" in store for us. Why? Civilization has so much going for it. It got its start because people wanted a Big Brother to protect their private property. It is still like that today. Anyone with an accumulation of private property has a vested interest in making sure the "system" survives. Holders of private property are trapped by the things they love just as a monkey is caught when he puts his hand into the monkey trap to grasp the bait and then can't remove the larger fist that is grasping the bait. The only way he could get free is to let go—but he won't. The same applies to us. The way things are going it truly seems we are destined to become robotic serfs under this new, anti-Earth, feudal-corporate empire that has no future because it is anti-Earth.

But there is light at the end of the tunnel. If we really want freedom, equality, world peace and a clean environment we must let go of many things. We would have to outlaw private property. We would have to shun cities and the stock markets. We would have to relearn how to live in harmony with the Creation we are a part of. We would have to become self-sustaining on the land in communal groups while holding all things in common. But we have to have a system in place that will allow that kind of world order to happen. And this all brings us back to that earlier reference about a home-grown, constitutionally backed federal government. In history books my people have been referred to as the "Iroquois" and our form of government has been referred to as the "Iroquois" Confederacy. We refer to ourselves as Hodenoshonee (people of the Longhouse) and to our constitution as the Gayaneseragowa (The Great Law of Peace).

Because of the sterilized condition of history books, it will probably come as a surprise to you to know that all of the requirements for global peace existed here in the "New World" before Columbus. Of course sharing, caring, freedom and equality are already inherent in communal societies. But communal groups can still have internal and external conflicts and that was/is the whole purpose of the Great Law of Peace. This federation is not a myth. It functioned for hundreds of years and some of its activities are well documented (in sometimes biased history books). Its governmental organization was the pattern the Yankees used to link their 13 separate colonies together into a United States. Henry Steel Commager wrote: "If Americans did not actually invent federalism they were able to take out an historical patent on it." Both Marx and Engels studied the Hodenoshonee League of

Peace with these observations: "And what a wonderful constitution it is. The Confederacy has no head or chief executive officer, no soldiers, no gendarmes or police, no nobles, kings, regents, prefects or judges, no prisons, no lawsuits—and everything takes its orderly course. There cannot be any poor or needy. All are equal and free—the women included."

If we compare the Great Law of Peace to a flowering plant, I would say that the United States took the stem to provide structural strength to its government, and the Soviet Union took the "niceness" of the flower to provide a wonderful new social reality for its people, but they both rejected and left behind the spiritual roots that produced this unique plant in the first place.

In conclusion, I'll say that global peace can only be possible under some sort of world order, but it has to be a world order that can justify its existence by being good for *all* people, and by being kind to the Earth Mother. And this, of course, is why I advocate a "New World" order.

REFERENCES

Berry, Thomas. 1988. *The Dream of the Earth.* San Francisco: Sierra Club Books.

Bodley, John. 1982. *Victims of Progress,* Palo Alto: Mayfield Publishing Co.

Engels, Frederick. 1942. *The Origin of the Family, Private Property and the State.* New York.: International Publishers.

Heilbroner, Robert. 1986. *The Essential Adam Smith.* New York: Smith Norton.

Held, Robert. 1985. *Inquisition.* Florence: Qua d'Arno Bilingual Publishers.

Mann, Michael. 1986. *The Sources of Social Power.* New York: Cambridge University Press.

Nader, Ralph, et al. 1993. *The Case Against Free Trade.* San Francisco: Earth Island Press.

Pleck, Elizabeth Hafkin. 1987. *Domestic Tyranny.* New York: Oxford Press.

Weatherford, Jack. 1988. *Indian Givers,* New York: Fawcett Columbine.

NOTE

1.   Younger Bear Clan, Cayuga Nation, Six Nations Confederacy.

Editor's note: Gawitrha passed away shortly before the 1999 World Order Conference, to the deep regret of the participants. He is sorrily missed.

Chapter 24

World Religion for the Coming Age

Hanna Newcombe
Director, Peace Research Institute, Dundas, Ontario

Transformation to unified humanity is not possible on the political plane alone. It requires a new symbolic environment, new values, new rites and ceremonies, new interpretations of reality—in other words, a new religion. In this new religion, the value of universality must play a key part. Universality is an extension of our horizons beyond the narrow self and its needs and pleasures (an extension that all religions require), and also beyond family, tribe and nation (which the great religions strive for, but have not achieved, being often actually divisive). Universality means an extension of consciousness, caring and sharing to all humanity, and indeed to all of God's creation, especially to the living planet Gaia herself.

The following chapter discusses some of the sources and ingredients of the new universal religion.

MEGASYNTHESIS OF THE GREAT RELIGIONS

The teachings of the existing great religions should by no means be discarded, but be built upon and properly applied in a non-doctrinaire manner in order to avoid the old divisiveness. Hinduism, Buddhism, Taoism, the American Native religions, Judaism, Christianity, Islam, Zoroastrianism, Sikhism, Jainism, Confucianism and others have achieved many great insights. Sometimes they are bound to a particular culture, but that would introduce all the more richness when we attempt a superecumenical synthesis. It is not clear if such a synthesis is possible in all respects, since some of the initial assumptions about the nature of God differ, but we might attempt to draw out the common elements. These certainly include the ethical teachings on the value of compassion and love; all religions teach the equivalent of the golden rule of "do unto others as you would have them do unto you." The synthesis should not be a watered-down least common denominator, but a combination of basic insights and elements, from which a new insight may emerge.

NEW UNIVERSAL HUMANISTIC RELIGIONS

There could arise new universal humanistic religions; in fact some have already arisen. The best example is the Bahá'í Faith, with its insistence on continuing progressive revelation (that is, acceptance of the prophets of all the previous great religions, plus the addition of the latest, Bahá'u'lláh), and its teaching that the content of this most recent revelation is precisely universalism. There is also Oomoto (whose other name and universal emphasis is Universal Love and Brotherhood), and World Goodwill (with its Great Invocation of Life, Light and Love, and its commitment of members to be "world-servers"). These new religions have brought and are bringing into being a new universal vocabulary, though "brotherhood" must be expanded to include "sisterhood." The Bahá'í Faith, for example, proclaims that "the world is one country and humanity is its citizens." However, there are still some doctrinaire and dogmatic aspects to some of these religions, too much emphasis on proselytizing which could lead to frictions, and features of esoteric doctrines in World Goodwill that may not be to everyone's liking.

RELIGION WITH SCIENCE

There must be consonance of religion with science. This is to be not just mutual grudging tolerance, each in its own realm without interference, nor only "peaceful coexistence of different systems" living side by side, but an active gaining of religious insights from the findings of science, and a re-enchantment of science with a sense of the sacred. This means a veering away in science from dead mechanistic materialism, as theoretical physics has already done to a large extent; the overcoming of dualism of matter and mind (body and soul), and a firm footing for religious faith in at least provisionally confirmed ideas and concepts, not total reliance on secondhand revelation (accepting the revealed message from a book, for example, without the possibility of a personal experience). As Thomas Berry said, we have a great new creation myth to tell, more wondrous than any we ever dared dream up before.

PANTHEISM

Pantheism, God in Nature and Nature in God (mutually), should replace the transcendence of God over Nature as in Western monotheism. (Perhaps "God" should be "Goddess" to emphasize intimacy and relationship rather than one-sided creation and dominance.) This mutual relationship involves more than a vague infusion of God(dess) into Nature and vice versa; it is a definite mechanism, which I call "the ultimate wrap-around": we, the products of Nature, create God, who creates Nature and us. The ancient sacred symbol for this idea is the Uroborus, the snake swallowing its own tail. The modern expression of it is Douglas Hofstadter's concept of "tangled hierarchies," in which A is greater than B, which is greater than C, which is greater than A, in a cycle of intransitivity. A simple example of intransitivity is the child's game "scissors cut paper, paper wraps stone, stone breaks scissors."

EMERGENCE (HOLISM)

The new religion should include theories of emergence and holism: the view that new qualities and new entities arise as more and more complex "wholes," wholes (or systems) being more than the sum of their parts.

Thus a proton is more than the sum of three quarks, a hydrogen atom is more than a proton plus an electron, a water molecule is more than one oxygen and two hydrogen atoms. On the macro scale, water is very different from a mixture of two colorless gases that may explode or burn, and an organism is more than the sum of organs, tissues and cells, and a society (community) is more than the sum of individual persons or citizens.

Similarly, Roger Sperry postulates with some plausibility that the brain is more than the sum of neurons, glia and neurotransmitters; and that consciousness is an emergent (that is, new) quality of the brain, emerging from its supercomplex relationships (networks), one of the emergent qualities also being ethical values.

The theory of emergence, first formulated by Henri Bergson as the "elan vital," leads to several other ideas: (a) holism as opposed to reductionism; (b) panpsychism, or radical vitalism; and (c) the primacy of relationships over materiality or substance. The latter two points are elaborated below.

PANPSYCHISM

Panpsychism, or radical vitalism, postulates that everything is alive and conscious to some degree, even atoms and stones; but the degree of aliveness increases as we ascend the evolutionary scale; it gets brighter, just as wakefulness is brighter than sleep. Thus mind and matter always coexisted, primordially; neither is prior or superior to the other; neither are they separate "essences." As Descartes's dualism would have it, they are two sides of the same coin, the inner and outer aspect, the subjective and the objective, how it sees itself and how others see it.

Another view is that there are really four entities: matter, energy, information and meaning. Energy is the ability to move matter, information is the ability to move energy (or matter), and meaning makes of information a mental quality. Matter and energy are interconvertible, as Einstein showed; energy and information are also interconvertible, through the entropy-probability relationship, as Boltzmann showed. So the three can operate as a relay: even though information is extremely dilute energy, which is extremely dilute matter, yet information can move matter through the relay. But information in the form of "bits" or "yes or no" choices is only "mere" information, unless it also has meaning in the sense of being in the context of either trying to understand the present or the past or aiming at some purpose in the future, both of which presuppose the presence of a mind. Thus mind and matter can be seen to be related (perhaps interconvertible) through the relay.

LOVE AS PRIMORDIAL PRINCIPLE

The attractive forces, which pull together objects from subatomic particles to galaxies, can be equated to Love at higher levels of consciousness; thus Love becomes a primordial universal principle. It is as if even the elementary particles were trying to organize themselves into wholes or systems, but succeed only partially because of the countervailing influence tending toward disorder or increasing entropy. Slowly, over the ages, they succeed to form real systems in the form of complex living forms, which then have ever higher consciousness, emergent new forms of mental functions, and thus greater capability to actualize Love at higher levels.

There is also the dark side, namely forces of repulsion, which would be equated to Hate; this is also one of the "principalities and powers" (as the Devil used to be called). Yet attraction and repulsion are both needed to hold crystals and other structures together and give them coherence and beauty, just as figure and ground give coherence to a picture in a work of art.

RELATIONISM

Relationships or connections become ever more important than material substances as we ascend the evolutionary scale from particles to atoms to molecules to macromolecules to cells to multicellular organisms. In an organism, the materials (atoms and molecules) are rapidly exchanged in metabolism; they are only passing through, like water in a river or burning gases in a flame. It is the *form* that remains constant, is preserved as long as life persists; in fact it is the definition of life. The particular chemical processes and reactions and the structures of cells, tissues and organs guide the passage of matter through the system, under the overall direction of the genes, and the promoters and inhibitors that turn them on and off.

In Aristotle's terms, the formal cause is more important than the material cause. It is also true that the final cause is more important than the efficient cause (or what we more narrowly call "the cause") in living systems. That is, purpose (looking to the future) predominates over (narrowly defined) cause (pushing from behind); or, put still differently, free will appears as an emergent quality to outrank determinism. Biologists should, in my view, no longer shun teleological arguments; they are often obviously the simplest explanations, rather than long circumlocutions pushing the evolutionary-selection view.

THE GAIA THEORY

Very important in the new religion should be the Gaia theory, the message that the Earth is alive. James Lovelock concluded this on the basis of analyzing components of the Earth's atmosphere, when he was asked by NASA to devise a test that would show the presence or absence of life on Mars and the other solar planets. The atmospheres of all the planets except Earth are in chemical equilibrium, but in Earth's atmosphere oxygen and methane coexist. Since they normally react quite quickly to give carbon dioxide and water, their presence together shows that they are being continually produced at least as fast as they are reacting together, and they can only be produced by life forms (for example, oxygen by photosynthesis and methane by certain bacteria). The presence of these gases in the atmosphere is detected by infrared spectrometry, and Lovelock poetically declares that Planet Earth sings of life in an infrared melody to broadcast its message into space.

The Earth maintains these gases in a steady state (not equilibrium) by homeostasis, which is a well-known mechanism in the metabolism of organisms. Since the planet as a whole practices homeostasis, it is in some sense alive. Homeostasis also exists on Earth in other aspects: a steady temperature in spite of the solar energy output increasing over the geological ages, a constant salinity of the oceans in spite of the fact that the rivers keep washing in salt from the rocks.

The Gaia theory has obvious connections to ancient Mother Goddess religions. In fact, Native American tradition has a central belief in Mother Earth. I once heard a Native speaker remark, about the new belief in Gaia, that "people now accept it because a white man said it." However, it is of some value to have a scientific basis for it.

The modern symbol of Gaia is, of course, the picture of Earth from space, a powerful symbol of the unity of life and ecological consciousness as well as world citizenship. It caught on immediately in popularity, showing that it corresponds to the emerging needs of humanity, to the spiritual soil in the collective unconscious from which our transformation must spring. If the NASA space program produced nothing more than that picture, it would have been worth it. Essentially we went into space just to get a look at ourselves. That picture is being distributed to every classroom (as far as possible) by the Planet Project of the World Federalists.

TEILHARD DE CHARDIN

Another part of the new religion is the great scheme of Teilhard de Chardin, the great prophet of the confluence of science and religion, the extender and generalizer of evolutionary concepts to the spiritual realm. An enemy of dogmatic or fundamentalist religions, evolutionary thought becomes a great friend and interpreter of universalist religion. Teilhard postulates that life evolves from an Alpha Point (creation) to an ultimate Omega Point (union with God, or becoming like God). Gradually, the evolving Earth is being covered, not only with a biosphere on top of the lithosphere and hydrosphere and in the atmosphere, but also with a noosphere (a word he coined), which is an envelope of increasing information with meaning, knowledge with wisdom.[1]

SELF-ORGANIZING STRUCTURES

Another important ingredient is the theory of self-organization in structures far removed from thermodynamic equilibrium, as explained in Erich Jantsch's *Self-Organizing Universe*. The basis of this is Nobel laureate Ilya Prigogine's concept of the "dissipative structure," an open system far from equilibrium, which, surprisingly, can seemingly defy the second law of thermodynamics by evolving a highly organized (low-entropy) structure within itself. However, it does so only at the expense of increasing the entropy of the surroundings, so that the total entropy does increase (sometimes considerably) and the second law is not violated. Dissipative structure foreshadow living forms, but there are examples of simpler systems: a chemical "clock" system that periodically turns blue at regular time intervals only to fade out again; or the patterns that form if a liquid in a large shallow dish is heated from below.

Dissipative structures are closely related to the new theory of chaos, a seeming disorder from which a new order can emerge. Simple examples are as common as turbulent flow of water in a mountain stream or waves breaking on an ocean beach; yet scientists until recently have not tried to explain such systems, because they are non-linear and therefore more difficult to solve. They could not even analyze the smoke rings coming from a pipe.

CRISIS TRANSITIONS

Crisis has to be seen as both danger and opportunity, as seen in the Chinese symbol for it containing the signs for both of these ingredients. Since humanity *is* in a crisis, this fear-hope perception is profoundly meaningful to us. For example, Dorothy Baker has carried out a remarkable comparative study of the patterns of world civilizations converging to a decision point in our time, which she entitled *Catastrophe or Transformation.* Her study is based on the pattern of the Greek drama, with its phases of exposition, inciting action, progression, climax and resolution; but the same pattern is present in Arnold Toynbee's scheme of history, where he calls them genesis, challenge and response, rise or growth, zenith or apogee, and breakdown and disintegration. "Resolution" of the dramatic or historic conflict does not have to mean "disintegration," but so far that has been the pattern for all previous civilizations. Such a scheme of "cultural lifetimes" may be all right in Toynbee's scheme, where there is always another civilization waiting in the wings to continue history, but if, as Baker claims, we now have an integrated "world civilization," there would be nothing waiting in the wings.

The concept of crisis brings images of development in stages, like a staircase composed of a series of vertical rises and horizontal runs. The runs are plateaus of tranquillity, integration, maturity, consolidation of previous gains; the rises are the crises, times of troubles and turmoil, chaos, an accumulation of fluctuations in Prigoginian structures. Instances are: (a) Toynbee's image of the mountain climber (successive civilizations ascending to a ledge where they are arrested, and from which the next civilization resumes its ascent; or his alternative image of a wheel rolling along the road; any point on the rim ascends and descends, but the carriage moves forward. (b) Gesell's or Erikson's stages of child development, which show successions of growth spurts and plateaus of consolidation. (c) Piaget's stages of cognitive development as stages of basic reorganization of intellectual functioning. (d) A similar scheme of moral development stages outlined by Kohlberg.

In evolution, we mostly lack a fossil record of transitions between species, because the "missing links" go through their period of crisis/transformation too quickly in terms of geological time. The viability (fitness) of transitional forms must be rather low—a jump between two highly adapted plateaus. This is why Jay Gould speaks about "punctuated evolution," the same staircase-like pattern that we have been describing.

REVERENCE FOR LIFE

The center of gravity of our new ethical orientation must be reverence for life, the ethic of Jainism and Albert Schweitzer. This has been called "Polaris for the Spirit" (that is, the guiding star for our navigation) by Carl Casebolt. The principle springs partly from scientific insight: all life on Earth is based on DNA rather than RNA (except for a few retroviruses, like the HIV that causes AIDS), on proteins with "levo" amino acids, on sugars with "dextro" orientation. These are all symmetry-breaking choices; it could have gone otherwise, and on some other planet perhaps did. This shows the unity or at least the "cousinhood" of all life forms, from bacteria at the base to the various pinnacles of the evolutionary tree, the flowering plants, the insects, the vertebrates. (I think that we should abandon the idea that humans are the only pinnacle—pride goes before a fall.)

MYSTICISM

After all the science-based theorizing, we must return to the spiritual basis of all religion, in what Aldous Huxley has called "the perennial philosophy." Basically this is mysticism, a direct religious experience of God as the ground of all being, which has its place in all religions. This ineffable and inexpressible "peak experience" is achieved only with great spiritual effort by saints and those "pure in heart." (The medieval book *The Cloud of Unknowing* describes the effort and the struggle to reach this stage.) But a lesser degree of this different kind of knowledge is achievable by all with only a little reflection and concentration; I call it "the sense of the Sacred," which can be felt in nature and all things beautiful, and which lifts one's spirit above the level of the mere humdrum secular humanism that some would tell us is sufficient. Sure, a moral life is totally possible at that level; but it leaves one's spirit unsatisfied in its yearning for spiritual sustenance on which to thrive.

Various concepts are related to the mystical experience: Carl Jung's "individuation" (which he sees as the inclusion of certain unconscious contents into the narrow ego, thus creating the wider self), Buddha's "enlightenment," in which the meaning of everything becomes totally and immediately clear (does not require intellectual explanation) and Sri Chinmoy's "self-transcendence." The path to this higher consciousness is meditation, now recognized, even by physiological measurements of heartbeat, breathing rate, metabolic rate, and so on, to produce a distinct state of consciousness different from both wakefulness and sleep. Other "psycho-technologies" (Marilyn Ferguson) can be used, and the paths through knowledge (Jnana Yoga), loving worship (Bakhti Yoga) and good works (Karma Yoga) are well recognized in Hinduism, besides the path through meditation (Raja Yoga).

Mysticism has been a part of all the great religions, though sometimes an unrecognized, unofficial, even a subversive or heretical part; since, as a highly individual practice, it undermines the authority of priest and church, and eliminates the role of all intermediaries and intercessors between the human soul and God. George Bernard Shaw in his play *Saint Joan* thought that Jeanne d'Arc was burned at the stake mainly because she heard and followed direct voices rather than being an obedient child of Mother Church.

ARCHETYPES OF THE COLLECTIVE UNCONSCIOUS

Related to mysticism is the realm of the archetypes in the collective unconscious, as postulated by Carl Jung. The collective unconscious is the ancient (perhaps timeless) gathering place of human and prehuman cultures and archetypes. The latter are seen as the deep expressions of the basic schemata within which human mental and spiritual experience is framed. Archetypes are vehicles of cultural and spiritual heredity, just as genes and chromosome are vehicles of physical and biological heredity.

We might picture consciousness like a spotlight in the middle of a darkened room. We can see what is going on under the spotlight as things and events move in and out of it, but many events are also happening at the dark edges and corners of the room, quite unseen. In the shadowy, half-lit area in between, which corresponds to the subconscious, we might discover some moving shapes if we look away a bit from the bright central light that usually blinds us to the shadow happenings.

The dark room with the central spotlight is not all there is, however; there are doors in the dark walls that lead to other rooms and secret passageways. Through Door A, the ordinary unconscious may connect to the deeper layers of the neural mind, the mammalian and reptilian brain, and beyond that to the hormonal, epigenetic, genetic and metabolic minds postulated by Jantsch, that is, to the body with its physiological processes that we normally do not control or know about, but perhaps could, as advanced mystics do when they control their pulse rate or their blood pressure. (We can all learn how to do this through biofeedback methods.)

Door B might lead to the higher realms of the spirit, which can be entered by meditation, as noted in the previous section. There we might find the Inner Light of the Quakers, the Atman that is Brahman of the Hindus, or the enlightenment of the Buddhists, probably all different names for the same divine reality.

Finally, Door C might link one's mind with other human minds; first, to perceive the "Thou" of persons close to us with whom we are interacting with some intensity and intimacy (family members, lovers, friends); then with other human minds known through books and other communications media; and finally with all human minds throughout the world, present and past, throughout the existence of our species, and perhaps dimly beyond. Some of this connection is still conscious (the interaction with people personally known to us), but the connection with those far away in space and time must take place through some common unconscious medium that remains somewhat mysterious, as if there were hidden passageways connecting the mental "rooms" of different individuals, even across space and time, non-locally and non-temporally.

This collective unconscious, as Carl Jung explained, is inhabited by the archetypes of good and evil, larger-than-life figures of heroes, angels, devils, dwarfs, giants, fairies, witches, nymphs, sirens and monsters—all creatures we know from myths, legends, fables and fairy tales, as well as dreams. They represent an accumulation of human experience, different in quality from a library or an encyclopedia, in that they include the emotional as well as the cognitive content of that experience; and because of that added richness and complexity, they evoke a sense of awe, a sense of the numinous or sacred; they resonate with the emotional and spiritual content of billions of minds.

EXISTENTIAL RESPONSIBILITY VERSUS NON-ATTACHMENT

Then there is the tension between existential responsibility and Buddhist-type non-attachment. There is this dizzying realization that it is we, as free individuals, who make decisions at the crossroads between catastrophe and transformation, without necessarily always knowing the consequences of our actions, because these consequences may be counterintuitive. The full realization of this responsibility is so awesome that it cannot be endured undiluted. It must be tempered with non-attachment, in which we do not fervently hang on to the object of our desires, no matter how noble and altruistic. We finally say "let it be" or "Thy will be done," even about human survival.

In this tension between responsibility and non-attachment we teeter on the knife-edge between being the "destroyer of worlds" (as Oppenheimer quoted the Rig Veda after the first atomic bomb test at Alamogordo) and being "children of the Universe who have a right to be here," feeling that "the Universe unfolds as it should," flowing with the rhythms of the Eternal Tao. Non-attachment, yet commitment; surrender to the Everlasting Arms, yet remembering that "God has no hands but yours to do His work on this Earth, no eyes but yours, no feet but yours" (as St. Theresa said). The tension is brought out in many other images: the Church Militant and the Church Triumphant, the yogi and the commissar (Arthur Koestler), mystics and militants (Adam Curle).

HUMILITY

A somewhat unlikely, but nevertheless vital, ingredient in the new religion is humility, traditionally a great Christian virtue (pride being the most deadly of the deadly sins). The catatonic children of Arthur C. Clarke's science-fiction novel *Childhood's End,* who deflected the Sun, the Moon and the planets from their courses, are not the Son of Man or Daughter of Woman, not the spiritual evolutionary successors of humans, because they lack the main attribute of God, which is Love, not Power; the power of love, not the love of power. The gentle and humble Francis of Assisi is more along the true upward path toward the Omega convergence.

Some recent advances in game theory help to tell us why. In Robert Axelrod's computer tournament of prisoner's dilemma games, Anatol Rapoport's short and simple "tit-for-tat" program won—not because it could defeat any other program (in fact it could not), but because the more sophisticated programs killed off each other. Similarly in a truel (a three-cornered duel), the two best marksmen tend to kill each other, leaving the worst one as the winner (or, better, the survivor). "The meek shall inherit the Earth." Humility may be closer to the meaning of evolutionary fitness than strength. One thinks of the children's story of the ten billion cats, who fought about which was the most beautiful, until all were dead—except the one who knew she was not beautiful and so stayed away from the fight; she was then recognized as the most beautiful cat after all.

In spite of Nietzsche's attempt to revaluate the values and his apotheosis of Superman, the old Christian and Buddhist ideal of humility stands scientifically vindicated, as we now understand the mechanism.

SYNCHRONICITY

Synchronicity is illustrated by the "hundredth monkey" phenomenon. The basic myth (a true story) is that one monkey, and then another, learned to wash her sweet potato before eating it, as observed on the Japanese island of Koshima in 1952–58. The practice spread slowly, in linear fashion, until the hundredth monkey was reached. This exceeded some threshold of criticality, and the practice then spread exponentially, like wildfire, even jumping from island to island where monkeys could not even observe each other. It is this last point, learning without direct contact, as if frequent enough performance of the act had smoothed the way somehow for its own repetition, that constitutes synchronicity.

The mechanism is thought to consist of "morphogenetic fields" (Aristotle's "formal cause")—fields that orient growing tissues in embryos and emerging behavior in monkeys along predetermined lines of force, like iron filings around a magnet. The field is formed by the first few tissue cells, or by the first 100 monkeys (the pioneers, like the leader stroke before the main stroke of a lightning flash, which preionizes the path), and then influences the successive units directly but invisibly, not by imitation.

This helps explains such puzzling phenomena as (a) the ease of crystallizing certain new chemical compounds with increasing rapidity after previous successes in crystallizing them, even in widely dispersed laboratories, although crystallization is extremely difficult to induce the first time around; (b) the frequent occurrence of new inventions or discoveries simultaneously in several places by different researchers, as if somehow "the time is ripe" ; (c) the observation that we sometimes encounter a new word, sight, sound or smell, if we have experienced it once, in quick temporal succession, again and again.

Above all, the phenomenon gives us hope that transformation to a peaceful, just and sustainable world order could occur much more rapidly than the linear extrapolation of the present slow rate would suggest. We are still pushing the rock uphill like Sisyphus—but unlike Sisyphus, we may find the top of the hill and then the rock will roll down the other slope without further effort. This hopeful implication makes this a valuable component of the new religion, especially since the aspects of the crisis model are so awesome.

And so we have it, the 18 ingredients of a new religion for our age: (1) megasynthesis of the great religions; (2) new universal humanistic religions; 3) consonance of religion with science; (4) pantheism; (5) emergence (holism); (6) panpsychism; (7) love as a primordial principle; (8) relationism; (9) the Gaia theory; (10) the teachings of Teilhard de Chardin; (11) self-organizing structures; (12) crisis transitions; (13) reverence for life; (14) mysticism, the perennial philosophy; (15) archetypes of the collective unconscious; (16) existential responsibility in tension with non-attachment; (17) humility; (18) synchronicity.

We have the 18 ingredients, but not yet an overarching founding myth or unifying concept or charismatic leader. "Charisma" means "grace," and grace is a free gift of God. In the extreme of our crisis, may it come to us soon.

NOTE

1. Exponents of Teilhardism in our time are multiplying and becoming more eloquent: from Donald Keys *Earth at Omega* to Robert Muller *New Genesis*, Marilyn Ferguson *The Aquarian Conspiracy*, Mark Satin *New Age Politics* and Theodore Roszak *From Person to Planet*. With the metaphor of humans as the Earth's emerging nervous system (Teilhard's noosphere), Teilhardism finds its culmination in Peter Russell's book *The Awakening Earth*, and especially his powerfully beautiful videotape *The Global Brain*. One of its points is the magic number 10 billion: 10 billion atoms make a cell, 10 billion nerve cells make a human brain, and 10 billion humans will form a unified human society. Already we are being linked by rapid-communication technology, and the spiritual links are to follow shortly.

Chapter 25

The Bahá'í Conception of World Order

Cheshmak A. Farhoumand
York University, Toronto

and

Charles O. Lerche
Vesalius College, Vrije Universiteit Brussel

INTRODUCTION

The Bahá'í conception of peace and world order is a combination of a profound vision of a united world and, even more important, a cogent plan for translating that vision into reality. The foundation of this world order is based on the twin pillars of the material and the spiritual. By this we mean that Bahá'u'lláh not only discusses spiritual and moral principles necessary in the formation and maintenance of world order, but He also provides an outline for the institutional foundations necessary to promote, uphold and safeguard these principles.

A short introduction to the Faith is in order to provide a context for the subject of the Bahá'í approach to world order. The Bahá'í Faith is the youngest of the world's independent religions. Its Prophet-Founder Bahá'u'lláh (1817–1892) taught that religious truth is relative and not absolute and that God through a succession of Messengers such as Krishna, Buddha, Zoroaster, Moses, Christ and Muhammad has revealed to humanity guidance appropriate to the needs and understanding of the age in which they appear so that humanity can advance to a higher level of spiritual and moral maturity. Bahá'ís believe Bahá'u'lláh to be the latest of these Manifestations, and regard His Writings as divinely inspired.

Bahá'u'lláh enjoins His followers the primary duty of an unfettered search after truth; He condemned all forms of prejudice, declared the purpose of religion to be the promotion of amity and concord; proclaimed its essential harmony with science and recognized it as the foremost agency for the pacification and orderly progress of human society. Moreover He unequivocally maintained the principle of equal rights, opportunities and privileges for men and women; insisted on compulsory and universal education; cautioned against and called for the elimination of the disparity between rich and poor; abolished the institution of the clergy; exalted any work performed in the spirit of service to the level of worship; encouraged the concept of an auxiliary language and delineated the outlines of those institutions that must establish and perpetuate the general peace of humanity.

In His lifetime, Bahá'u'lláh revealed over a hundred volumes of works, much of which address the subject of peace and world order. His claim of divine emissary status and His teaching led to a massive persecution of His followers and His own imprisonment, banishment and exile for the entirety of His 40-year ministry. His final destination was the Ottoman Empire's penal colony of Akka, where He spent the last 24 years of His life and passed away in 1892.

Bahá'u'lláh's vision lives on, however, in a community that is dedicated to working worldwide to give His teachings practical effect through transformation and service. Only 100 years after Bahá'u'lláh's passing, this community of 5.5 million individuals has become the second most widely spread religion geographically with adherents in 21,058 localities within 195 countries and 45 territories, representing over 2,100 ethnic, national and tribal affiliations. Despite its diversity, however, the Bahá'í community is united under the banner of Bahá'u'lláh's teachings and their experience of community-building is a source of encouragement to all who share their vision of humanity as one global family and the Earth as one homeland.

PEACE AND UNITY

According to the Bahá'í Writings, world peace is not only possible but inevitable, representing the next stage in the evolution of the planet and its citizens. In other words, for the first time in human history the foundations of peace are attainable and if implemented will propel humanity into realizing the unification of the human family. The Bahá'í call for peace began in 1870, when Bahá'u'lláh Himself wrote to the leaders of the world, such as Queen Victoria, Napoleon III, and Wilhelm II, inviting them to reduce their armaments and seek peace. He said,

> Take ye counsel together, and let your concern be only for that which profits mankind and betters the condition thereof . . . We see you adding every year unto your expenditures and laying the burden thereof on the people whom ye rule; this verily is naught but grievous injustice. Burden not your people beyond that which they can endure. Be reconciled among yourselves, that ye may need armaments no more save in measure to safeguard your territories and dominions. Be united, O concourse of the sovereigns of the world, for thereby will the tempest of discord be stilled among you and your people find rest.[1]

Disarmament, though important, does not eliminate the root causes of war and violence. Bahá'ís believe that true and lasting peace necessitates the eradication of the underlying sources of hatred that lead to violence and war. These include racism; the disparity between rich and poor; unbridled nationalism; and religious strife. The Writings also indicate that there are important prerequisites to peace such as the equality of rights and opportunities between the sexes; universal education; improved global communication; human rights and socioeconomic development. With this guidance, Bahá'í individuals and institutions are busy with projects that promote these principles both within the Bahá'í community as well as within the larger world community.

In addition to these important principles, Bahá'ís propose that world order can only be founded on an unshakable consciousness of the oneness of humanity, a spiritual truth confirmed by all the human sciences. Recognition of this truth requires the elimination of all forms of prejudices based on race, class, color, creed, nation, sex, degree of material civilization, or any other distinctions that would create a perceived sense of superiority among individuals, groups and nations. Moreover, universal acceptance of this spiritual principle is essential to any successful attempt to establish world peace and is a fundamental prerequisite for reorganization and administration of a world order based on justice and equality. Hence, this recognition "calls for no less than the reconstruction and demilitarization of the whole world. . . ."[2]

Bahá'u'lláh's great-grandson, Shogi Effendi (1897–1957), the appointed Guardian of the Faith from 1921 to 1957, explains that the concept of the oneness of humanity does not mean the subversion of the existing foundations of society, but rather that this oneness

> seeks to broaden its basis, to remold its institutions in a manner consonant with the needs of an ever-changing world. It can conflict with no legitimate allegiance, nor can it undermine essential loyalties. Its purpose is neither to stifle the flame of sane and intelligent patriotism in men's hearts, nor to abolish the system of national autonomy so essential if the evils of excessive centralization are to be avoided. It does not ignore, nor does it attempt to suppress, the diversity of ethnic origins, of climate, of history, of language and tradition, of thought and habit, that differentiate the peoples and nations of the world. It calls for a wider loyalty, for a larger aspiration than any that has animated the human race. It insists upon the subordination of national impulses and interests to the imperative claims of a unified world. It repudiates excessive centralization on one hand, and disclaims all attempts at uniformity on the other. Its watchword is unity in diversity.[3]

INSTITUTIONS AND GOVERNANCE

The institutional foundation of world order was also enunciated by Bahá'u'lláh. It assumes the curtailment of national sovereignty and promotes collective and common security for the peoples and nations of the world with a system of administrative bodies. Bahá'ís believe that their own administrative order also represents a pattern for the future world order. Authoritative decision making is carried out by elected counsels at the local and national levels, currently called "Spiritual Assemblies" and later to be called Houses of Justice, and by a world administrative body called the "Universal House of Justice."

Similarly, the institutional bases of the future world order were framed by Bahá'u'lláh: "The time must come when the imperative necessity for the holding of a vast, and all-embracing assemblage will be universally realized. The rulers and kings of the Earth must needs attend it, and, participating in its deliberations, must consider such ways and means as will lay the foundation of the world's Great Peace amongst men."[4]

Concerning the workings of this world-gathering, Abdu'l-Bahá (1844–1921), the son of Bahá'u'lláh and authorized interpreter of His writings, offered these insights in 1875:

> They must make the Cause of Peace the object of general consultation, and seek every means in their power to establish a Union of the nations of the world. They must include a binding treaty and establish a covenant, the provisions of which shall be sound, inviolable and definite. . . . In this all-embracing Pact the limits and frontiers of each and every nation should be clearly fixed, the principles underlying the relations of governments toward one another definitely laid down and all international agreements and obligation ascertained. In like manner, the size of the armaments of every government should be strictly limited, for if the preparation for war and the military forces of any nation be allowed to increase, they will arouse the suspicion of others.[5]

Abdu'l-Bahá'u'lláh goes on to advocate the Pact's enforcement through collective security, and to promise unequivocally that "Should this greatest of all remedies be applied to the sick body of the world, it will assuredly recover from its ills and will remain eternally safe and secure."[6]

The Bahá'í scriptures also promote federalism as the most effective and just institutional structure for a unified world:

> Some form of a world super-state must needs be evolved, in whose favor all the nations of the world will have willingly ceded every claim to make war, certain rights to impose taxation and all rights to maintain armaments, except for purposes of maintaining internal order within their respective dominions. Such a state will have to

include within its orbit an international executive adequate to enforce supreme and unchallengeable authority on every recalcitrant member of the commonwealth; a world parliament whose members shall be elected by the people in their respective countries and whose election shall be confirmed by their respective governments; and a supreme tribunal whose judgment will have a binding effect even in such cases where the parties concerned did not voluntarily agree to submit their case to its consideration.[7]

These institutions will be supported by a world culture and economy, and facilitated and stimulated by an efficient system of global communications and a universal auxiliary language—all of which will contribute to the emergence of a world commonwealth "in which the fury of a capricious and militant nationalism will have been transmuted into an abiding consciousness of world citizenship . . . ."[8]

Thus, the Bahá'í vision of world order incorporates a model of governance that transcends most contemporary concepts of democracy, accountability or transparency:

Governance must be guided by universal values, including an ethic of service to the common good. It will need to provide for the meaningful participation of citizens in the conceptualization, design, implementation and evaluation of programs and policies that affect them. It should seek to enhance people's ability to manage change and should offer opportunities to increase their capacities and sense of worth. It will need to provide mechanisms for equitable access to the benefits of programs and policies, to education and information, and to opportunities for lifelong learning. Moreover, it must help to ensure that the news media are active, vibrant and truthful.[9]

From a Bahá'í perspective, governance at the global level also requires that the masses of the world's peoples be actively involved in setting new goals and formulating strategies of change, since

international institutions cannot develop into an effective and mature level of government and fulfill their primary objective to advance human civilization, if they do not recognize and nurture their relationship of mutual dependency with the people of the world. Such recognition would set in motion a virtuous cycle of trust and support that would accelerate the transition to a new world order.[10]

Finally, while promoting the eventual creation of a fully developed and authoritative planetary government as the best long-term goal for world order, for the immediate future it is suggested that

> in accordance with the principles of decentralization...international institutions should be given the authority to act only on issues of international concern where states cannot act on their own or to intervene for the preservation of the rights of peoples and member states. All other matters should be relegated to national and local institutions.[11]

"UNITY IN DIVERSITY" AND HUMAN RIGHTS

The Bahá'í model of world order incorporates a commitment to human rights based on the following principles:

- Human rights have a spiritual foundation, in that they represent the conditions necessary for the human spirit, through a process of individual investigation of reality, to develop its inner potential.
- Human rights should be anchored in the principle of the oneness of humankind, and world unity requires universal respect for human rights.
- Human rights are indivisible, since all categories of rights are necessary for human dignity and fulfillment.
- Human rights require a sense of collective responsibility, an awareness that an injury to any member of humanity is an injury to the whole. This is a responsibility not just of governments but of every person as a divinely created being.
- The "adversarial paradigm" of human rights—government versus individual citizens—should be replaced by a cooperative paradigm, where all elements in society work together for the promotion of human rights.
- The primary obstacles to progress on human rights are unfettered national sovereignty, adequate enforcement mechanisms,

and the general lack of awareness of human rights—particularly at the local level.[12]

In regard to the fourth point, the Bahá'í International Community (BIC)[13] has explained that

> Since the body of humankind is one and indivisible, each member of the race is born into the world as a trust of the whole. This trusteeship constitutes the moral foundation of most of the other rights— principally economic and social—which the instruments of the United Nations are attempting similarly to define.[14]

They go on to argue that this trusteeship involves a number of obligations of society toward its members, among which are "employment, mental and physical health, social security, fair wages, rest and recreation . . ."[15] The BIC has on a number of occasions also emphasized the necessity of insuring cultural diversity and of reconsidering aspects of prevailing economic orthodoxy:

> The principle of collective trusteeship creates also the right of every person to expect that those cultural conditions essential to his or her identity enjoy the protection of national and international law. Much like the role played by the gene pool in the biological life of humankind and its environment the immense wealth of cultural diversity achieved over thousands of years is vital to the social and economic development of a human race experiencing its collective coming-of-age. It represents a heritage that must be permitted to bear its fruit in a global civilization. On the one hand, cultural expressions need to be protected from suffocation by the materialistic influences currently holding sway. On the other, cultures must be enabled to interact with one another in ever-changing patterns of civilization, free of manipulation for partisan political ends.[16]

The classical economic models of impersonal markets in which human beings act as autonomous makers of self-regarding choices will not serve the needs of a world motivated by ideals of unity and justice. Society will find itself increasingly challenged to develop new economic models shaped by insights that arise from a sympathetic understanding of shared experience, from viewing human beings in relation to others, and from a recognition of the centrality to social well-being of the role of the family and the community.[17]

These arguments highlight the central importance of justice, which is

> the one power that can translate the dawning consciousness of humanity's oneness into a collective will through which the necessary structures of global community life can be confidently erected. An age that sees the people of the world increasingly gaining access to information of every kind and to a diversity of ideas will find justice asserting itself as the ruling principle of successful social organization. With ever greater frequency, proposals aiming at the development of the planet will have to submit to the candid light of the standards it requires.[18]

A sincere commitment to global justice helps to counter "the temptation to sacrifice the well-being of the generality of humankind—and even of the planet itself—to the advantages which technological breakthroughs can make available to privileged minorities"[19] and implies that only those global initiatives that "are perceived as meeting their needs and as being just and equitable in objective can hope to engage the commitment of the masses of humanity, upon whom implementation depends.[20]

Only trust in the fairness of rulers' motives and policies can elicit the support those policies require to succeed:

> The relevant human qualities such as honesty, a willingness to work, and a spirit of cooperation are successfully harnessed to the accomplishment of enormously demanding collective goals when every member of society—indeed every component group within society—can trust that they are protected by standards and assured of benefits that apply equally to all.[21]

A better world order requires a new style of leadership in both the public and private sectors, and the BIC has outlined a new model of leadership for the next millennium; a leadership that shuns elitism, adheres scrupulously to high moral and ethical standards and thinks and acts globally.

> Above all else, leaders for the next generation must be motivated by a sincere desire to serve the entire community and must understand that leadership is a responsibility; not a path to privilege. For too long,

leadership has been understood, by both leaders and followers, as the assertion of control over others. Indeed, this age demands a new definition of leadership and a new type of leader. This is especially true in the international arena. In order to establish a sense of trust, win the confidence, and inculcate a fond affinity in the hearts of the world's people for institutions of the international order, these leaders will have to reflect on their own actions ... Through an unblemished record of personal integrity, they must help restore confidence and trust in government. They must embody the characteristics of honesty, humility and sincerity of purpose in seeking the truth of a situation. They must be committed to and guided by principles, thereby acting in the best long-term interests of humanity as a whole.[22]

CONCLUSION

Over one hundred years ago Bahá'u'lláh declared that the human race had come of age and was embarking on a new, divinely ordained, stage in its collective evolution; a stage that would witness the gradual emergence and fruition of a fully integrated, truly planetary civilization. He also stated unequivocally that the "prevailing order" was "lamentably defective,"[23] that it would "soon" be "rolled up ... and a new one spread out in its stead."[24]

Yet Bahá'ís do not turn a blind eye to the world's current problems, but see them as a part of a transition.

> The turmoil now convulsing human affairs is unprecedented, and many of its consequences enormously destructive. Dangers unimagined in all history gather around a distracted humanity. The greatest error that the world's leadership could make at this juncture, however, would be to allow the crisis to cast doubt on the ultimate outcome of the process that is occurring. A world is passing away and a new one is struggling to be born. The habits, attitudes, and institutions that have accumulated over the centuries are being subjected to tests that are as necessary to human development as they are inescapable.[25]

To Bahá'ís there is no "going back": far-reaching vistas of challenge and opportunity stretch out before us. This great vision inspires the world Bahá'í community with optimism about the future.

National rivalries, hatreds, and intrigues will cease, and racial animosity and prejudice will be replaced by racial amity, understanding and cooperation. The causes of religious strife will be permanently removed, economic barriers and restrictions will be completely abolished, and the inordinate distinction between classes will be obliterated. Destitution on the one hand, and gross accumulation of ownership on the other, will disappear. Economic barriers will have been removed and the interdependence of capital and labor recognized. The enormous energy dissipated and wasted on war, whether economic or political, will be consecrated to such ends as will extend the range of human inventions and technical development, to the increase of the productivity of humanity, the extermination of disease, the extension of scientific research, the raising of the standard of physical health, the sharpening and refinement of the human brain, the exploitation of the unused and unsuspected resources of the planet, the prolongation of human life, and to the furtherance of any other agency that can stimulate intellectual, moral and spiritual life of the entire human race.[26]

In conclusion, what should be reemphasized is that for Bahá'ís a more peaceful and positive world order can only come about through a synthesis of inner and outer transformation, the transformation of values into virtues through action in the form of service. We are reminded that there is a difference between the impossible and the yet to be experienced and assured that "these fruitless strifes, these ruinous wars shall pass away and the most great peace shall come."[27]

NOTES

1. Bahá'u'lláh, *Gleanings from the Writings of Bahá'u'lláh*, trans. by Shoghi Effendi (Wilmette, Ill.: Bahá'í Publishing Trust, 1976), p. 254.
2. Shoghi Effendi, letter of November 28, 1931, to "Fellow-believers in the Faith of Bahá'u'lláh" and entitled "The Goal of a New World Order," in *The World Order of Bahá'u'lláh* (Wilmette, Ill.: Bahá'í Publishing Trust, 1969), p. 43.
3. Ibid., pp. 41–42
4. Bahá'u'lláh, *Gleanings*, p. 249
5. "Abdu'l-Bahá, *The Secret of Divine Civilization,* trans. by Marzieh Gail (Willmette, Ill.: Bahá'í Publishing Trust, 1977), pp. 64–65.
6. Ibid.

7. *World Order of Bahá'u'lláh*, pp. 40–41.

8. Ibid., p. 41.

9. "Valuing Spirituality in Development: Initial Considerations Regarding the Creation of Spiritually Based Indicators for Development," a concept paper presented to the "World Faiths and Development Dialogue," hosted by the President of the World Bank and the Archbishop of Canterbury at Lambeth Palace, London, England, February 18–19, 1998. Source: http://www.bic-un.bahai.org/98–0218.htm.

10. "Turning Point For All Nations: A Statement of the Bahá'í International Community on the Occasion of the 50th Anniversary of the United Nations," New York, October 1995, http://www.bic-un.bahai.org/95–1001.htm

11. "Turning Point."

12. Gleaned from various BIC statements on human rights, which can be found at: http://www.bic-un.bahai.org./i-e-hr.htm.

13. The Bahá'í International Community (BIC) is an international non-governmental organization that both encompasses and represents the worldwide membership of the Bahá'í Faith. Registered with the UN Department of Public Information (UNDPI) since 1948, the Bahá'í International Community was granted consultative status (category II) with the UN Economic and Social Council (ECOSOC) in 1970, consultative status with the United Nations Children's Fund (UNICEF) in 1976, and working relations with the World Health Organization (WHO) in 1989. The BIC has offices at the United Nations in New York and Geneva and representations to regional United Nations offices in Addis Ababa, Bangkok, Nairobi, Rome, Santiago and Vienna. Its United Nations Office now includes an Office of the Environment and an Office for the Advancement of Women. Source: http://www.bic-un.bahai.org/bic-e.htm.

14. "The Prosperity of Humankind," a statement prepared by the Bahá'í International Community Office of Public Information, Haifa, first distributed at the United Nations World Summit on Social Development, Copenhagen, DenmarkHaifa, Israel, March 3, 1995. Source: http://www.bic-un.bahai.org/95–0303.htm.

15. Ibid.

16. Ibid.

17. Ibid.

18. Ibid.

19. Ibid.

20. Ibid.

21. Ibid.

22. "Turning Point."

23. Bahá'u'lláh, "Lawh-i-Maqsud," in *Tablets of Bahá'u'lláh Revealed after the Kitab-i-Aqdas*, compiled by the Research Department of the Universal

House of Justice and translated by Habib Taherzadeh with the assistance of a Committee at the Bahá'í World Centre (Haifa: Bahá'í World Centre, 1978), p. 171.

24. *Gleanings*, p. 7.
25. "Prosperity."
26. Shoghi Effendi, *The World Order of Bahá'u'lláh*, 204.
27. Shoghi Effendi, *God Passes By* (Wilmette, Ill.: Bahá'í Publishing Trust, 1965), p. 194.

Chapter 26

The Inner Role of the United Nations

Sri Chinmoy
Leader of Sri Chinmoy:
the Peace Meditation at the United Nations

Editor's note: The U.S. State Department invited Sri Chinmoy to come to Washington on June 6, 1980, to address its "Open Forum," a policy discussion group inaugurated during the Vietnam War to acquaint policymakers with different points of view on critical issues of the day. Sri Chinmoy, who has been conducting meditations at the United Nations since 1970, was asked to speak on the inner role of the United Nations.

Javier Perez de Cuellar, Secretary-General of the United Nations (1982–91) commented on Sri Chinmoy's vision of the United Nations: "You concentrate on the truths and ideals which unite all mankind: the longing for peace, the need for compassion, the search for tolerance and understanding among men and women of all nations."

When I speak *of* the United Nations, my mind, heart and soul immediately compel me to speak of the United States in the same breath. When I speak *for* the United Nations, my mind, heart and soul are immediately blessed by the prosperous and generous soul of the host state—the Empire State, New York.

The term "united" has always had a special appeal to all human souls, and this transcendent idea has remained in vogue down the sweep of centuries. There was a time when America was under the repressive yoke of Great Britain. Then America fought dauntlessly and sleeplessly for its rightful independence. At first, the newly liberated Americans and their beautiful, vast land were sadly wanting in oneness. But there came a time when a new dawn of oneness-glory broke upon the glowing and illumining horizon. Americans felt the supreme necessity of a united country, and the thirteen colonies gradually, steadily, unerringly and selflessly became unified. Similarly, although at the present time peace is not reigning supreme in the United Nations, there shall definitely come a time when peace-flood will inundate the "united" nations around the globe.

Who could have envisaged that the thirteen colonies would one day develop into such a powerful country—fifty states standing indivisible, united by none other than the Hand of the Supreme Being? For the United States, the heart-throbbing and life-illumining song "united" had its birthless and deathless origin in the hearts of the great Americans whose names are synonymous with the lofty principles of liberty, justice and oneness. The founder of the nation, George Washington; the vision-luminary, Thomas Jefferson; the wisdom-sun, Benjamin Franklin; and the tireless fighter, John Adams: these powerful luminaries, along with others, bravely dreamt of unity for the thirteen colonies.

Again, it was a great son of the United States, Woodrow Wilson, who had the pioneer-vision of the League of Nations—the hallowed source of the United Nations. Some people are of the opinion that the League of Nations totally collapsed and failed, but I cannot see eye to eye with them. The League of Nations did not fail. We must view the League of Nations as the loving mother and the United Nations as her most promising child. When parents leave the earth-planet, their children often manifest more aspiration-light, more vision-power and more manifestation-delight than the parents themselves were able to do. Unmistakably, it is from the dying parents that a bright new light comes to the fore. When the children successfully offer much more than their parents to the world at large, we never think that the parents were hopeless and useless in comparison. On the contrary, we perceive a most significant inner connection, a link founded upon inner growth. We see that the children are marching and progressing in their parents' footsteps. For this reason we can safely say that Woodrow Wilson's League of Nations actually offered its wisdom-light to its future child, the United Nations.

The United States and the United Nations are divinely destined to run abreast. Not in vain is the headquarters of the United Nations in the United States—in New York, the capital of the world. This dynamic and fascinating world capital draws the world's attention at every moment. Is there any place that can be more appropriate than New York City to house the vision of universal oneness, which is in the process of being realised and manifested in the heart and soul of humanity?

True, at times the United States and the United Nations are not on good terms. But each knows perfectly well that the one adds tremendous value to the other in terms of prestige, recognition, self-awareness and oneness-perfection. Inwardly they know that they truly need and deserve each other. In silence, unreservedly the United States gives the United Nations confidence-light. In silence, unreservedly the United Nations gives the United States oneness-height. Being a seeker, in my silence-heart I feel that the concept of the United Nations has verily come from the United States, unconsciously if not consciously, for the United States had this united feeling two hundred years ago, whereas the United Nations is only a few decades old.

At the present moment of evolution, the United States says to the United Nations, "If you take my help, you have to use it in my own way." The United Nations says to the United States, "I am ready to take your help and I shall remain most grateful to you. But if I use your help in your own way, then I will be totally lost in the comity of nations. Whatever you can afford to give me, please give me unconditionally."

The United States immediately responds, "Oh no, I do not want to give you my help unconditionally. I have a right to know whether or not my momentous and generous offering is being utilised properly. As it is my bounden duty to help your supreme cause, O United Nations, I feel that it is also your bounden duty to accept my wisdom-sun on rare occasions."

The United Nations says, "Sorry to stand firm in my belief, O United States. One day you will be blessed with the real joy of unconditional self-giving, which is always without a second."

The inner role of the United Nations amuses the intelligentsia, inspires the world-peace lovers and nourishes the world-oneness-servers. God has showered His choicest Blessings upon the inner role of the United Nations. When we contemplate on the idea of "role", we immediately think of either responsibility or challenge. But when it is a matter of inner role, there is no such thing as responsibility or challenge; there is only one self-giving Divinity which is breathlessly growing into a self-becoming Reality.

The United Nations is often misunderstood. Perhaps its fate will always remain the same. But is there anybody who is not misunderstood, including poor God? Misunderstanding is the order of the day. But that does not and cannot prevent the United Nations from making its soulful self-offering in the creation of a Oneness-Home for all.

The United Nations has been marching resolutely and triumphantly toward its inner goal. Indeed, the remarkable leadership of its four Secretaries-General has made its outer success and inner progress not only convincing but also fulfilling. Secretary-General Kurt Waldheim throws considerable light on the inner role of the world organisation: "we are not faced with many separate problems, but with different aspects of a single over-all problem: the survival and prosperity of all men and women, and their harmonious development, physical as well as spiritual, in peace with each other and with nature. This is the solution we must seek. It is within our power to find it."

Secretary-General Waldheim's predecessor, the Supreme Pilot of the United Nations—U Thant—valued unreservedly the inner or spiritual obligations of the United Nations. Him to quote: "I have certain priorities in regard to virtues and human values. . . . I would attach greater importance to moral qualities or moral virtues over intellectual qualities or intellectual virtues—moral qualities, like love, compassion, understanding, tolerance, the philosophy of live and let live, the ability to understand the other man's point of view, which is the key to all great religions. . . . And above all, I would attach the greatest importance to spiritual values, spiritual qualities."

Secretary-General Dag Hammarskjöld offered the hallowed message-light that each individual has a responsibility to his own inner role. According to him, each individual must strive inwardly as well as outwardly to achieve abiding peace: "Our work for peace must begin within the private world of each one of us. To build for man a world without fear, we must be without fear. To build a world of justice, we must be just. And how can we fight for liberty if we are not free in our own minds?"

Illumining leaders from all over the world who are serving the United Nations remind us of the undeniable fact that the earth cannot exist without the world body—the United Nations—in spite of its apparent failings and problems. Secretary-General Trygve Lie's precious message ran: "The one common undertaking and universal instrument of the great majority of the human race is the United Nations. A patient, constructive, long-term use of its potentialities can bring a real and secure peace to the world."

The outer role of the United Nations is greatness remarkable. The inner role of the United Nations is goodness admirable. The supreme role of the United Nations is fulness adorable.

Greatness our mind desperately needs. Goodness our heart sleeplessly needs. Fullness our life breathlessly needs.

Greatness surprises the curious world. Goodness inspires the aspiring world. Fullness fulfills the serving world.

Greatness is blessed with an outer challenge. Goodness is blessed with an inner promise. Fullness is blessed with an integral perfection. Challenge awakens, promise expedites and perfection immortalises our varied capacities.

Greatness is sound-amplification. Goodness is silence-enlightenment. Fullness is God-Satisfaction.

The pillars of the United States, its Presidents, call upon us to dedicate ourselves to the most significant cause that the United Nations embodies. Needless to say, the world organisation is God's gracious experiment and precious experience. Such being the case, we must feel an inner obligation to participate in this aspect of God's cosmic Drama. The late President John F. Kennedy spoke not only to his fellow Americans but to all his fellow beings when he proclaimed: "My fellow inhabitants of this planet, let us take our stand here in this assembly of nations. And let us see if we, in our own time, can move the world towards a just and lasting peace."

President Carter has also powerfully encouraged his country to remain part and parcel of the United Nations. He tells us that real leadership and continuous service to mankind are inseparable: "There is no possible means of isolating ourselves from the rest of the world, so we must provide leadership. But this leadership need not depend on our inherent military force, or economic power, or political persuasion. It should derive from the fact that we try to be right and honest and truthful and decent."

The favorite son of New York, Senator Daniel Moynihan, former United States Ambassador to the United Nations, expresses his country's sincere awareness of the sublime necessity of the United Nations: "While there have been some calls to boycott the General Assembly, or not to vote in it, there have been but few calls for withdrawal from the United Nations. It is almost as if American opinion now acknowledged that there was no escaping involvement in the emergent world society."

The United States' Special Ambassador to the United Nations Law of the Sea Conference, Elliot Richardson—a heart of peace and a life of light—encourages, strengthens and spreads a global viewpoint: "The inter-dependence of the world is an increasingly visible fact, and I believe that out of that fact is bound to emerge in due course a compelling—and comparably inspiring—concept of the opportunities for global cooperation."

A staunch supporter of the United Nations, indeed, the donor of the land upon which the UN stands, Nelson Rockefeller vividly draws the parallel between the roots of the United States and the roots of the United Nations: "The federal idea, which our Founding Fathers applied in their historic act of political creation in the eighteenth century, can be applied in this twentieth century in the larger context of the world of free nations—if we will but match our forefathers in courage and vision. The first historic instance secured freedom and order to this new nation. The second can decisively serve to guard freedom and to promote order in a free world."

As the Declaration of Independence of the United States is an unparalleled discovery, so is the Charter of the United Nations. The U.S. Declaration of Independence and the UN Charter are humanity's two aspiration-dedication-realities. The beacon-light of the Declaration of Independence shows countless human souls the way to their destined Goal: "We hold these truths to be self-evident, that all men are created equal, that they are endowed by their Creator with certain unalienable Rights, that among these are life, liberty and the pursuit of happiness. That to secure these rights, Governments are instituted among men, deriving their just powers from the consent of the governed . . ."

The United Nations Charter bravely and heroically proclaims these rights for all of humanity, and speaks to "reaffirm faith in fundamental human rights, in the dignity and worth of the human person, in the equal rights of men and women and of nations large and small, and to establish conditions under which justice and respect for the obligations arising from treaties and other sources of international law can be maintained, and to promote social progress and better standards of life in larger freedom . . ."

Concern for and satisfaction in the towering achievements of the United Nations may be a confidence-trip into the unknown, but never into the unknowable. The great messenger of the Catholic world, Pope Paul VI, during his visit to the United Nations in 1964, eloquently expressed the inner role of the United Nations: "The Church considers the United Nations to be the fruit of a civilisation to which the Catholic religion . . . gave the vital principles. It considers it an instrument of brotherhood between nations which the Holy See has always desired and promoted. . . .

The convergence of so many peoples, of so many races, so many states, in a single organisation intended to avert the evils of war and to favour the good things of peace, is a fact which the Holy See considers as corresponding to its concept of humanity and included within the area of its spiritual mission to the world."

When Pope John Paul II visited the United Nations in October 1979 and spoke to the General Assembly, Secretary-General Waldheim introduced him thus: " . . . your presence among us on this historic occasion is particularly encouraging since it dramatically reaffirms the great spiritual values which you represent and which inspire the Charter."

Pope John Paul II indeed reaffirmed the value of the inner United Nations and the spiritual dimension of world politics when he told the General Assembly: "An analysis of the history of mankind, especially at its present stage, shows how important is the duty of revealing more fully the range of the goods that are linked with the spiritual dimension of human existence. It shows how important this task is for building peace and how serious is any threat to human rights."

The composer of the immortal "Hymn to the United Nations," the late Maestro Don Pablo Casals, reminds us that individuals and their countries undeniably need the United Nations. He gives an inspired call for us to selflessly play our parts in the inner and outer roles of the United Nations: "Those who believe in the dignity of man should act at this time to bring about a deeper understanding among people and a sincere rapprochement between conflicting forces. The United Nations today represents the most important hope for peace. Let us give it all power to act for our benefit. And let us fervently pray that the near future will disperse the clouds that darken our days now."

The outer role of the United Nations is a colossal hope. The inner role of the United Nations is a generous assurance. The supreme role of the United Nations is a prosperous satisfaction.

Hope is a growing plant. Assurance is a blossoming tree. Satisfaction is a delicious fruit.

At the present stage, the United Nations is a growing plant which is only decades old. Is it not absurd for us to expect the United Nations to solve the overwhelming problems of centuries? Let the child-plant grow and glow, smile and cry. Then there shall come a time when this tiny plant will grow into a huge tree, with countless leaves, sleepless flowers and spotless fruits—sheltering, inspiring and nourishing all those who desperately need its protection-shelter, rejuvenation-inspiration and satisfaction-nourishment.

Chapter 27

The Caledon Declaration on Building a Foundation for Peace in the Third Millennium

Editor's note: These recommendations for action were developed independently by eight Working Groups formed at the Interdisciplinary Conference on "The Evolution of World Order: Building a Foundation for Peace in the Third Millennium," whose Roundtable Session was held on June 8, 1997, at the Soka Gakkai Centre in Caledon, Ontario, Canada.

The well-being of Planet Earth needs our attention. There have been many calls for action and we are eager to add our own here. The participants in the World Order Conference urge the adoption of new approaches and thinking for swift progress towards a safer and more just world order.

UN REFORM, AND PEACE AND SECURITY

The UN, in its present form, cannot secure global integration. Its Security Council is dysfunctional and undemocratic. We believe that there should be no veto powers in that body. There should better representation of the world as a whole. The UN must also better reflect the balance between civil society and states. The UN must be made stronger, more effective, relevant and representative. To this end we recommend that several actions be taken:

1) Membership in the Security Council should be contingent upon full and timely payment of dues, the signature and ratification of basic international conventions, and the fulfillment of moral and legal obligations created through General Assembly resolutions and declarations.

2) The Security Council must become more representative of current global, regional and national interests through appropriate changes in membership. We suggest that the UN explore possibilities of subsidiary continental assemblies.

3) The international community should limit the use of the veto to matters of relevance to international peace and security with the aim of the eventual and permanent removal of the veto.

4) A common, auxiliary language should be considered in order to promote efficiency, foster dialogue and facilitate global understanding.

5) Effective means to foster compliance with all UN membership obligations and responsibilities should be introduced. One measure is citizen reporting for verification of state behaviour under such obligations.

6) We strongly support the speedy creation of an effective and independent International Criminal Court, and the expansion of the compulsory jurisdiction of the International Court of Justice, so that the force of law replaces the law of force.

7) We propose the establishment of a "Civil Society/NGO Forum" that meets annually to provide input into the UN General Assembly deliberations.

8) We support the establishment of a Rapid Deployment Force to allow a rapid response from the UN and allow it to relieve certain nations from a policing role in the world.

DISARMAMENT AND THE ARMS TRADE

Many nations, including Canada, have a not-quite arms-length dependence on weapons of mass destruction, including nuclear weapons. To maintain respect for international law or moral principle, NATO and NORAD must reduce their reliance on nuclear weapons. Governments must increase their reliance on the UN for keeping the peace.

We recommend that all governments recognize the July 1996 International Court of Justice advisory opinion on nuclear weapons by supporting the establishment of a nuclear weapons convention through the UN with time-bound steps to global nuclear disarmament under effective international controls.

We call upon nations such as Canada to give notice of termination, in due course, to any allies or alliances which entail such indefinite dependence, including NATO and NORAD. In particular and in preparation for the above, Canada should:

— terminate NATO flight training at Cold Lake, Alberta;

— not renew arrangements for low-level flight training over the Innu territory in the Labrador-Quebec corridor;

— collaborate as necessary with the government of British Columbia to bring an end to the use of Canadian waterways for routine U.S. naval operations torpedo testing in Nanoose Bay.

To help control weapons, Canada and other weapons-exporting states should adopt an open accountability process on weapons exports with a view to total elimination of such exports. The process should include:

— establishment of fiscal-use standards which will exclude export, whether direct or indirect, of all weapons (including dual purpose devices) to repressive regimes and human rights violators;

— inclusion of NGOs, as observers, in the determination process for all weapons exports;

— a schedule to drop to zero for all weapons exports;

— active promotion of industrial conversion from military to civil production.

POPULATION AND DEVELOPMENT

True development means progress towards an equitable sharing of resources, ecological and cultural carrying capacity, and empowerment of populations. Women, in particular, should be empowered in the development process. Women's voices have to be assured rather than simply encouraged.

We feel that every issue is a population issue because of the effects of one population on another, and of the environmental difficulties associated with population increases.

One of the challenges of global citizenship is to see everyone as an equal part of that citizenship with the right to determine their own future.

We propose that nations double their funding (e.g., Canada to 100 million dollars) and rigorously meet their commitments which were made at the Cairo conference and reaffirmed at the Beijing conference.

THE ENVIRONMENT

The current focus of the resource extraction industry is on the export of "raw" resources. Most countries suffer from using an unsustainable "industrial model" for such extraction (large-scale activities carried out by multinational corporations). We encourage companies and governments to engage in:
— green-energy accounting;
— diversification to value-added industries;
— the use of additional tariffs on raw lumber exports to the U.S. to support value-added activities, which will promote individual quality of life and responsibility for sustainable development;
— much more research and implementation of alternatives to the unsustainable "industrial model".

We strongly protest the weakening and elimination of environmental ministries and regulations in Canada and other countries and urge that such protests be addressed to all levels of government.

BIODIVERSITY

Of the 20 million species on this planet, 120,000 perish every year due to pollution, ozone depletion and loss of habitat, which is driven by human population growth and industrialization.

We appeal for:

— the preservation and expansion of wilderness areas, including world parks, national parks, regional parks, municipal Parks, peace parks and UNESCO biosphere areas;

— the establishment of "Creature Corridors" that accommodate all forms of seasonal migration, which are short and long range;

— a system of planetary accounting of living species;

— the gathering together of scientific data—life zones, biological food niches, geological structures, etc., with carrying capacity limits to be enforced for all land use reforms;

— the modification of educational curriculum to include learning for a sustainable civilization and to strengthen existing environment education and outdoor education programs; one goal would be to sensitize children and teachers to local and global biodiversity;

— a recognition that the preservation of species, and the proper use of parks and natural corridors is a source of recreation and peace;

— a system of citizen feedback to monitor the implementation of recommendations such as the above. Questionnaires can also be sent with questions such as: What measures have been taken to protect biodiversity? Do you observe any effects of the measures? What is missing from the measures?

SUSTAINABLE ENERGY SOURCES

There is a great need for research, education and promotion of alternative energy sources and systems, particularly solar energy. We recommend that

— a demonstration plant be built for solar/hydrogen fuel for transportation;

— a data base on solar energy success stories be created, and its information be widely distributed;

— an "Exciting Energy" program be adopted as a millennium project.

ECONOMICS AND SOCIAL JUSTICE

The disparities in wealth between rich and poor are growing internationally. We must reduce these disparities, both within and between nations. The Working Group proposes five areas for reflection and consideration:

1) The OECD Multilateral Agreement on Investments (MAI). Agreements on international investment, which are being considered by the members of the Organisation for Economic Co-operation and Development (OECD), threaten democratically elected governments with usurpation of the power to enforce international agreements or to control the activities of transnational corporations in their countries. The agreement puts transnational corporations above the national law, in the sense of having no obligation to benefit the economic development or protect the human and natural resources of host countries. This agreement sets the stage for increasing disparities due to wealth accumulation by transnational corporations at the expense of the host countries. As such, we recommend that the OECD nations should not finalize or implement the MAI or any similarly unbalanced agreements or unregulated markets.

2) Taxation and Custom Duties. Changes in taxation and custom duties should be considered on the principle that these should serve the purpose of the redistribution of wealth. Three changes are proposed:
— tax a fraction of one percent of each international currency transaction, in order to reduce speculation which increases international wealth disparities;
— domestically, each government should work toward introducing or reinforcing effective progressive income tax on individuals and corporations, while simultaneously phasing out of regressive sales taxes;
— domestically, each government should protect agriculture and agricultural processing, if need be through custom duties, to ensure control of local food production.

3) Domestic Capital Formation Versus Foreign Investment. International economic equality would greatly benefit from determined encouragement of domestic capital formation, in preference to, and as a replacement of the injection of foreign capital with the goal of increasing domestic productive/reprocessing capacity and reducing the dependence of less developed countries upon rapid exploitation and export of raw natural resources.

4) Social Auditing of Corporations. We support and encourage improvement of current efforts to develop social auditing of corporations with respect to environmental protection, job creation and contributions to the public good in the communities where they operate.

5) The Impact of Developing Technology. We are concerned about the development of technology which may have diminishing returns for society, to the point of possibly becoming negative. Technology can lead to unemployment and environmental damage and may even reduce total economic output. This issue should be given more study.

A HOLISTIC VIEW OF THE HEALTH OF PLANET EARTH

Human activity is disrupting the natural processes in the biosphere. There are many serious planetary disorders and imbalances which are not being diagnosed and communicated adequately to enable proper therapy.

1) Ownership and Stewardship of Property. In so far as absolute private property is seen as a virus[1] which has caused illness for this planet, we have to, as a first step, change our perception towards it. In fact, people do not own property outright. Owing to restrictions on its use—in terms of zoning bylaws and other social covenants—a human being's actual role in relationship to land and the life forms on it is that of a steward.

It is proposed that:

— land deeds and legislation be reworded so that the word ownership is replaced by the word stewardship;

— a statement be included on relevant land use documents

recognizing, for example, that the Earth is a living being, and is not subject to ownership;

— the legislative language related to the relationship between people and the land be re-examined.

2) Planetary Communication. From a cybernetics point of view there is a need for, and a lack of, a reliable integrative feedback loop at the level of the whole world. Informing all literate world citizens of the most important facts and trends as these affect the future of mankind on Earth will help create such a feedback mechanism. We are the eyes and the ears of the planet, we are the brain that needs to decide action. All world citizens must be on a 'neighbourhood watch', and observe and report imbalances. Regular reports on planetary wellness should be published, and include facts and commentary on issues of population, health, environment, economics, human rights and duties, rights of all life, and other desiderata for world order, guided by values as set out in the Earth Charter (q.v. Benchmark Draft).[2] The non-profit letter will offer a combination of theoretical basis and points of practical implementation.

3) Making use of such technologies as the Internet, perhaps enhanced by a common auxiliary language for all, a more integrated communications system could become the "nervous system" to promote a global consciousness and help bring about the wellness of Planet Earth. There is need to establish an educational mechanism which could serve the interests of the whole planet using systems specifically designed to provide information of importance.

4) The Earth Charter. The benchmark draft of the Earth Charter[2] should be given the widest possible circulation. This should be done by individuals, starting with the conference participants and by the sponsoring organizations.

NOTES

1. This metaphor is derived, in part, from a talk and paper presented by Gawithra in which ownership and the defense of property are cited as the root of much conflict in Western civilization.

2. The Benchmark Draft of the Earth Charter is included in this book as an annex to Chapter 10 by Rosalie Bertell and the latest version is available at «www.earthcharter.org».

Index

ment, 49; and Gulf War, 130; and International Criminal Court, 110, 115; and Iroquois Great Law of Peace, 218; and League of Nations, 9, 119; and United Nations, 23, 87, 120, 123-25, 127, 129, 155; and Vietnam War, 65

UNSCOM. *See* United Nations, Special Commission

verification, 26-31, 85, 101-107, 126-28
Vietnam War, 65, 246

Waldheim, Kurt, 249, 252
war: accidental, 57-62; civil, 67, 70, 73-75, 175; costs of, 152-53; crimes 30, 111-13, 126, 152; international, 64, 67-68, 87, 175; just, 20, 191, 215; law of, 19; spirit, 65-68. *See also* Gulf War, nuclear war, Thirty Years' War, Vietnam War, World War I, World War II
weapons: biological, 30-31, 85, 102-03, 106-07; chemical, 9, 27-28, 30-31, 85, 102-04, 126-27; electromagnetic field, 91; land mines, 153; nuclear 13, 21, 57-58, 60, 66-67, 85, 101-3, 157, 182, 202, 255. *See also* arms control, disarmament

Westphalia, Treaty of, 6, 10, 19, 100
Wilson, Woodrow, xvii, 119, 247; Fourteen Points, 127
women, 81, 93-94, 97; Decade for, 147; employment of, 37; rights of, 80, 148; UN conference on (Beijing conference), 14, 93, 147, 151-154, 165-168, 256; violence against, 148, 152, 167. *See also* education
World Bank, 75, 92, 150
world citizenship, 94, 172, 225, 238, 256, 260
World Court. *See* International Court of Justice
world order, 7, 9, 12-13, 46, 48, 53, 58, 67, 92, 119-120, 213, 217-18, 232-43; Conference, 253; economic bases for, 35, 42, 45-46, 51; evolution of, 8, 172-72, 179-80; types of, 3-4, 6
World Trade Organization (WTO), 49, 86, 90-93, 122, 155
World War I, 8-9, 65, 119, 121
World War II, 4, 9, 65, 119-21, 124, 174, 187

Yamoussoukro Declaration on Peace in the Minds of Men, 161-165